Scottish Writers Talking 1

Scottish Writers Talking 1

George Mackay Brown
Jessie Kesson
Norman McCaig
William McIlvanney
David Toulmin

Interviewed by
Isobel Murray
and Bob Tait

Edited by Isobel Murray

Kennedy & Boyd

Kennedy & Boyd
an imprint of
Zeticula
57 St Vincent Crescent
Glasgow
G3 8NQ
Scotland.

http://www.kennedyandboyd.co.uk
admin@kennedyandboyd.co.uk

First published 1996 by Tuckwell Press, ISBN 1 898410 78 x
Reprinted 2008.
Copyright © Isobel Murray 1996, 2008.

ISBN-13 978-1-904999-89 8 Paperback
ISBN-10   1-904999-89 1 Paperback

This volume is dedicated to the happy memory of

Jessie Kesson,

1916-1994,

writer of the sma' perfect.

CONTENTS

PREFACE

SCOTTISH WRITERS TALKING is the first of a series of volumes which will feature in-depth interviews with Scottish writers. Isobel Murray and Bob Tait undertook the interviews primarily to record and preserve the voices and opinions of Scottish writers in a Sound Archive, but a major aim was always to edit selected interviews for publication in a way that would interest readers of Scottish writing, help or provoke students of that writing, and highlight the importance and achievements of postwar Scottish literature.

A minor negative impetus for this series has been the publication by Penguin of the *Writers at Work* series of volumes of interviews from *The Paris Review*, of which six volumes had appeared when we began, with a total of 75 writer interviews. These have *not* been used as models of method, but their choice of American and English writers, supplemented to different degrees by French, Irish, Russian, Danish, Chilean, Colombian, German and other writers, without a single Scottish writer ever being featured, was an inspiration by default.

The interviews presented here are of different lengths and often cover different areas: the length of the interviews has often been determined by circumstances, while it is the aim of the interviewers as far as possible to let the writer determine the direction of the conversation. They have been pruned of incidentals, but the editor has tried to retain the sense of the speaking voice of each writer, and not to pretend to present the material as if the subjects had written them. It seemed necessary to indicate when writer - or writer and interviewers - laughed (L): otherwise, serious misunderstandings might ensue!

The writers selected for the first volume include two, George Mackay Brown and Norman MacCaig, who tend to be very chary of talking about themselves and their work in interview, and therefore fairly lengthy selections from these rare and illuminating occasions are included.

The death of Jessie Kesson in 1994 was a grave loss to Scottish letters, and a personal grief to the interviewers, who found in Jessie not only a splendid interviewee but a good and lasting friend.

Her work is achieving ever increasing attention and ever higher praise. Her extraordinary background is well known - she was daughter of an Elgin prostitute, inmate of an Aberdeenshire orphanage and cottar wife in the North-East of Scotland - and this forms the basis or background for her highly praised fiction. Here it is interesting to compare her account of all this with the conversation of David Toulmin, author of *Hard Shining Corn*, *Blown Seed*, *Straw into Gold*, *Harvest Home* and others. Toulmin, as farmworker and autodidact, at one stage pursued his solitary writing career only three miles away from Kesson, each unaware of the other's existence.

The geographical spread of the volume is fairly wide: Kesson and Toulmin hail from the North East, and Mackay Brown is internationally identified with Orkney; McIlvanney comes from Ayrshire and bases his work there and in Glasgow, while MacCaig, who was born and lives in Edinburgh, also has a deep attachment to the wilds of North-west Sutherland.

ACKNOWLEDGMENTS

The editor owes heartfelt thanks to George Mackay Brown, the late Jessie Kesson, Norman MacCaig, William McIlvanney and David Toulmin for their patient and gracious co-operation, and to Iain Crichton Smith, who helped interview Norman MacCaig on his last tape: also to Bob Tait, whose contribution as sound engineer was invaluable throughout, and whose occasional well-judged interventions in the interviews prompted some of the most interesting responses from the writers.

This project could not have been undertaken without the financial help of the University of Aberdeen Development Trust, and the advice of its first two Directors, Alistair Smith and Elizabeth Hall. Grateful thanks are also due to Mrs Anne M. Robertson, Fiona Insch, Paul Bohan, Thomas Wratten and Professor David Hewitt.

Isobel Murray
December 1995

A SEQUENCE OF IMAGES

GEORGE MACKAY BROWN

We visited George Mackay Brown in his native Orkney in a little council flat in the heart of the port of Stromness. He was most kind and hospitable, but we knew that the interviews would not be easy for him. He did not hold anything back—indeed at times he offered remarks not directly prompted by questions: but he was uncomfortable, and at times rocked away in his old rocking chair, as if trying to get further away from the microphone. He hates talking about himself, and is allergic to modern technology, but he persevered with good temper.

BT   Stromness, Orkney interview with George Mackay Brown. April 10th 1984.

IM   Present: George Mackay Brown, Isobel Murray and Bob Tait. We all know each other a little bit, from the past. George and I were undergraduates together in Edinburgh, 1956-1960, and George also knows Bob, because he was editor of *Scottish International*.

GMB   Yes, that' s right. I' ve had a drink or two with Bob.

BT   This is true! (L)

IM   But we' ll try to fill in facts and so on. We've come to Orkney to talk to George partly because he doesn't really like leaving Orkney, and one doesn' t entirely blame him. George, would you like to tell us a little about your parents, what they did, the circumstances of your childhood?

GMB   Well, I was the youngest of six children and my father was one of the local postmen, and he was also a tailor actually, to trade, but he had to be a postman too to supplement the family income. And my mother came from Strathy on the north coast of Sutherlandshire, and she was a Gaelic speaker and came to Stromness to work in the local hotel when she was oh, just a girl, sixteen or seventeen I suppose. And that's it. I've stayed in Stromness all my life since, in this house or that.

IM   Did you learn Gaelic at all, when you were little?

GMB   No. No, I'm very ashamed to say I didn't.

IM   Did your mother want you to?

GMB   No, she didn't. (L)

IM   Oh well, you needn't be ashamed.

GMB   I'm very lazy you see about these things, otherwise I might have done.

IM   Your father, I think, was quite a lot older than your mother?

GMB   He was fifteen years older than my mother. He was about thirty-four when they got married and my mother was nineteen.

IM   And you lost your father when you were quite young?

GMB   Well not really. He died in 1940, just soon after the war was started. He was sixty-four when he died.

BT   And you were eighteen?

GMB   Yes I was, Bob.

IM   So, you went to school in Stromness, did you?

GMB   Yes, when I was five. I went very unwillingly to school. (L)

IM   Even before you got there, you weren't in favour of the idea?

GMB   Oh no!

IM   Why not?

GMB   Oh I don't know. I was a very sort of timorous child, and I didn't like to be away from the front door of the house, you know. (L)

IM   Did you get on well with your elder brothers?

GMB   Yes, fairly well. There was the usual little family quarrels and tussles and that, but no bad feelings.

IM   And when you did get to school, was it that bad? You did describe it in *Chapman* as 'the dark prison'. [See *Chapman*, Vol. 4, Summer 1976, p. 21.] Was it really that bad?

GMB   It was pretty bad. I think we all felt it, as far as I know. It was pretty bad. Much better now. But ach, there must have been one or two gleams too, I'm sure there must have been. But the overall memory when you look back—it was just like a prison house right enough.

IM   Did you enjoy things like reading when you were quite little?

GMB   Yes, I read, but I only read pulp magazines, you know, like the boys' papers that D.C. Thomson in Dundee put out: *Wizard* and *Rover* and *Hotspur*: I liked it best.

IM   And *Adventure*!

GMB   And *Adventure* yes! I didn't like the *Adventure* but we read them. We couldn't afford to buy them all, but the boys—my contemporaries—changed the magazines with each other you know. (L)

BT   Have you ever wondered, looking back, what you made of that peculiar world of the comic stories, because it was all about English boys—middle class, a different world?

GMB   I know! It's a different world altogether. It might have been on Mars, you know, and yet we were enthralled by these stories, we thought how wonderful—what a wonderful life these boys had: but as it turns out their lives were hellish you see, in these places. (L)

IM   You also at some stage were very attached to Grimm's fairy stories?

GMB   Oh yes, I loved them.

IM   Was that at the same time as you were reading the pulp magazines and so on?

GMB   That's right. Yes, I liked them. Then somebody gave me, or told me about, Andersen's stories you know, but I didn't like them so well at all. Of course, I was maybe a bit too young, eight or nine, they're a bit more sophisticated than Grimm's stories.

IM   I think sometimes also they're somewhat on the sentimental side.

GMB   Yes.

IM   I think children perhaps see through some of them. (L)

GMB   That's right.

IM   So, did you leave school then as soon as you reasonably could?

GMB   No, I went on to sit—they called it the Higher Leaving Certificate in those days, in 1940, it must have been, and I passed at the second attempt. I must have tried in 1939 too, but I did pass in 1940, and then it was a question of what happens then. I wasn't very keen on going to university really and that was the same year that my father died too, so I suppose it was thought that I should stay at home and find a job in Stromness, and I had no objections to that. And I worked for a few months in the Post Office, but then I got TB, and that put me out of the game for a few years you see. Off and on.

IM   The right years to be out, in a way, wasn't it?

GMB   Yes, oh yes. (L)

IM   Your father was very anxious that none of you would be involved in the war, or sent to France, all the rest of it ...

GMB   Well, that's right. He was horrified at that and we couldn't understand it you know, because we thought it would be a great adventure too—going to the war—but the old folk knew better, didn't they?

IM   Did any of your brothers go?

GMB   Three of them went, yes. And they all came back too.

IM   Well that was fine. Was the TB something completely unexpected, or had there been any in the family?

GMB   Absolutely. No, nothing, nothing. It was very strange. But then you see when I was about twelve I began to smoke quite heavily, Woodbines too—(L) a very strong tobacco and inhaled them you know, and I think that ruined my lungs in a way. I'm sure it did. Because before that I was quite an athletic little boy, and I was quite a good footballer and all that sort of thing, but about the age of fifteen or sixteen I couldn't run for anything because the wind was so very much restricted. (L)

IM   This is a very moral tale, George! (L)

GMB   It ended up to be tuberculosis anyhow.

IM   And did the illness make a big difference to your life in any large kinds of ways? Did it make you decide well I must have this kind of a life, or I mustn't do that?

GMB   I never thought about it really, I just lived from day to day. And in fact I wasn't very seriously ill either, you know. I was able to go about, and I wasn't confined to bed, well, after the first few weeks I could get up and about, and go anywhere I liked. But I began to read quite a bit then too. I'd stopped the *Wizard* and the *Hotspur* long before that, of course! (L)

IM   Did someone advise you what to read, or—

GMB   Not really. I just sort of ...

IM   Investigated the library shelves.

GMB   And bought some Penguins if I had a shilling or something to spare.

IM   And who were the people, if you remember, that most pleased you at that time?

GMB   Well, the one that first struck me I think was Forster's *Passage to India*; and that was a real revelation to me because it was so beautifully done and so perfect in form and everything. And then I went on to read them all—but there was only five of them, wasn't there? And short stories. And I thought they were all wonderful really.

IM   Alan Bold in his little book about you gives us a long list of writers he says have particularly affected you—I'm not quite sure whether this is a list that you gave him or ... [Alan Bold, *George Mackay Brown*, Edinburgh, 1978.]

GMB   I probably did—

IM   OK. Well I'll just ask you then, if you've got any particularly vivid thoughts about any of them? Forster was on it, and another one was Thomas Mann.

GMB Oh yes, Thomas Mann. I read *The Magic Mountain* in the mid-forties and I thought that was—

BT Very suitable for a man suffering from TB!

GMB Well, that's right, that's right. (L) And I thought it was a *wonderful* book too, and then of course you read all the other books. One or two let me down. I was very bored by one called *Lotte in Weimar*. I couldn't get on with that at all, but all his other books ...

BT What about *Faustus*?

GMB Oh, *Faustus*, yes. That was about 1949 it came out, and I liked that too, immensely. I've read it several times since.

IM And the others? Oh, Borges ...

GMB Borges, yes—but I think that's a later attraction. But I liked his stories too, so marvellous and economical, beautifully shaped, very mysterious stories too.

IM So when you were developing your own reading taste did you find yourself reading poetry?

GMB Oh yes, I read a lot of poetry. *The Golden Treasury* and ...

IM *Parnassus*?

GMB *Parnassus*, I read *Parnassus*, that's right. And I didn't like T.S. Eliot to begin with, but in the late 1940s—it's as if you've found a key, you know, into it and I admired him enormously too. And Yeats, of course.

IM Dylan Thomas is the other poet on this list ...

GMB Yes, ah well, not to the same extent, because I think he wrote a sizeable amount of trash too, but his best poems are absolutely magnificent, I think—wonderful. It seems to me to be either a hit or a miss with him, don't you think?

IM Indeed, indeed.

GMB Some of the misses are dreadful too. (L)

IM Oh, while I'm here—what about Scottish authors?

GMB It's rather embarrassing to say—but I liked Neil Gunn's *Morning Tide*—I don't like anything that he wrote after that.

IM Not even *The Silver Darlings*?

GMB No. In fact I made the mistake a few months ago of trying to read *Morning Tide*—I should have left it alone. I didn't like it much. It's a sad thing to say that too. Compton MacKenzie: I don't like him at all: I could never read him.

IM Grassic Gibbon?

GMB Yes, the first part of *Sunset Song*, I thought, but then, I don't know, it seemed to sort of degenerate into caricature, you know, and melodrama and that. But they say that he had to write at a tremendous pace to make a living and that, and he didn't have time to go back over his work.

IM   He finished it within a very few months of dying.

GMB   Well, there's no doubt about his talent all the same: when he was writing well, he could do marvellously.

IM   And what about these amazing Scottish poets, who if you didn't meet in your reading in the '40s you certainly, I'm sure, met in Edinburgh in the '50s?

GMB   Ah, yes. There was quite a few of them there, yes.

IM   Any of them whose work particularly impressed you?

GMB   Well, MacDiarmid's *Drunk Man Looks at the Thistle* ... I think it's far too long, but he should have given it to Ezra Pound, as T.S. Eliot did with *The Waste Land*, (L) because there's a lot of dead wood in it, I think, but it's magnificent in parts too, wonderful. And MacCaig, I like him too: but he worked on a very small scale, of course, but it's very good. But on the whole Irish writers, you know, have influenced me and given me more joy than the Scottish writers really.

IM   Isn't that interesting?

GMB   Yes, it might be the Celtic blood on my mother's side; I don't know.

BT   It's interesting about Gunn. Have you been able to put your finger on why Gunn put you off? I mean he is a Caithnessian, isn't he?

GMB   I know. I dunno what put me off: I was certainly enormously impressed when I read *Morning Tide*. I must have been about fifteen or sixteen then.

IM   When did you come across either the person or the work of Edwin Muir?

GMB   Not until about '46 or '47, and I think I read one or two poems in *The Listener*—that's where he published quite a few of his poems. And I found him difficult to begin with, but again once you got the key to it everything was simple and ... well, more or less, there's still depths there that's hard to plumb sometimes but I really was attracted to his verse ...

IM   And was it because you were attracted to his *work* that you wanted to go to Newbattle, or by the time you decided to do that, had you met him? [Newbattle Abbey College, a residential college for adult education, was founded in 1937. Its government grant was withdrawn in 1988.]

GMB   Well, I went to Newbattle because I was bored you know hanging about at home—and idle and that, and reading and drinking beer and that. So the Director of Adult Education, Mr Doloughan—he asked me if I would like to go to Newbattle because they were trying to get—the attendance at Newbattle was very low at the time.

IM   This was when it had just reopened after the war really, and I suppose ...

GMB   That's right. 1950. But I went to the second year, 1951, and that's the only reason I went. I think I thought a change would do me good. And to meet a few other folk.

IM   So Muir wasn't particularly a motive for going there, but he was a very important part of the experience.

GMB   Yes. Edwin had to interview all the prospective students, you see, and he happened to be on holiday that year in Stromness was it?—or Stenness—anyhow I had a meal with him in the Stromness hotel. That was the first time I met him: and that's it. He was very kind to me always, and, in fact, I suppose if he hadn't taken a sort of interest in me I wouldn't have offered anything to publishers at all.

IM   Yes, he did really most of the work about starting getting you published.

GMB   Yes he did. He sent a sheaf of my poems to the Hogarth Press, and I didn't have any struggle—birth-struggles—at all: it was amazing! (L)

IM   And that started a publishing marriage which has gone on uninterrupted really, hasn't it?

GMB   Ever since, yes: they've been very good to me too these publishers, I must say. [Mackay Brown remained with Chatto & Windus' Hogarth Press until 1987 when he moved to John Murray.]

IM   And did Muir at all inspire you to *write* this poetry? Or was it being at Newbattle that did it? Or ...? How do you think it started?

GMB   I liked Newbattle very much and it widened my horizons a good bit too, I must say. And then, every month or so we were required to submit an essay to Edwin. He was in charge of the English and an essay could take any form, you see—a poem, or a little play, or a story—anything: that was an essay. So I showed Edwin one or two poems, and he seemed to like them quite well, and that was that.

IM   So you started off very much as a poet; prose caught up quite a lot later.

GMB   That's right, I think that's true.

IM   It wasn't that Muir didn't like your prose, it was that you were writing poetry and he admired it, so you went on writing poetry?

GMB   That's right, yes. Occasionally I would sort of churn out a story too, you know, but I didn't attach much importance to the stories—or the poems.

IM   But it reminds me of the little story about Oscar Wilde and Walter Pater. When Wilde was at Oxford Pater said to him: 'Why do you always write poems, Mr Wilde? Why do you not write prose; prose is so much more difficult?' (L) Would you agree with that?

GMB   No, much easier to write a story than a poem, very much easier, oh, yes. I don't agree with Mr Pater about that at all. (L)

BT   Why is that? Why is it so much harder to write a poem?

GMB   Oh, because a much more complex thing I think, Bob, you know, so many more senses come into play, and it's difficult. Well, of course, it's so much shorter than a story, the average poem. It's got to be, well it's got to approach something like perfection before it's any good, whereas you've got more leeway in a story haven't you, there's a lot more slack to take up. (L)

IM   There is a different kind of difficulty though, if you try to write a sustained long piece of prose isn't there, a novel, because the difficulties of structure and so on are very considerable?

GMB   Yes. Oh that's right.

IM   You've written, you've *published* two novels at this stage, and I believe we're expecting another one fairly soon.

GMB   Next month. [*Time in a Red Coat*, 1984.]

IM   Do you find novel writing particularly difficult?

GMB   Not really.

IM   So why only three, is it just when a 'long idea' comes to you? (L)

GMB   Well, I'm sort of basically lazy I think, (L) and the thought of approaching another novel is well, it makes you sit up and think, but once I get going I quite like it then. It sort of hives off by itself and takes charge of itself and you follow dutifully behind, that's the good thing about it.

IM   Do you think when you're writing at all about your potential readership?

GMB   No, not at all.

IM   Or does your publisher ever try to persuade you to think about them? Simply on the grounds that conventional wisdom would say these days that novels were easier to sell than short stories, and that short stories were easier to sell than poems, for example. I think that's true, isn't it?

BT Yes, it *is* true, yes, there's no getting away from it.

GMB Yes that's right. Well I don't think I would ever have undertaken *Greenvoe* unless Mrs Smallwood—she was the Managing Director ...

BT Norah Smallwood.

GMB Yes, Norah Smallwood. She suggested that I should try a novel, so I'm open to any suggestions, (L) I sat down and sort of thought about *Greenvoe*.

IM Well, *I* think that *Greenvoe* is a very fine and interesting and innovative piece of work; are *you* reasonably pleased with it?

GMB No, I think it's awful in parts, you know, I'm so ashamed. (L) I really am ashamed of some of it, but on the other hand if I dip into it again, you know, which I do well maybe once or twice in the year, there's good things come floating to the surface that you'd forgotten about too, so I think it all sort of evens out in the end.

IM Just for my personal satisfaction can you give me an example of the things you're ashamed of or you don't like about it?

GMB Well I think probably in our next session I can.

IM OK. Well we've argued quite strongly that it's a very finely worked piece. [Isobel Murray and Bob Tait, *Ten Modern Scottish Novels*, Aberdeen, 1984. See pp. 144-67.] OK, we'll come back to that.

IM Let's go back momentarily to Muir, because, apart from anything else, among all the various pieces of your oeuvre which I've managed to read and usually buy, one of the things which is very difficult to get hold of is the little thing you wrote about Muir. [*Edwin Muir*, West Linton, 1975.]

GMB Oh yes.

IM So I daresay like me anybody listening to the archive may have a similar thing.

GMB It's a very slight piece you know, it's of no value at all. There was a French student and she came up to Orkney because she was doing her thesis on Edwin Muir, you see, and somebody sent her along to me, because she didn't know anything about Edwin at Newbattle. And it was a kind of anecdotal thing that she wanted, so I wrote this just in an afternoon or so, a few impressions you know of Edwin, and how he got on with his students and the other tutors. I sent it to the French student and that was that, (L) but there's a man in West Linton, what's his name? Anyway he prints these rare, not rare editions, but limited editions, yes, and hand-made paper and that, and another friend suggested, is it Frizzell?

BT   Yes, Alex Frizzell.

GMB That's right. Kugan Duval suggested that Alex Frizzell might do this essay, so he did about two or three hundred copies sort of numbered and signed.

IM   What aspect of his work is most important to you?

GMB His poems; but also some of his essays, I think, are wonderful. *Essays on Literature and Society.* There's two in particular: 'Politics of *King Lear*' was one of them: it's a marvellous examination of the motives behind *King Lear*, and 'The Natural Man and the Political Man': that's a fine essay too. He wrote some novels but I didn't like, well I read one of them, but I didn't like it at all.

IM   Did Willa Muir figure much in your acquaintance with Edwin?

GMB Well, she was a very kind woman you know. She had quite a sharp tongue in her head, but she could be enormously kind to people, very generous; and I liked her too, very much. She sort of guarded him right enough, all his life.

IM   As regards his work, one of the things which traditionally affects everybody, and I think it *does*, is the extraordinary autobiography he wrote, particularly in the first version *The Story and the Fable.*

GMB Yes. I know that one.

IM   Which seems to me on the surface to have a lot of resemblance to the ways you write and think. The idea that you've talked about—I can't remember where—about the pattern of things, and how in the simple story every battle becomes The Battle and every quest, The Quest and so on. [In fact, in *Magnus*, 1973, in Magnus' long meditation the night before his death, pp. 136-44.]

GMB Oh, that's right. That is very like Edwin, the same sort of idea was always there, in fact he called a lot of his poems 'The Good Town', 'The Transfiguration' and 'The Labyrinth' ...

IM   'The Combat'.

GMB And 'The Combat', as if there was one and only you see, but of course it covers every situation.

IM   Had you ever thought yourself of writing anything autobiographical?

GMB No, no fear. Oh no. (L)

IM   If you read Muir's autobiography, it's not because of anything that happened to him or anything he *did* that it is actually interesting, and I don't think one has to have a particularly varied or exciting life to write a fine autobiography.

GMB   No certainly not, there's that Irish one called *Twenty Years A-Growing* written by a young man, is it the Blasket Islands off the south-west of Ireland and he'd never, well he went across to the fair, but you know it's a beautiful book. [Maurice O'Sullivan of the Great Blasket wrote *Twenty Years A-Growing* in Irish. It was first published in English in 1933.] But I don't know, I think a lot of autobiographies are very distorted, they're all concerned to put themselves in a good light, and I think they nearly all must be distorted unless they're a good artist like Muir, you know, who can see himself objectively.

IM   You also seem in general very anxious not to speak out in the first person in your writing.

GMB   No, I don't like that at all.

IM   Even in poetry where many, many poets, including Muir of course, stand up and say 'I', you don't really. Have you ever?

GMB   I think I probably must have occasionally but it's not the normal thing at all.

IM   But the critics, the commentators, the reviewers, and the students, all tend to agree that 'The Tarn and The Rosary' is perhaps near to an autobiographical thing ...? [*Hawkfall and Other Stories*, London, 1974, pp. 168-200.]

GMB   Well, there is a sort of similarity here and there, but it's by no means a self portrait; it's just one or two facets that are the same. But no, I'm quite different from this man in that story.

IM   And for example, the long letter he writes in that story, to his friend, to try to explain why he became a Catholic. People have taken that as a kind of *apologia*, an explanation of your own position.

GMB   No, it's quite different; well, one or two things are similar I suppose.

IM   So you're fairly determined to keep your own self as tucked away as the ballad maker or the skald, or whatever.

GMB   Yes, I won't be writing any autobiographies.

IM   One other aspect of Muir—I wonder whether you're particularly influenced by his poem 'Horses'? I can't remember which of the Horses poems ...

GMB   There's three Horses poems, I think.

IM   Yes, exactly.

GMB   There's one very early one—about the farmboy watching the—

IM   The 'lumbering horses at the heavy plough ... '

GMB   Yes, it's a very good poem too.

IM   Yes, but I was more thinking of the post-atomic war one, because it occurred to us, when we were writing about *Greenvoe*, that there was at least a nice harmony between that poem about the war, and ending up with the horses, and the whole threat in *Greenvoe* countered all the time by the Horsemen and the Mystery of the Horsemen and all the rest of it—that it seemed *something* very vaguely in the same area, and also in *Fisherman with Ploughs*, is it not?

GMB   Ah yes, it is. I think, probably, that a little bit of Muir *did* get into these things, you know, I'm quite sure it did.

IM   It's quite interesting. It's such a powerful poem, I mean, it would not be surprising—

GMB   Oh it is. It's a very beautiful poem and a marvellous—one of the best he ever wrote, I think.

IM   And once he's given the horses in that poem that symbolic weight—it's somehow almost natural to take all horses as having it thereafter, isn't it? (L)

GMB   Oh absolutely, yes!

BT   Did a lot for horses! (L)

GMB   That's right! Edwin's story of his childhood is very beautiful, in that *Story and the Fable*—it's wonderful.

IM   His red christening dress!

GMB   That's right. (L)

IM   You didn't have a red christening dress?

GMB   No, no, we didn't have any christening at all.

IM   Really?

GMB   No. My parents—they went to the local church, you see, but they never became members or anything—and my father didn't believe in christening or anything like that.

IM   Didn't he? That's interesting. So rather like Sandy Stranger in *The Prime of Miss Jean Brodie* you didn't have something to rebel against?

GMB   No, no.

IM   You didn't have Calvinism to rebel against?

GMB   Well yes, when we went to the church every Sunday you see. And sat through these dreadful sermons on a Sunday after-noon—oh God! it was awful! (L) Because the sermons then were much longer than they are now—they were about twenty-five minutes or half an hour.

IM   And I bet it seemed longer!

GMB   Ah it seemed endless, eternity—and the bluebottles buzzing in the panes and that. Good God! (L)

IM   And did you have to dress up in your best clothes?

GMB   Oh yes. Sunday suit. They were never worn except on Sundays. That's right.

IM   Something one can detect in your work, as again in Muir's, not so much a positive dislike of the best aspects, or the most living aspects of Calvinism, but a sense of sadness and sometimes desperation at the damage that the psychological effects of Calvinism have had on Orkney, and Scotland.

GMB   I think it must have done, on the whole of Scotland.

IM   It's quite a strong thing in the portrait of Mrs McKee in *Greenvre* for example, I think.

GMB   Oh yes?

IM   All her struggling with all her guilts and all the rest of it.

GMB   Ah yes, I know. But occasionally I get the same sort of mental trouble as her, you know. Extraordinary. Not to the extent that Mrs McKee had it, but slightly, you know. And it makes a whole day unhappy—something from your past rises up—something that you've said or done. Very strange.

IM   And is it something that you *know* at a different time wasn't really a serious thing?

GMB   Oh it's not ... not serious at all.

IM   I mean obviously when Mrs McKee has these terrible states about whether or not Flora's teapot should have been given back to her ... This was obviously a very trivial thing to worry about.

GMB   Oh yes. Absolutely. All these things are very trivial, that you worry about. Terrible.

IM   But it seems to me that one of the advantages of moving from Calvinism to a religion like Roman Catholicism is that you can take things to a confessional and at least in theory leave them there.

GMB   That's right.

IM   The human psyche doesn't always, of course, work like that, but—

GMB   You never really get rid of Calvinism all the same. It's sort of bred in your bone, you know, and you're born into it, no amount of other religions will shift that, I know quite well. It's very difficult.

IM   Nonetheless, you did become a Roman Catholic.

GMB   Oh yes.

IM   When did you start being attracted to that?

GMB   Well, since a long while back. Since I was in my middle or late teens, I think, you know.

IM   And was it the services, the language ...?

GMB   No, it wasn't the services at all, because there's only one little Catholic church in Kirkwall you see. I'd never been inside that. No, it was just reading, I think, you know, things that I'd got from—well, rather like the character in 'The Tarn and The Rosary' I would— ... But the first thing that enthralled me— well, it's a kind of anti-Catholic essay by Lytton Strachey—you know his *Eminent Victorians*—the one on Cardinal Manning? And he obviously dislikes Cardinal Manning, and he plays him off against Newman, of course, and Newman is a sort of saintly man and Manning was a sort of political, ruthless priest. But anyhow when he goes back over the dogma of the Popes and how they contradict each other in this century or that—I found it absolutely fascinating, the whole thing. I got hooked in a very strange kind of way.

IM   Did it send you to reading it all up?

GMB   Not really. I read Newman's *Apologia*, but he deals with so many personalities, you know, round about Oxford in the early nineteenth century that I found some bits of it were very illuminating, but most of his reminiscences were pretty boring—you didn't know the people.

IM   So it was all literary Catholicism? But not wishing it any ill to start with, yes?

GMB   That's right.

IM   Were you affected by any particular Catholics, priests or lay-people?

GMB   No, I didn't meet any until I was 30 or so. I knew one or two Catholics, but they didn't influence me one way or the other.

IM   So that was just something that was going on under the surface.

GMB   That's right.

IM   Perhaps as much in reaction to some of the darker aspects of the Calvinism you knew ...

GMB   Yes, that's right.

IM   Almost you were sympathetic to Catholicism before you quite knew what it was?

GMB   That's right. It's true. I'd never liked the services, or the rituals, in that Presbyterian church; never appealed to me any time at all!

IM   Fine. Well, after you'd been to Newbattle, you took a little time out, I think, and then?

GMB   Well, I got another attack of tuberculosis, you see. I think some of these things were psychosomatic, you know, you just wanted for some reason to be ill, and you were. (L) I don't know, I'm sure that there's some truth in that, you know. After I left Newbattle, well, they don't hand you any certificates, there's no passport to a job or anything, and well, I don't know, I just became ill anyhow, for another year or two years or something.

IM   Were you still smoking?

GMB   Now, I think I was smoking a pipe by that time—yes, I was. (L)

BT   Compromise! Compromise!

GMB   Yes, I was smoking a pipe but I don't even smoke that now.

IM   Good. Do you miss it?

GMB   No, I don't miss it at all.

IM   That's another fine moral point. Give up smoking.

GMB   I missed it terribly to begin with for a month or two I must say.

IM   So you were ill and what, back here?

GMB   Yes.

IM   And when you left Newbattle did that mean that you knew that you could if you wanted go to university, although you didn't have bits of paper?

GMB   Well, in fact, I *did* have the Highers.

IM   Oh, of course, yes.

GMB   I had enough Highers to get into Edinburgh University in '56. Higher Latin and Higher Maths—you couldn't get into English unless you had Higher Latin in those days, Isobel.

IM   I remember, George, I remember! (L)

GMB   I did manage to scrape that at school anyhow.

IM   Yes. So you did Latin and Maths and English at school?

GMB   Yes and French and History.

IM   So, after the first Newbattle experience and after the second TB experience, you did eventually decide to go to university: were you meaning from the beginning to study English?

GMB   Well, yes, I thought I would, you know. Apart from everything else it was an extra year, you know, out of time—out of my time. (L) [An Ordinary MA would take three years, Honours in English, four.] I had no wild ambitions or anything.

IM   But it mattered in those days, didn't it? We had to know, a bit, because as I recall we had to do British History if we wanted to do Honours in English.

GMB   Ah, that's right.

IM   And we also had to do either Latin or Logic and Metaphysics or Moral Philosophy.

GMB   Yes.

IM   If you were like me you didn't know the difference between the last two. (L)

GMB   Oh, God, no! Philosophy—terrible. And they told us to read a thing by Kant—called the *Groundwork of the Metaphysical ...*

BT   *The Groundwork of the Metaphysics of Pure Reason.*

GMB   Aye, that's right. And I read it and it could have been written in Chinese for all it meant to me. (L) But anyhow I came by luck on a book—it was a kind of examination of this essay by Kant by a Jesuit priest—was it Copleston?

IM   Yes. [See Frederick Copleston's *A History of Philosophy*, 8 vols, 1946-66.]

GMB   And he was so lucid, you know, he was far more lucid of course than old Kant, and he took it to pieces and explained it so wonderfully, so I just read this Copleston and got through all right. (L)

IM   We had an amazing History course which as I recall was British History from 55 BC to 1914.

GMB   Yes, it could have been, Isobel.

IM   Did you pass that, George?

GMB   Yes.

IM   Well done! So did I, just. (L)

GMB   Some of these History lecturers were very good. There was a chap—he became a Labour M.P. later on—Mackintosh?

IM   John Mackintosh, yes.

GMB   —and he—the First World War and the early twentieth century—he was super.

IM   Superb on that, and he was speaking then to an audience of about 400 in a totally unsuitable—

GMB   The Pollock Hall, yes.

IM   Yes, Pollock Hall—a dreadful place, and yet he held his audience for 50 minutes at a time with no problem. So you felt you got quite a lot out of something like doing History there?

GMB   Oh yes.

IM   And in our second year of course as well as doing English Literature again you had to do English Language. How did you get on there?

GMB   Ah, not very well to begin with. The grammar of Old English and that threw me, I must say, but it was just a question of sitting there and grinding it up and once you mastered the grammar it became quite enjoyable then, I thought.

IM   And did you ever think, coming from Orkney and all the rest of it, of trying Old Norse?

GMB   I went to one lecture and then—it's just pure laziness you know—and I *do* regret now that I didn't persevere, but I thought I had enough on my plate anyhow. But I would have been pleased to know a bit more about Old Norse—because all the sagas are written in Old Norse you know.

IM   Yes. Does it worry you to read books in translation, essentially? Do you think that there are some things that are just so untranslatable that you lose ...

GMB   Well, poetry, I think is almost untranslatable, but I think you get a good lot out of novels in German and Russian; there's always *something* lost inevitably.

IM   I remember going to that first Old Norse thing and as I recall what happened was that we were given a wonderful advert for it—from Dr Schram, who told us how interesting the sagas were and everybody tore along because it all sounded so great, and the first thing Hermann Palsson said was that we all had to buy the grammar book and it cost a lot of money, and I think almost nobody arrived at the next time.

GMB   Yes, that put me off too I think. (L)

IM   So we finished our degree in Edinburgh. I found I got a great deal out of the Honours years in particular, with the very small group teaching, that kind of thing: did you like that?

GMB   Yes I did.

IM   I was a nervous lassie and didn't much like groups of ten or twelve, but by third year when there were three or four of us just, it was better. And obviously you enjoyed the Honours teaching a lot because after, I think, being ill again, is that right? Were you ill after you ...? Or did you just take time off?

GMB   What happened after 1960? I sort of hung abroad for a year or two doing very little. Living on Social Security and that (L), and drinking far too much; far more than was good for me.

IM   So when did the notion of doing some postgraduate work come up? Was it your idea or ...?

GMB   No, I don't think so, but somebody suggested it to me and I thought this was marvellous—you see another *two* years I got out of it. (L) That's right! I was so delighted and they gave you quite a good grant too, I mean I could live easily on it. Well, not in affluence or anything, but you got by.

IM   And was Hopkins a totally free choice ?

GMB   I chose it myself, because he's the writer in the smallest bulk you see. He's only written about fifty poems. (L) That was one of the reasons, but I did admire his poetry too, enormously.

IM   So what kind of thing were you trying to do with Hopkins?

GMB   Well, Miss Maynard was my tutor, and it wasn't a thesis, nothing
      like that. All she wanted was a kind of essay once every month or
      something like that, and they were pretty rough-hewn these
      essays I must say. I don't think she liked them very much. She
      was a nice woman but you could tell by the tone of her voice
      when she was disappointed. 'I don't think you've approached
      this in just exactly the right way.' (L)

IM   Do you remember what kind of way you *had* of approaching it?

GMB   Well, she would suggest, I *think* this is what happened, she
      would suggest a sort of a new line, or a new aspect of Hopkins so
      I just accommodated myself to that and ...

IM   And did you find yourself going away and reading critical books
      and all that or just ...?

GMB   No, I hate these things.

IM   Quite.

GMB   I read his letters, and there's a lovely Oxford edition in three
      volumes of his poems and letters and something else—

IM   Journals.

GMB   Journals, yes.

IM   Yes, he's one of the poets, I think, whose letters are extraordinar-
      ily useful. The times when he did write down a prose paraphrase
      of a poem, I find them often very useful.

GMB   That's right. But I'm still at sea about Inscape and—what was
      the other?

IM   Instress.

GMB   Instress, yes. (L) And I puzzled my brains over it and then he did
      sort of accent a few words, you know, a few lines, and it's not the
      way that I read it at all that Hopkins meant it to be read, you
      know, it's like a musical score or that. (L)

IM   Sprung rhythm, yes.

GMB   Sprung rhythm. And outrides was another thing. Outrides, I
      couldn't get the hang of that either! (L)

IM   And sonnets with six stresses to the line and eight stresses to the
      line.

GMB   And curtal sonnets and ...

IM   And did you find that sort of technical aspect of it less rewarding
      ...?

GMB   It wasn't rewarding for me at all, no. But I really enjoyed the
      poems very much. Looking at them in depth like that.

IM   I find the late sonnets very distressing, and I find myself lectur-
      ing on them to eighteen to nineteen-year-olds hoping they won't

understand them.

GMB Yes. Oh, I know!

IM Because the message of them is so desolate.

GMB Yes, absolutely. Terrible sonnets, really.

IM Yes. So you never thought of writing something for publication about Hopkins?

GMB No.

IM I suppose another reason why you might have been attracted to Hopkins, taking us back again to the religious question, was that he was not only a Roman Catholic but a Jesuit priest. Did you find him interesting from that point of view?

GMB Oh yes.

IM We haven't really talked about the time coming up to your being received into the Catholic church, have we? Can you remember what were the sort of ...?

GMB Well, let me see now: I was very late, you see—I was convinced more or less for a long time, and then I went to see the priest in Kirkwall, who was a very good man, a Jesuit, too, Father Cairns. We always had Jesuits in Kirkwall, and in Shetland and in the Hebrides, they send them to these desolate outposts, you know. (L)

BT Quite right!

GMB Yes. But there's something about them, Jesuits, I like them very much. Some of these Irish priests are a bit narrow, I think. (L)

IM So you went to the priest. You were received into the church in 1961, as I recall,

GMB Was it '61—I think that's right. It was just before Christmas I remember.

IM Yes. I was just wondering, you know, whether being an undergraduate, being in the city, having available a much wider range of churches, priests, services, and all the rest of it, made a difference?

GMB Well, yes it did.

IM Did you take advantage of your time in Edinburgh to investigate a bit?

GMB That's right. That's right. And—yes. I can't remember very much about it. But I used to go to Mass, you know, most Sundays right enough. And of course I had quite a few friends among the Edinburgh students who were Catholics too.

BT Was it a case of having a belief in God and trying to find the religion that most closely fitted it?

GMB I think probably that's right, Bob.

BT   And having for reasons that we've already gone into, to some extent discarded Calvinism.

GMB   It didn't take much discarding because I discarded it when I ... from the age of six or seven.

BT   So, I mean, in a way, Catholicism was there, kind of waiting—but were there very *positive* reasons why you chose to become a Catholic rather than say—

GMB   An Anglican or something?

BT   An Episcopalian—which would not be an unnatural thing in Scotland.

GMB   That's right. No. I never was much attracted by them. But it's really a mystery, because it hasn't sort of made me a better person, you know. (L) I don't know, but nevertheless.

IM   You talked about doing some reading and being—wouldn't he be furious—moved towards the Church by Lytton Strachey of all people. (L)

GMB   Lytton Strachey, that's right. Reading that essay was just like a—like the light opening—extraordinary.

IM   And he was making difficulties, and you passed that point, but when you decided to become a Catholic—were there any difficulties left, were there any things that worried you or ...?

GMB   Not really. I suppose there *were* one or two, but—but then it's impossible to be a hundred percent sure, you know, you've got to...

IM   And the Second Vatican Council which changed such a deal in the Catholic church: was that something that on the whole you welcomed or ...?

GMB   No, I didn't welcome it at all. The Mass in the vernacular and that—it's robbed the whole thing of all its sort of majesty and mystery and I don't know. So many things—it's wiped so many things away. Well, I suppose the heart of the thing is still there, but, I don't know, so much of its glory has been sort of shed—all of a sudden too. There was something very mysterious about the same language being used all over the world, you know, the Latin and you could drop into a Catholic church in Poland or the Argentine, you know, or anywhere, you had the same Mass all over the world.

IM   Does the concept of the Pope mean much to you?

GMB   I suppose it does—a sort of universal pastor and that. Yes it does, and vicar of Christ and that—quite exciting to think about.

IM   And so the ideas of authority and the importance of Popes and Councils: in a sense you're caught, because the Second Vatican

Council was a Council like the others, wasn't it? Could it be that much mistaken?

GMB   I know, supposed to be—yes, yes. The Holy Ghost is supposed to speak in the Council, I suppose.

IM   Or prevent serious error anyway.

GMB   Yes, that's right.

IM   So, now that you've been happily inside the church for more than two decades, is it something you just comfortably inhabit, or something that you still think about, worry about ...?

GMB   I don't worry about it.

IM   You don't belong to one, as it were, wing inside the Church rather than another wing?

GMB   No—no room in Orkney for wings you see, (L) you just go there and listen to Father Spencer.

IM   Well, O.K. so much for Religion. Meanwhile back at the ranch—even in Orkney—Politics.

GMB   Politics, yes.

IM   Somebody who's been reading your books might well say that there's quite a lot of overt sympathy for people over the centuries who have been oppressed, exploited and so on.

GMB   I suppose so, yes.

IM   A certain amount of anger against the, particularly absentee, landlords and things like that.

GMB   Oh yes.

IM   Yet when you come actually to concentrate on a laird (I never know how to pronounce it) in the short story 'Tithonus'—

GMB   I don't know how it's pronounced. (L)

IM   But when you actually concentrate on him, he's a very pathetic, sad figure and one feels sympathetic.

GMB   That's right.

IM   Despite the fact that he is certainly helping the community to die and doing nothing about it.

GMB   No, but he can't do anything about it, that's the way he's placed. He has a fixed annuity that gets steadily eroded in value as the years pass.

IM   Your father was quite strongly political, wasn't he?

GMB   Well he never joined any Party or anything, but I suppose you would call him a sort of Socialist you know—more a kind of emotional Socialist than an intellectual one.

IM   And would you call yourself one?

GMB   Oh well, very sort of vaguely, I think, yes.

IM   The one political, in the widest sense, subject that seems to me to pervade a lot of your work and to be the one contemporary issue on which one is always clear what you think, is the possibility of atomic or nuclear war.

GMB   Well everybody must think about that, surely, but specially since there's deposits of uranium, you know, just round Stromness mainly, and they might open a mine there any time I suppose, if they want to.

IM   And would you *do* something about that?

GMB   No, I'm too lazy to do anything. (L)

IM   You might write about it but that would be it?

GMB   Yes, I wouldn't march in any processions or anything like that, or fling myself in front of the guns or the horses and that. (L) Nothing like that.

IM   So the big political act was putting your name to the Scottish Writers Against the Bomb poster?

GMB   Oh, yes. Both of your names are on it. (L)

BT   Yes.

GMB   I've got it in the kitchen. (L)

BT   So have we!

IM   So you think of yourself as being too lazy to do anything about that; do you think there's anything to be done? A lot of people argue that we are just, you know...

GMB   Too apathetic?

IM   Hopelessly in the control of forces who will control us.

GMB   It's very frightening.

IM   Is there any point in being a Greenham Common woman, for example?

GMB   I admire these women enormously, I do. Though they have a bad press sometimes, but I think they're real heroines, these women, amazing.

IM   Do you think there is going to be a nuclear war?

GMB   God, I hope not! Well, I don't know. When you think of the road that we've taken since the beginning you know, and seen so much fear and uncertainty, I don't know. I think it's just actual fear that's keeping one or other of them from ... I can't see the Russians wanting to start a war: God knows they suffered enough in the last two wars, didn't they?

IM   You'd have thought so.

BT   Do you feel that it's more or less likely? I mean, do you feel that there's kind of an in—built attraction towards wars?

GMB   Well, there seems to be in the human race.

BT   Some people feel like the Greenham women that unless something is done then it is going to happen. Would you share that feeling?

GMB   Well, I must say I'm a bit of a pessimist about it, but still I think there's probably a Begetter up above—He's got some tricks up His sleeve surely, that we can't—that we know nothing about.

IM   But you said a minute or two ago surely everybody thinks about it: I think one of the tricks of getting by at all is that people manufacture ways of *not* thinking about it.

GMB   Oh they do, yes.

IM   And, that for a writer who is not in any obvious way politically committed, you've actually written *more* about that particular subject than most contemporary writers have.

GMB   It's such a fearful thing.

IM   And you've actually faced in *Fishermen with Ploughs* in particular, the concept of the whole thing happening,

GMB   Oh yes, that's right.

IM   And looking to see if there could be an after.

GMB   Yes.

IM   That's a frightening idea.

GMB   Terrible, terrible.

IM   And it's not by any means a simply optimistic piece, is it?

GMB   No.

IM   Muir's poem 'The Horses' is a single statement and it becomes very positive ...

GMB   Oh yes, that's right.

IM   But *Fisherman with Ploughs* is a very much more ambivalent and grey thing.

GMB   Dark grey.

IM   On the whole you don't write about contemporary subjects, but that is *one* that you come back to.

GMB   That's the one that overshadows everything, I think.

IM   And you talk somewhere about why you didn't write about the seventies, and I found it very unconvincing. When you do write about contemporary things I find it very interesting, and wish you'd go on. I was re-reading 'The Winter's Tale' I think it was, the other day.

GMB   Oh yes?

IM   A story that is told by the doctor and the minister and the visitor, I can't remember what he was, but you just talk in this doctor's voice and he's a *very* contemporary voice and I wanted to know more about him. (L)

GMB   Yes. I feel more secure, you know, writing, distancing myself a wee bit, and seeing things as they were maybe fifty years ago. I think it's a kind of cowardice right enough, but I find it difficult to write about Stromnessians or contemporary Orcadians, you know.

IM   Well, that was another thing I was going to ask. Do you find yourself using either all or part of people you know in the creation of character, or is that something which, if it happens at all, is so subconscious that ...?

GMB I think so. Yes, it's very difficult, but, yes, I think so, I don't understand how it happens that way.

IM   Well I think very often there's something to be said for leaving it that way. When you are starting to write something, do you know in advance whether it's going to be a poem or a story or whatever?

GMB Sometimes you do, I think, but it's a very mysterious kind of business. Of course, once you've started something that takes maybe a week, or two or three weeks maybe, there's no problem there once you get going, but if you're starting something new it's very strange, because you sit there and it's almost like a spiritualist séance you know. (L) And you sort of make your mind a blank, and you have a blank sheet of paper, and it's extraordinary! There's a kind of maybe a rhythm or an image that comes into your mind and takes root and everything grows out of that. It's very strange, I can't explain it, but that's the nearest sort of simile that I have for it.

IM   And sometimes the image or the character is something that recurs quite a lot in your work.

GMB Certain types do occur I think, Isobel, yes.

IM   For example, the tinkers.

GMB Yes, the tinkers, that's right. (L)

IM   I think you're very fond of those tinkers?

GMB Yes, but they're banished from the scene too you see, or at least they've become respectable. They used to live in tents, you see, all the year round, and come round the doors selling bootlaces and trinkets and everything, but now they've all got council houses or built houses of their own and they have shops and everything, and little businesses, (L) so that's another type that's vanished from Orkney. It's not quite so interesting you see as it was fifty years ago when I was a boy.

IM   But given you're writing about, say the Orkney of fifty years ago, the tinkers have a terrific appeal for you. Is it because you think that their view of everything else is somehow detached, somehow truer?

GMB   Well they're on the edges of society, they're not part of the establishment, you see, and they have a sort of wild freedom of their own, I think. And they're able to behave in a distinct way from us, who are part of the framework of the community. We are sort of restricted compared with these people.

IM   You almost sound envious. (L)

GMB   Well, I don't know. I couldn't live in a quarry, in a tent, in December and January, Isobel. (L)

IM   It doesn't sound ideal but you're envying some aspects?

GMB   Oh, yes.

BT   On the one hand there's a very strong feeling from your work of a desire for a very stable social order, where everybody does have their place and their function, and they're known from generation to generation almost *by* their function, and on the other hand, this interest, this appeal of those who are on the margins and enjoy a freedom. Are you conscious of playing this paradox?

GMB   I think so, I think you're quite right, Bob. And then the fishermen, the local fishermen too, well they *are* part of the community, but are still in a way, they are not quite so free as the tinkers, but they behave in their own—they have their own rules and laws, you know—they fight and get drunk and all that sort of thing but they're fascinating people too, you know, and their wives. But there too, you see, they go out to sea in bigger boats now, and they don't seem to me to be such rich characters as their fathers and grandfathers. And the language of Orkney of course, the dialect has been eroded—it's approaching more and more to sort of common English you know, and all the delightful bits are getting cut out and ironed out.

IM   You don't, though, *write* in dialect at all, do you?

GMB   No. Nobody would understand me. Well, I would feel that I wasn't free to. I couldn't do like Grassic Gibbon does, for example.

IM   He, I think, was particularly successful in managing to open out his dialect for the generality, but I was amazed to find the last time we were up even in Shetland, people writing in the Shetland dialect knowing that it was obviously going to be for a very small readership.

GMB   Yes. Well, but they have a much higher regard for their own culture and arts than the Orcadians do, strangely enough. Though funnily enough too they don't produce many writers: it's strange you know. Well the *New Shetlander* and that have some quite good writers, but most of their energy seems to have gone into music, and they're much better at that sort of thing than Orcadians.

BT   Nonetheless music's very important to you.

GMB   Well in a way, I don't understand any technicalities of it, Bob, but—

BT   But the musician as a type—

GMB   Oh yes, that's true.

BT   Is really very important.

IM   The fiddler, very often.

GMB   The fiddler, that's right.

BT   Why do you think that is?

GMB   I don't know. The blind fiddlers that used to come to the Lammas Fairs and that. Well, the Lammas Fairs have gone too, you see, but when I was a boy there was always this blind fiddler: I suppose it must have been the same man that came back year after year, and he would wander through the crowds playing this fiddle and I was fascinated by this man, you know, that couldn't see and produced, well it sounded marvellous music to me. And he would have a little cap and people would put pennies into it.

IM   Do you remember the music?

GMB   No, I don't remember the music. I think it must have been just sort of strathspeys and reels and that. Yes.

IM   I just wondered whether the strongest thing was the paradox of the blind man playing the music or the visual thing of seeing him, but not particularly the sound.

GMB   That's right. I think just seeing him, Isobel, is—that's the thing!

IM   Well before going on to ask you about Peter Maxwell Davies, just in an ordinary way: do you listen to music much?

GMB   Not much. It doesn't mean so much to me as literature, for example, and I know nothing, as I said to Bob, about the technicalities of it, but I don't really have an extensive knowledge of music.

IM   So, how did the relationship with Peter Maxwell Davies start?

GMB   Well he lives in Hoy, and I used to meet him occasionally, and he asked me once if I would object to him setting some poems, some of my poems, to music. And then the St Magnus Festival began away back about '76 or '77, I think, and he wanted to use that novel of mine called *Magnus* for the libretto of this opera that he was writing for the first Festival in Kirkwall, in St Magnus Cathedral too. But it wasn't really a 'cooperation, because he just took the words that he wanted, and I didn't really contribute, well, except that I'd written the novel, but I didn't work *with* him as it were, you know. He's put quite a lot of my stuff to music, but then I just provide the words, you know, and—

IM   And does he consult you in the course of it?

GMB   No.

IM   He just goes away with the words and adds what he likes.

GMB   That's right, yes.

IM   And do you recognise the finished product? Do you feel it's partly yours?

GMB   I suppose I do, yes. (L) He's very avant garde, Maxwell Davies, and to begin with I really didn't understand that atonal music, as they say. But I found that the more you listen to it, the more familiar you are with it, the easier it is.

IM   What about the perhaps analogous experience of seeing a television rendering of one of your stories? I'm thinking particularly of Bill Forsyth and *Andrina*.

GMB   Ah, yes. Well that's quite surprising too, I think, because they don't see it the way that I see it at all, you know. So it is very interesting to me from that point of view. And, of course, they've got to leave so much out. They were going to come this summer and do *Greenvoe* for BBC television, but I think they're short of money or something, for they postponed it for a year, I was quite pleased anyway. (L)

IM   And did Bill Forsyth consult with you when he was making *Andrina*?

GMB   No. No, he didn't consult with me. He knew exactly what he wanted to do. It was very strange, most film-makers want to exploit the natural scenery, but Forsyth did just the opposite, you know, he kept to dull backgrounds and that, fields and a few uninteresting—

IM   And so much of it inside the little house.

GMB   Yes, that's right.

IM   But, given that it wasn't the way that you'd seen it, did you enjoy seeing it?

GMB   Yes I did. I think he made a very good job of it.

BT   In what main respects did it differ from the way that you see it?

GMB   Well, I don't know, really you just see a sequence of images in your mind, you know, when you're writing the thing, and this was seeing some—I don't know how to explain it, but it's a different approach to the same thing. A different road to get to the same place.

BT   But you find this fact quite interesting in itself?

GMB   Ah, yes.

BT   You've also worked with John McGrath, another director, haven't you?

GMB   Ah, yes.

BT   Some years ago.

GMB   That's right. 1970 or something.

BT   Did he come close to seeing the same kinds of thing as was he too very different?

GMB   Not very different, but one or two bits were, you know.

IM   What was he doing?

BT   Again short stories; I don't remember—

GMB   Three short stories, that's right. One was 'A Time to Keep' and the other one was 'Celia' about the alcoholic girl.

BT   That was it. That one's coming back to me now.

GMB   And 'The Whaler's Return'.

IM   Partly because it's just occurred to me while we were talking about it, I was wondering whether Andrina herself, the girl, is a clear image in your mind, or whether it's partly her mystery that makes her very effective. It suddenly occurred to me that she's really somewhat like the Thora character in 'Tithonus' when we only see her through the laird, you know, and he never actually makes the big connection, he never speaks,

GMB   He never speaks to her.

IM   He never relates to her at all, and it's all about might-have-beens. There is a sense in which 'Andrina' is a story about might-have-beens as well, isn't there, very much?

GMB   That's right. It was a story I didn't particularly like, you know— it was written very quickly—in about half a day or something like that—and I sent it to Maurice Lindsay's magazine, *The Scottish Review*, and he must have picked it out of there you know, at random, but I think there were far better stories and more worthwhile ones to film but anyhow that's the one that Forsyth wanted—and I must say he did a good job of it.

IM   You talked about 'Andrina' being published as a short story—in a magazine: how much attention do you pay when you're putting together a volume of short stories—is it you that decides to do it?

GMB   No.

IM   Is it Chatto that comes along and says, give us a new volume?

GMB   Yes.

IM   And do you say OK here they are, or do they choose what they want? Is there any question about giving the thing a form?

GMB   I usually select about a dozen or so, but no, they have no form or pattern at all: and they just usually accept them you know, but there's no sort of underlying unity at all in any group of stories.

IM   Well George, just before we started to tape today you said wryly that you rather wished that you had held on to some of your books a bit longer—some of them you are less pleased with than others?

GMB   Yes, some poems and stories I wish I hadn't written or else kept them, you know, for a year or so. I rushed them too quickly into print and it's rather embarrassing ... (L)

IM   But didn't you also say in the introduction to the new volume of *Three Plays* that you write at your best when you just write, when you don't revise and rethink and all the rest of it?

GMB   Some things come fairly spontaneously right enough, and I think they tend to be the best things really, you know. I know if I work too hard on a thing I usually spoil it. I think a good thing is to let it lie for about a year, you know: if you come against some terrible knotted difficulty. And look at it again and you see at once where you've gone wrong. It's a very strange thing this— the subconscious mind, you know, was working on the problem all the time.

IM   So that's the sort of thing that happened with the Brandon the Voyager play: you worked on it and then when it wasn't working right you just put it aside? [See *The Voyage of Saint Brandon* in *Three Plays*, 1984.]

GMB   That's right. I just picked it up, you know, off and on. Every few months or so I did a piece or struck a piece out and it's still not wholly satisfactory. There's pieces you know that could be a lot better. (L)

IM   Brandon strikes me as a most delightful character.

GMB   Oh, yes, a wonderful man.

IM   Very warm and approachable though. I find him easier to relate to, for example, than Magnus, and it struck me that it's interesting what you're doing with the medieval account there, because there's a sense in which you've got a very twentieth-century kind of gentle scepticism operating on some of the medieval material...

GMB   Ah, yes. I know, there's a great gap between their minds and our modern minds, it's very strange. And yet children you see would be able to take that sort of thing and believe it wholly, but adults

	like us, well, we tend to probe and want to know why and ...
IM	Yes, very often you look for the child's response.
GMB	Yes.
IM	To all sorts of things. Is it the simplicity, or the freshness, or ...?
GMB	Oh, of course it is, yes. I think most writers and artists have that inbuilt in them somehow, or at least they don't lose their innocence in a way. They keep their childhood vision and perceptions all their days, if they're lucky!
IM	But you do write sometimes specifically for children?
GMB	Oh yes. I've done three books for children.
IM	And is that something different in itself, George?
GMB	Well, in that case you do sort of imagine the little audience of children you know. I've had lots of friends and their children, and relatives too, and I know all about telling them bedtime stories.
IM	Did you enjoy that?
GMB	Oh yes I loved it. But they were impromptus you know, you made them up as you went along, but it got me on the right wavelength for writing children's stories, I think.
IM	Although you often refer to or actually produce a child's response in an adult situation in your adult books to indicate where the adults are perhaps going wrong, you do write in a different way when you are actually specifically writing for children?
GMB	Oh yes, yes.
IM	One of the things that interested me, whizzing through a great deal of your work before coming here, was how some subjects seemed to come up more than once, and I was wondering whether on the whole that happens because you don't *like* what you did with it the first time, and you know you got it wrong and want to try again, or precisely there was more in it than you thought. For example, 'The Seller of Silk Shirts'.
GMB	Ah, yes. That's right.
IM	Which is a fine little short story.
GMB	(L) Yes, I know. And we expanded it in *Greenvoe* to form a huge chapter.
IM	And Indian Johnny's part in *Greenvoe* is really very important, isn't it?
GMB	Yes it is. The other one, the short story, was pretty slight, I think.
IM	Delightful, but not intended to be more than a little balance in contrast.
GMB	That's right.
IM	Whereas Johnny provides a—it's almost like the words at the

end of *The Waste Land*, he comes in with an Eastern kind of
religious vision.

GMB Yes, that's right.

IM   And guides the reader, I think, a bit, what to make of the people
of *Greenvoe*.

GMB Oh that's right. Sure! Seeing them from another viewpoint
altogether. Of course these Indian silk sellers used to be quite a
common thing, you know, when I was young, and even after the
war for ten years or so, they could come from door to door with
their heavy cases, you know, and by a mixture of cajolery and
superstition they would browbeat—they were very charming,
some of them—but nearly everybody bought something from
them, you know. (L) Like the blind fiddler, they were sort of
constant in my mind somehow—stand for *something* ...

IM   And there's a tinker couple, sometimes called Jock and Mary.

GMB Oh yes. (L)

IM   Sometimes not called anything, and they're very recognisable as
well. They recur, I think, because you're fond of them, and
because as we said they maybe represent something on tne edge
of society that has both a more liberated existence of its own, and
a more clear sight on the establishment.

GMB Yes, and they were very poor too, and they were on the edge of
poverty and destitution all the time, these people. And yet, they
had great style and character with it.

IM   And then, one of the other things that does repeat itself a great
deal is this fascination with Magnus.

GMB Yes.

IM   If I've got it right now, we start with him in *The Orkney
Tapestry*?

GMB Oh yes.

IM   Yes? And then you *wrote* the play, which has only just been
published, in 1984, as *The Loom of Light*.

GMB That's right.

IM   And only after that you wrote, more or less wrote to order, the
novel.

GMB Well, yes, the play was the sort of bare bones of the novel.

IM   And you've also written at least one short story, I suspect more—
there's one about his mother waiting for him to come back.

GMB Yes, 'The Feast at Paplay', yes, that's right.

IM   So it's obviously not just a question of being economical with the
material: you have a genuine fascination?

GMB Oh yes, I do have a great fascination for him right enough. He's a very mysterious character all the same, it's difficult to get to real grips with him. He's a medieval character. I suppose our outlook now is so different from theirs that there's a great chasm between us and them. But still, it's interesting sometimes to try and throw a bridge across it and enter into their situation.

IM His being a medieval character and his being a saint, are those differently important? Are there many saints in whom you are interested, or is it only the Orcadians?

GMB Well, I suppose I'm interested in them in a way, but Magnus is the one that is nearest to us and in place, and I wouldn't, I don't think I would tackle any other saints after Magnus. (L)

IM Well I don't mean necessarily writing about them. But with your sympathy with, and interest in, the tinkers, and the poverty, one might have thought Francis, for example, would have interested you.

GMB Oh, Francis, yes, yes. But he's too far away you see—you'd have to enter into the spirit of Italy at the time and that's impossible for me, I really would never dream of doing anything like that.

IM Brandon, on the other hand, do you think of him as importantly saintly?

GMB Well, I think he had this sort of childlike vision, you know, to a great degree and that was very interesting too. But also, I suppose, they would say he was such an old man—I suppose that a rationalist would say that his wits had gone astray, he was in his dotage but I don't entirely believe that either.

IM You marvellously refrained from being totally clear when directing the reader or the listener to that play about who's right and who's wrong. (L) To my mind when you're reading it, there is a sort of *sublime* lunacy about Brandon, because he comes to these very ordinary, almost squalid little scenes and *invests* them with his belief that this is the ideal.

GMB He throws the shining garment of the spirit over them. (L)

IM Yes. And, *I* thought that poor Malachi had the bad end of the stick—he was the theologian.

GMB That's right.

IM Who knew perfectly *well* that what Brandon said was this, that or the other *wasn't*; he could see it in all its everyday boringness.

GMB That's right.

IM But he gets punished with the long salt drink; doesn't he?

GMB That's right.

IM Is that fair? (L)

GMB But it's not me that punished him, it's the tellers of the original tale. (L)

IM   And all this business of seeing things differently from what they clearly are, is that all quite manifest in the medieval version?

GMB   Oh yes, it's very much more surrealist than that version that I've done there. Because it never questions anything, it accepts them, just as a child would do, you know. A good story this! But of course in literature Blake had the same, well, the same *kind* of vision as old Brandon, you know. He saw what really mattered in everything, all the objects and things that he saw around him.

IM   Yes, it's almost like: 'What is truth, said jesting Pilate'. The nature of truth in this play is what interests me because it starts off, and again I'm not sure whether this is in the original, with Brandon confusing two people, the Abbot Birnius, a very holy man, and the poet Byrne, who is some kind of brother to your tinkers.

GMB   That's right, well he's a wandering sort of fairground man, yes.

IM   And your blind fiddler, and all the rest of it.

GMB   Exactly, he is.

IM   He's an artist.

GMB   Exactly. That's right. He doesn't come into the original story at all, of course, no, but Birnius comes in, you see, and tells Brandon about this wonderful place that he's been to, the land of the young, and Birnius [slip of the tongue for Brandon?] is fired with the desire to go there too but Byrne doesn't come into it.

IM   So that's an addition that *you've* made?

GMB   That's right.

IM   Brandon's vision then is partly a religious vision, and partly a— very much a secular poetic one.

GMB   Yes.

IM   The two brought together, and yet at the very end when Brandon *has* begun to realise, partly with the death of Malachi, I think—

GMB   Oh, that's right. That shatters him, of course, and lets in the light of common day and that, and common sense. Yes, yes. (L)

IM   Then, he gets to 'the isle of the young'—and what does he find there but a—?

GMB   Just an ordinary island of ordinary people.

IM   And the longest speech of the play I think by a long way—from a very self-pitying laird.

GMB   Well, I don't know if he's self-pitying—but he is a sort of greedy man and he rules his islanders with a rod of iron. That's right. But, of course, in the medieval account, it was glorious beyond description, this place that they came to.

IM   So you changed it dramatically?

GMB   Oh yes. Well it is glorious in old Brandon's mind you see and ...

IM   This is what interests me—he says at the end something like 'Man, in his little kingdom, in all his frailty and glory' [142]. Are we then to think that he has—that what we've seen, real life, ordinary people, *is* man in all his frailty and glory, or is it only Brandon in his kind of sublime vision that has seen that?

GMB   Oh yes, but of course to the saints everything is afire with God, as they said. Even the commonest objects and people.

IM   And, at the end when Brandon is dying, and he comes to the, is it the fourth name that begins with a 'B'?—it's all very confusing—Brian.

GMB   Oh yes, the scribe, yes.

IM   He is told not to insist on putting too much truth into his story.

GMB   Yes, that's right. Well, what common or garden folk regard as truth—nonsense, after all. Yes. But all these names are similar to one another, Byrne and Brian and Birnius, so that he confuses them in his sort of wandering—he's dying, I suppose, and he keeps confusing them in the last scene of all, just as he did in the first scene, of course.

IM   It seems to me an absolutely marvellous subject for a play for voices.

GMB   Well it's going to be broadcast on Easter Day, actually, on Radio 3.

IM   But a play for voices is exactly right because—

GMB   Oh yes.

IM   Because you wouldn't want to have it on stage.

GMB   Oh no, it could never be staged. Oh no, no, that's impossible.

IM   Or even filmed, or anything, because what the mind can do— seeing the two things at once; what Brandon is seeing and what everybody else is seeing—you couldn't actually have that operating on any medium except radio.

GMB   That's true.

IM   I think it's an ideal one. You have written plays for the stage though, haven't you?

GMB   One or two. But they weren't conspicuously successful! I don't think they worked very well. I think to be a good dramatist you have to actually work at theatre, work and be a part of a group or something, like Shakespeare or Ibsen and Molière. They knew the whole craft, from the beginning and all the techniques available to them. But I don't know anything about that at all, so I think that's why my plays never take off. (L) I think they're probably better read than seen on the stage.

IM   Yes, almost pageant in some ways, I think, from time to time.

GMB   Yes.

IM   One of the things, it seems to me, endearingly to crop up in almost everything you write in different ways is comedy. You've never been somebody who thinks that there is only one place for comedy and when you're being serious it's no use.

GMB   I suppose that's right!

IM   Do you enjoy comic writings by other people?

GMB   Oh yes. Evelyn Waugh, for example. And Wodehouse, I used to read him when I was a boy. And, who are the other ones? Brecht, of course, has got a great streak of humour in him too. I like his plays very much, by the way.

IM   Yes, oh we haven't mention Brecht. No.

GMB   Although I'm diametrically opposed to him in beliefs and outlook, but he's a master dramatist all the same. No doubt.

IM   And do you enjoy going to the theatre?

GMB   Well we don't get much opportunity here you see Isobel, but when I was in Edinburgh maybe once or twice I went to the theatre but I'd rather go to the pub.

IM   So you're talking mainly about *reading* Brecht?

GMB   That's right. That's right. I went to the pubs rather than to the theatre. Course you see plenty of theatre sometimes in the Abbotsford and Milne's bar too ... (L)

BT   Indeed!

GMB   Spontaneous theatre! Yes.

BT   Well scripted!

GMB   Wild, melodrama and comedy and farce of every kind.

IM   A place too where a writer could perhaps find a lot of material?

GMB   Oh yes, sure!

IM   You haven't set anything in a pub yet.

GMB   One or two stories.

IM   Yes, of course.

GMB   'The Whaler's Return'. Of course that boy gets drunker and drunker as he tries to get home from Birsay to Stromness (L)— 18 miles and he's sort of dragged into every alehouse along the way or he goes there voluntarily. (L)

IM   And there's the story in which the girl lives in the pub and it's in *A Calendar of Love*, isn't it? [The title story in *A Calendar of Love*, 1967, pp. 9-40.]

GMB   That's a pretty awful story. I wish that one had never been published.

IM   Why?

GMB   I quite liked it at the time but I can't bear to read it now. I think
        it's so phoney, somehow.

IM   Can you at all put your finger on it?

GMB   Well, I don't know. (L) I think the people seem to be sort of
        caricatures and the dialogue's not good.

IM   Well now I would have said they were certainly not the most
        realistically complex, but neither did they seem to be meant to
        be. On the one hand you've got a very converted fisherman
        Peter, and on the other hand a right roisterous womaniser.

GMB   Terrible, and they're both after the same girl, of course.

IM   Yes, it seemed to me to be an example of your enjoyment of
        pattern.

GMB   Well, I suppose it was really, that started it off but the end result
        as a whole is not really very good. If anybody wanted to put it in
        an anthology I would withhold permission. (L)

IM   Would you? Ah, that's strong. Are there many stories that you
        would feel that strongly about?

GMB   Maybe a dozen or so, I suppose, yes.

IM   And you said that there were some things in *Greenvoe* that you
        much disliked now?

GMB   Yes, that's true. I think that most of them were sort of caricatures
        too you know, and the only real person, as far as I'm concerned,
        was the minister's mother, Mrs McKee; she was a sort of
        rounded character, and I much enjoyed writing about her, but
        lots of the other ones you know, they were just—they're not real
        people at all—card-characters and shadowy.

IM   Yes, but I'm sure ...

GMB   Maybe they serve their turn, I don't know, but Mrs McKee—

IM   They were not intended to be the same kind of character as Mrs
        McKee.

GMB   No, but she was supposed to be one of these sort of minor
        characters too, but she suddenly took off by herself, and began to
        grow and develop in all kinds of ways, so I really enjoyed writing
        that.

IM   But I find her a most powerful character and the whole idea of
        her and her internal story, her mental assize—I would love to see
        you writing *more* about people having this kind of internal
        turmoil and experience of it. Those of us who come from the big
        city and just envy you your wonderful pastoral Orkney may
        sometimes feel that characters in Orcadian, often historical,
        situations are delightful, but not close to us, whereas it seems to

me that we recognise in Mrs McKee, everybody to some extent, some of ourselves.

GMB Yes, I think so, too. And I could write about her more convincingly because to a much lesser degree I sort of suffer from the same mental situation myself, you know. Occasionally, just off and on, you go through black periods and that, for no apparent reason.

IM I find Mrs McKee one of the most fascinating things you've done. You know?

BT Indeed.

GMB Yes, I liked her too, I'm not ashamed of Mrs McKee.

BT She's an intrusion into your usual scene with this tormented Calvinist guilt.

GMB Yes.

BT She's very unusual in that respect. You don't often have characters who have that sort of problem.

GMB No not really, Bob.

BT Isn't that interesting? And she took off and developed into this very large part of *Greenvoe*. And associated also with the other theme. I mean, she blames herself, at the end of the day, for the coming of their apocalypse.

GMB That's right. Of course in that situation everything bad that happens around you—you're to blame for it, you see. It's very strange.

BT It's as if she had spirited it up.

GMB Yes, that's right. Yes, yes.

IM Astonishing powerful lady! And I don't think there's anything *at all* wrong—I think it's very interesting, the way you construct that book; with some characters so simple that you call them caricatures, but they're not intended to be anything else.

GMB No, not really.

IM When you've met Mrs Evie for two pages, you know everything you need to know about her, but she remains entertaining.

GMB Oh yes.

IM And a very economical way of telling the story.

GMB There are plenty of Mrs Evies around here—not plenty but there are a good few. I don't want to libel my fellow-islanders. (L)

IM Perhaps one of the harshest pictures in *Greenvoe* is the appalling Miss Fortinbell, who comes along with the seed pearls in her hair and her kilt to distribute the welfare clothes. (L)

GMB Oh, yes, the Laird's sisters and aunts and that, we've got *them* too. She's a particularly awful example of it, and most of them are much nicer than that actually, though they do speak with that sort of English public-school accents, you know, and they tend to shout. You can recognise them in the streets in Kirkwall or Stromness because most of the Orcadians speak in quiet voices you know, but they don't, they shout as if they were roaring into a tempest. (L) It's very funny: whether it's the schools they went to I don't know, or maybe it's just that they think they're far more important than everybody else, I don't know.

IM   And you've got fishermen in *Greenvoe* who seem quite satisfactorily, I think, individual for the purposes of the story, and at the same time symbolically standing for all—Samuel stands for religious fishermen, whereas Bert Kerston stands for secular fishermen perhaps, and the Skarf for the political one, not that he does a lot of fishing. I was very impressed by the character of Samuel, and what happened to him.

GMB   Samuel, oh the religious fisherman, oh yes.

IM   And the strange experience he has when ...

GMB   Oh that's right, when he's almost drowned. Yes, yes, I suppose that's quite—I quite enjoyed writing that too, but—

IM   I thought it was a most interestingly sympathetic picture of a deeply Calvinist man.

GMB   Yes.

IM   Samuel never allows himself to say anything nasty about anyone when he's 'alive' but when he goes through his equivalent of Vanity Fair, when we think he's dead and he thinks he's dead, we learn what he thinks of all the people, his suppressed thoughts about them—

GMB   Yes, that's right.

IM   Interesting man.

GMB   I know. But when *Greenvoe* was published two or three reviewers said that it was—ach—that it was too like Dylan Thomas, *Under Milk Wood*, you know, to be really good; it was too derivative and imitative. But I had never really thought about *Under Milk Wood* while I was working on it at all. So it wasn't really. But I can see how some people might see a sort of a parallel in it.

IM   I can see how they would, if your characters were all on the same level: because the Thomas characters are all brilliant vignettes all about equally important. But it seems to me that one of the fascinating things about *Greenvoe* is that you make a mental compact to yourself that you can have someone tiny as Mrs Evie, something as uncomplicated as Mrs Evie, and you move through

considerably more complex characters like the religious fisherman Samuel, or the Skarf, and then you've also got this unexpected in-depth picture of Mrs McKee, so that *either* one might
argue that the whole thing is wildly disjointed—

GMB   Well, that's it! I think Mrs McKee unbalances the whole thing,
you know. She assumes too big proportions really for the shape
of the whole book, but I don't know: I wouldn't unwrite it
anyway or cut her out in any way.

BT   Oh no!

IM   Oh, no absolutely not. No, apart from everything else we've
written our chapter! We defend her. [*Greenvoe* chapter in *Ten
Modern Scottish Novels.*] (L)

GMB   Oh good.

BT   Oh, very strongly.

IM   In fact I think the character I would find hardest to cope with in
Greenvoe is the Skarf.

GMB   Yes. But there are people like him around too, strangely enough.
Very poor men and that, and they're very well read you know,
and they think deeply about things, though the Skarf I think was
on the wrong lines with his investigations and that, but there
are—I've met several Orcadians like that.

IM   Yes: it's more that perhaps you're trying to do too many things
with him.

GMB   Yes I think so, and this business about writing the sort of
impressionistic history of the island and that—that's a wee bit
far-fetched. (L)

IM   A wee bit far-fetched.

GMB   But it seemed to be a sort of unifying thing you know to bring
them all into the pub and get him to recite his pieces there.

IM   And it also goes with the things you say in *An Orkney Tapestry*
about how if you don't connect present-day Orkney to its roots
and its history you're not really telling the story. [See *An Orkney
Tapestry*, 1969, pp. 19-21]

GMB   Yes, that's right. It's so important, I think.

IM   But I felt that the Skarf—perhaps he had too many jobs—he had
to do this impressionistic history, which is fun and included
some things—some gentle anti-Catholic satire, anti-medieval
Catholic satire—is it wrong to eat whales in Lent?

GMB   Oh yes.

IM   That's fine. So perhaps you can also have him as this—what is it
he calls himself?—a Marxist-Leninist-Maoist—but he also
sometimes seems to me to have a touch of the authentic Mackay

Brown voice as well,

GMB   I suppose he does.

IM   When he starts describing the palace of Earl Robert Stewart: not a chapel anywhere. Why does the Skarf care? (L)

GMB   Oh yes. That's right.

IM   It is brought together in the end, I think, it says on his card in the card-index file that his ideas are 'tinged with mysticism'. (L)

GMB   That's right, yes. (L)

IM   And really, I think, I would like to have known more about him earlier on. I was sad when he committed suicide, and I think it was only after that that one heard about his illness and various other things. I'm being hopelessly unrealistic: on the one hand, I'm asking for him to be a more complex character and on the other hand I'm saying he's doing too much already! (L)

GMB   I know. He was quite a difficult character to work with right enough. But I quite enjoyed doing it, all the same. But I realise that he didn't come off like old Mrs McKee.

IM   No, I don't think so. You write every morning, yes, basically?

GMB   Yes.

IM   Do you know—well, say—do you know *now* what it is you'll be writing tomorrow morning?

GMB   Oh yes, because I've started something you see, that's no difficulty. It's when there's something new to be done that you sort of sit for a while and wait for the spirits to come into your séance. (L)

IM   Do you need, or at least, respond happily to deadlines?

GMB   Oh I respond quite well. In fact, they make me work very well you know, deadlines. It's a funny thing that. And I can produce what's wanted in very good time, usually a week or a fortnight before.

IM   So that almost you want people to ask you to do this or that?

GMB   Oh, yes. Well you see they tell me what to write or what the subject is. And it's a thing probably I would never dream of doing on my own bat. When it's given to you—there's a job and do it—I can respond at once. It's very strange.

IM   Could you give me an example?

GMB   Not at the moment, but maybe before the afternoon's out. (L) Well, you're asked to do things for the BBC sometimes, you know, stories and ...

IM   They would actually say would you give us a story about this or that?

GMB   Yes. And about 2000 words long or something like that.

IM   Yes, that's interesting. I mean, I knew, obviously they ask about—they give you a time—a word-length, because they're looking for times, but I hadn't realised that they would say, can you give us a story about, you know, fishermen or ...

GMB   No, they don't really set the subject, but somehow they spur you into action—you know, all these commands—do this for such and such a date! (L)

IM   You still do the journalism, weekly is it?

GMB   Yes, for the *Orcadian*, the newspaper. But it's just a bit of fun really you know, and you write it in about twenty minutes or something like that.

IM   And do you ever have a problem writing it?

GMB   No, never. Occasionally you sort of wonder for a couple of minutes (L) or so, but there's such a deep barrel of things—of course the seasons sometimes dictate it you know, or you write one or two little spring articles about this time of year, and coming on for Christmas you give them Christmas stuff and New Year stuff and all that sort of thing. (L)

IM   And do you get feed-back from that?

GMB   *No.* I never write controversially—I hate getting caught up in political arguments and religious arguments so I studiously avoid this.

IM   No but—it doesn't have to be argumentative—does nobody stop you in the street and say I was interested in what you ...

GMB   Oh yes, occasionally, yes, and say they didn't like that this week and it was rotten and things like that, and give us something that you did six months ago, or something like that. You always get some feed-back like that too.

IM   And do you like that?

GMB   Oh yes. It shows that somebody's interested, but very few people write letters to the Editor you know, strangely enough. Well not strangely enough, because they're not controversial at all.

IM   So you get more direct and more ordinary human feed-back from writing for the *Orcadian* than you do for writing for Chatto really?

GMB   Well, of course, you sometimes get letters too from readers and that. And if you've had something on the radio or the television. I was in bad odour when these three short stories were done about twelve years ago. People weren't speaking to me on the street.

BT   Really?

GMB   Oh, yes, that's right. But they forgot in a month or two, they came back again, it was quite nice.

IM   Did you give them a bad image?

GMB Absolutely! Some of them were really shocked about this—
     especially about this alcoholic girl you see, Celia, but the Doctor
     in Kirkwall said to me: 'My God,' he said, 'there's about twelve
     Celias,' he said, 'in my list, you know alcoholic young ladies.'
     (L)

IM   Part of the Mackay Brown legend, perhaps one of the central
     planks of the Mackay Brown legend, is a tremendous antipathy
     to progress.

GMB Oh, to progress. (L) Ah, well, if it wasn't for medical progress I
     would probably have been in my grave twenty years ago; so it's
     just a sort of stance that you take up really, in order to fight for
     something that you truly believe in. People are worshipping all
     these false Gods nowadays, progress and money and mammon;
     everything, even in Orkney. These television advertisements
     and that, you must get a better car, and a better washing machine
     and all that sort of thing, terrible!

IM   I was perhaps surprised to see the television set in this room at
     all.

GMB Ah well, the only concession I've made is that it's black and
     white you see. (L) I keep one step behind. I'm not in the
     vanguard of culture.

IM   You wouldn't see that as hypocritical compromise? (L)

GMB Oh well, I suppose it is. I do enjoy some plays and that, I must
     say. No, I'm not against progress, or I wouldn't have a coal
     fire—I suppose I'd have peats, and I'd be living in a little croft on
     the edge of the moor with a few hens around the door, so no. But
     it's just that you've got to take up a certain position I think, and
     keep people in touch with their roots and sources. They tend to
     forget them. They're way out on this wasteland of the twenty-
     first century.

IM   Do you think though some people have roots to be kept in touch
     with?

GMB Most of the Orcadians have you know, some of them have been
     on the same farm for nine hundred years you know, direct
     descent.

IM   Oh, of course. But I'm thinking more of people who—you're
     published in London, and very, I think, on the whole, very
     respectfully reviewed by national, international press, don't you
     think some people perhaps feel: this man is always telling us it's
     very easy and simple, get back to your roots—but I haven't got
     any.

GMB   Well I guess so.

IM   My parents bore me in a city, and they were born in a city, and ...

GMB   Yes, but still if you keep reminding them of the first essential things and the four elements and that, you can' t go very far wrong and you *may* do them a bit of good. (L)

IM   So it's not necessarily an insistence on Orkney itself. It's sometimes Orkney is a symbol of kind of basic simplicities and realities?

GMB   Not now, fifty years ago it was.

IM   O.K. It's precisely this Orkney of fifty years ago you're talking about. It's a symbol.

GMB   That's right! That's why I like to write about the people who lived then, that I knew when I was a boy, and their language was far richer then, most Orcadians still are. But I don't know: they've lost something that their grandparents had: there's no doubt about it.

IM   Don't you think that it's partly also, the coincidence of what you knew when you were a boy—the vision you saw them with—that everybody has perhaps a time when they see more clearly, more freshly, more intensely the people around them?

GMB   I suppose, maybe it's distorted a wee bit to that extent, you know, that you see through the rose-tinted spectacles and that. But I don't know ...

IM   Not distorted, that's a bad sense. It's more like the St Brandon thing. You see better, truer, perhaps.

GMB   Ah that's right, yes, I think you're quite right. Because the people were very much poorer in those days too. But somehow they were more real human beings than, well—I hate to make comparisons too—and the people nowadays are all right really, but it's just that they've let the world come in a bit too much you know. Maybe Alan Bold's right about that sonnet after all—'the world is too much with us'. (L) [See A. Bold, *George Mackay Brown*, pp. 3-4]

IM   It's a funny sonnet really for you, rather than for me, because I wasn't born by the sea. I mean there's something so extraordinarily artificial at the end of that sonnet about old Triton blowing his wreathed horn. I think the first part worked. (L)

GMB   It's fortunate, in a way, to be born near the sea and have farms in the hinterland and that, and it's the contrast between the farms and the fishermen—it's very stimulating all the time. I found that it has given any richness that my art has, you know, great constant streams coming out all the time. And then you'd get

quite a few of the poorer ones, you know, they were crofters and
they were fishermen at the same time too, you know.

BT   Fishermen with ploughs?

GMB   Fishermen with ploughs, that's right.

IM   Would you like to tell me a little bit about this forthcoming
        novel, *Time in a Red Coat*?

GMB   Well, the theme of it is war, and it's treated in rather a strange
        way, because there's this girl who was born in China, somewhere
        vaguely in the East, you know, and she was born during the
        beginning of a war after maybe hundreds of years of peace. And
        this same girl, she wanders through history for about two thou-
        sand years maybe, and gradually comes westwards through Asia
        and Russia and into Germany and all different parts of Europe
        about the time of Napoleon: and finally—she never seems to age
        very much—maybe just a year or two—and finally, she comes to
        Orkney in the last two chapters, and that's about the basic thing,
        but there are one or two sort of complications, you know, that it's
        very difficult to speak about (L) really, there's one or two
        elaborations you know, ...

IM   And she has a certain kind of second sight?

GMB   Yes, she does. She has enormous gifts of being able to penetrate
        into the sort of roots of situations and that, and she can see into
        the future; into the wars to come—which God forbid, because I
        don't think many of us will be alive to tell about it. But anyhow,
        in the end she becomes a crofter—fisherman's wife—(L) where
        else could I end it?—in some little island in Orkney. And in the
        end she does grow old—she does age—when she comes to
        Orkney, and she ends up as an old, old woman doing a kind of
        monologue or soliloquy.

IM   And really the whole book is that monologue or soliloquy, is it?

GMB   No, just the last chapter.

IM   And it's got this intriguing title *Time in a Red Coat*. Red, why
        red?

GMB   Well, red for war I suppose really. When she starts her journey to
        the west her coat is all white, and it gradually gets splashed and
        clotted with blood and rust and all kinds of soilings and in the end
        it is completely red.

BT   Just a point about that: a redcoat is a name for a British soldier—
        did you have that in mind?

GMB   No, I didn't, Bob, but now that you've said it, I'll lodge it firmly
        in the archives up on top here. (L)

BT   The thing is a lot of people are probably going to go off and say oh he's talking about the British army, imperialism and all that.

GMB   Not really, but it's very—I think it adds to the sort of weight of the tale right enough, now that you've remembered that. I should have said it, but it's too late now. Thanks to Bob Tait. (L) For enhancing the title so nicely.

IM   Are titles important to you?

GMB   No, I'm very bad at titles actually, Isobel, and I have to sit for long whiles and think about them.

IM   For each poem, each story, as well as for a collection?

GMB   Well, some of them are simple enough, like *Greenvoe*—write about the little village and *Magnus*, of course, that was simple too because it was about him, but this one was a bit more difficult.

IM   Right. Now, for example, your play about Magnus was called *The Loom of Light*.

GMB   That's right. It's weaving: that metaphor comes into it over and over again. And in fact that's part of the title for this new novel too.

IM   And some sorts of connections with the image of the seamless garment.

GMB   Yes, that Christ wore, of course, and so on.

IM   And also that New Testament parable about being invited to the wedding and the ...

GMB   That' s right. That certainly comes into the Magnus story, and the play.

IM   So, perhaps we can move on to say a little about the work that you said was quite a lot more difficult than the stories and the novels, and that's the poetry. By this time you've published really quite a number of collections of poetry. Are you conscious in any way of there being a development, a progression from say *Loaves and Fishes* to *Voyages*?

GMB   I've never really thought about it, you know, but I suppose there *must* be, I must cast a cold eye on the whole lot (L) sometime, but I think as you get older right enough your horizons widen a wee bit.

BT   Can I come in there—do you ever go through the exercise of looking over stuff you've written and summing up in your mind where it's going, what the tendencies are?

GMB   No, never, Bob. I never think about that, because sometimes I dip into some of these books and that, but I'm likely to get a rude shock, you know, (L) some poem that you assume is not too bad can go—it's awful ...

BT   Can I pressure you on that point a wee bit—why is that? Is it perhaps because the next one is still to come and you might be worried about disturbing the process by which it comes?

GMB   No, I'm never worried about that really. But I'm not conscious of any development, but I guess there must be; it must have gone in some direction or other.

BT   To the reader this is fairly clear.

GMB   Yes. Well the reader, of course, has a more objective outlook than myself. I think in the early ones the imagery was a lot denser than the newer ones for some reason—in fact they were clotted sometimes, disastrously: but that's just all in the game.

BT   So why is it that you—is it that you don't *like* reading stuff you've done? I mean, you obviously remember it very well.

GMB   Yes, I do.

BT   Throughout this conversation, you know, you've been telling us about stories and *precisely* what happened and what you think of them now. So you remember them all right.

GMB   I remember, yes, I remember most of them. Sometimes too you get a pleasant surprise, you know, something that you thought wasn't very good, you say, oh well, I was a good writer when I wrote that. (L) So it works both ways, you see.

IM   Poems on the whole, as you said again yesterday, these days tend to be short?

GMB   Yes. Well I never really wrote any long poems.

IM   Yes. Well, I mean, even more generally, I think, poetry is some kind of concentrated language. It would be hard these days to persuade people to read something like *Paradise Lost*. I can say it *is* hard these days to get people to read *Paradise Lost*! (L)

GMB   Oh yes, yes, but right enough, Eliot's *The Waste Land* I suppose is an epic condensed until it can be condensed no more.

IM   But you *do* sometimes write poems as it were, in clusters.

GMB   Yes.

IM   And you do that with short stories as well.

GMB   Yes, I do.

IM   You know, a collection of stories about poets, the Magi or whatever, as a group.

GMB   And they sort of reflect off one another you know, and if they come off they give you a sense of completeness, one leaning on the other like stooks in a harvest field. (L) They should be like that, but it doesn't always work.

IM   But, you have sometimes done a bit of experimenting. I think we

would agree that whether or not you wanted to write a long
poem, a straightforward long poem, you wouldn't do it, because
nobody would read it, and indeed you said before with hideous
rashness that *A Drunk Man Looks at the Thistle* was kind of on
the long side.

GMB Well, I think so. (L)

IM So, when you've done more extended things they've tended to be
experimental, I think particularly of *Fishermen with Ploughs*,
which is a kind of mixture of genres.

GMB Yes, it is. And yet they're supposed to cohere into a whole, the
whole lot, and I quite enjoyed doing that, coming through the
centuries and that. That's an old trick of mine, of course, that's
what happens in *Time in a Red Coat* too. And lots of stories and
that with that sort of development.

IM Well it illustrates this basic belief in the cyclic nature of so much.

GMB Yes, I think so and—I don't have anything more to say at the
moment.

IM You said that stories get written and then sooner or later there's
to be a book, so they get put together, but that you don't have a
strong sense of trying to impose a form on a book of short stories.
Is it any different when you produce a volume of poetry? Do you
see *that* as something with more form?

GMB Well, the only one was *Fishermen with Ploughs*, but all the other
books have just been a sort of scattering, you know, and a
gathering together, without any coherent connection at all.

IM There was a volume called *Poems, New and Selected*.

GMB Yes, it came out at the same time as *Fishermen with Ploughs*.
[1971].

IM What I was interested in was *who* selected them? Was it you?

GMB Yes.

IM Did you find it easy?

GMB No, I just left out the bad ones, what I thought were the bad ones
and kept the half-decent ones.

IM And then, not all that much later, this other one *Selected Poems*.

GMB Yes, that was in '77 I think.

IM Yes. Again it was you that selected them. Did you find yourself
selecting radically different poems?

GMB I left some of them out right enough that had been in before. (L)

IM So, basically you became a harder judge as time goes on?

GMB Oh, yes.

IM So there are presumably poems as there are stories, that if
somebody wanted to anthologise them you would say no.

GMB   They don't give you the chance sometimes. Well, I suppose, well
       I would rather they didn't do it, but you don't want to upset their
       anthology either, you know. But there are some that I would say
       certainly no!

IM   And choose something else. Right, that's interesting. Another
       little thing. We were talking about what you lose reading people
       in translation. I think I pinned you down to saying something like
       that poetry perhaps couldn't be translated?

GMB   It's very interesting, really, to see the attempts at translation, you
       know, so long as you realise that about 70% of the magic has
       gone in the translation. It must be the worst kind of translation of
       all to do, I think.

IM   But, you've done some yourself?

GMB   Sort of paraphrases ... no translation ... no. I wouldn't dare to do
       that.

IM   No, but I mean you've published things, for example in
       Winterfold, in that collection of poetry, you've got the twelfth-
       century Norse hymns of Rognvald Kolson.

GMB   Yes, that's right, but they're very free, you know, they're not ...
       they're just vaguely discernible as being the originals, but in
       some cases they just wander into ways that poor old Rognvald
       would never have dreamed of.

IM   And there's also a translation of the Old English poem *Deor*?

GMB   Oh yes, that's pretty free too, yes!

IM   That kind of translation presumably could just as easily be from
       a language that you don't read at all, from you know, really from
       an English translation of something else? So it's a sort of imi-
       tation or rendering or something like that.

GMB   That's right, yes. None of my translations are really translations
       at all. It's a sort of a jumping-off point.

IM   *Voyages*, your last, most recent, volume of poetry, has an
       interesting sort of anthology—indeed, it's *called* an anthology at
       the beginning: 'Seal Island Anthology'.

GMB   Ah, yes.

IM   Is Seal Island a particular place?

GMB   No, no, it's a mythical place, an imaginary place really, but I was
       thinking of a small island like Graemsay or Eynhallow, and
       trying to imagine the kind of life that went on there about fifty
       years ago (L)—a bit more, maybe seventy years ago. Because
       these islands, well, Eynhallow there's only about a tenth of the
       people that used to be—so it's not a real island, no. But I think
       the sort of themes and the people that appear in it are constants in

Orkney, in Orkney history and time and so on.

IM   And certainly these 27 short poems mean a great deal more put together than individually.

GMB   Oh yes.

IM   I don't know whether you would think of them as—or whether you wrote them—as individual poems and then kind of crafted them together—

GMB   No, no, I imagined this—I began with imagining this island, you see, and the kind of people, the kind of life they had, and their love affairs and fights and all that sort of thing. In fact there must have been about twice that number originally, but a lot of them got cut out—they fell by the wayside. Yes. (L)

IM   And do you destroy things that you cut out, or do you put them away in case you might want to work on them more?

GMB   I tend to put them away. If they're really bad I put them in the fire right enough; if I know that there's no sort of life in them at all; but sometimes things that you put in the drawer and find again after two or three years, you can see a sort of promise and you could possibly do something with them after all.

IM   One of the things that impressed me about the poems in *Voyages* is that you don't bring yourself, you know, the 'I' into them; they have characters in them, and they very often have plots or implied plots or suppressed plots. Dramatic situations, quite *strong* in some of the *Voyages* poems, I think.

GMB   Yes, yes.

IM   And the, what was it called, 'Letters from a River'?

GMB   Oh yes, that was a sort of a kind of a ...

IM   'Letters *to* the River', it was.

GMB   'Letters to the River', that was *pure* imagination, of course, putting myself in a kind of a Far Eastern situation, you know, nothing to do with Orkney at all.

IM   No, that's—it seems to me one of the things again that you've been doing a bit in recent years?

GMB   Yes, well I'm tired of ...

IM   In stories as well as in poems.

GMB   Yes, that's right. I got sort of tired of people saying oh, sooner or later he'll begin to scrape the bottom of the barrel you know, he can't do anything more, he's exhausted the whole subject. (L) But I don't think so, you know, there's so many themes here that you could live to be quite an old man and still only be a quarter the way down the barrel really (L)—and God forbid, some folk'll say. (L) So I said to myself, just to show these guys you know, I'll wander a bit further afield in my imagination.

IM   Well, it's interesting because you said earlier that in some senses, the Orkney you write about is only an image of what you're trying to talk about anyway, and it is perfectly possible to take it to, you know, these post-nuclear sort of settlements that you have in—is it?

GMB   *Fishermen with Ploughs*?

IM   No, I was thinking of the story where everybody's living in the little villages with 250 inhabitants, each with its own poet—is it 'The Seven Poets'?

GMB   Yes, 'The Seven Poets', that's right.

IM   Showing that what you are trying to do often is to write about the values and the virtues of small communities in which people have places and understood relationships, rather than that you're just saying, you know, Orkney is the best!

GMB   God forbid! It's quite a good community to live in right enough, but after all we have great sort of precedents for wandering around in the world, Shakespeare for example, we don't think he was ever out of London, well, out of England anyhow, some people say he came to Scotland to sample the air for *Macbeth*, nobody knows for sure, but he certainly wasn't in Venice or Rome, no, no, so it gives you a little holiday to use your imagination sometimes.

IM   And I found that 'Letters to the River' is a very powerful poem because it's got this implied story that the girl has been in some way enticed away from a fairly poor background.

GMB   That's right, yes.

IM   No doubt by somebody whose intentions are no good whatsoever, and she's been separated from implicitly the man she loved or was about to love ... it is, I think, deliberately vague, the actual details of the ...

GMB   Well yes, it is a bit vague, but you can guess that they were sweet on each other at one time.

IM   So that the poem is concentrating on the quality of her present state of mind, we're not told anything about the current lover or the old one, just about her kind of dither.

GMB   That's right!

IM   Between liking the new luxury, and missing the—

GMB   And she's always remembering the village that she came from and her boyfriend and ...

IM   Yes, I find that's very strong. I also found 'Sally: a Pastoral'—

GMB   Sally, oh yes. (L) That was written for a—Charles Causley's—

was it his sixty-fifth birthday? They produced a little book of poems you know by twenty poets or so, and that was sort of dashed off fairly fast for that.

IM   But again I think one of the things that strengthens it is this you know, implied plot, so that the reader enters ...

GMB   Yes, well I think it's rather strange because lots of my poems are sort of compressed stories and you could expand them and make a short story of them. Maybe a novel if you wanted to go to town. (L) And also lots of the stories could be compressed a good bit into a poem, you know, with all the inessentials left out. I think so anyhow, I've never really done it or tried to do it.

IM   Could you imagine for example writing a poem of Mrs McKee?

GMB   No, I don't think so, no. That would be too much. I think it's much better done in prose than in verse, that situation.

IM   But it *is* a very intensely felt one.

GMB   Yes.

IM   What is it—because of its complexity you think prose is better?

GMB   I don't know.

IM   There's another set of things, again I've been doing this rather unreal exercise obviously of reading or re-reading fairly quickly through your work, and one is struck not only by characters you return to, we've mentioned them, but certain images or certain ideas that seem absolutely unerringly to feed your imagination. One of them would be the Magi.

GMB   Oh, the Magi, yes. *All* the ... the whole Christmas story sort of excites me you know, and every Christmas or about the beginning of December I churn forth half a dozen poems and two or three stories. (L) I don't know why that should be but Christmas has always been a magic time to me, you know, since childhood on. And still is—when you'd think you would forget about it, but no! No, it still has power to produce poems and stories anyhow.

IM   And sometimes the stories about Magi are quite a long way from our traditional thinking about the Three Wise Men that followed the star, and sometimes, almost, you get the feeling that the Magi story in, O Lord! I won't remember it now, I think it's in *Andrina*. ['Magi—The First Magus, The Second Magus, The Third Magus' in *Andrina and Other Stories*, 1983, pp. 87-104.]

GMB   Ah, yes. There's three, a group of three stories.

IM   There's a group of the three and the first of them is again some kind of oriental prince.

GMB   That's right.

IM   Suddenly become a king and sent off with a gold plate, and he's

	told to give it to the poorest child he can find. But it's almost as if the Wise Men ...
GMB	Yes, that's right. Christ was at the end at Bethlehem, and Christ was at the end of his journey.
IM	Almost that *every* birth is Christ's birth and *any* poor child is ...
GMB	Well, I suppose, yes.
IM	Is that there as well?
GMB	Yes. And in these three stories the Magi are all boys of course, and that's the sort of unity that keeps them and one of them comes from Eskimo-land, the Baffin Bay area, somewhere up there, and the other one's a Negro I think, yes ...
IM	Traditionally, that's in the traditional thing isn't it? The Caspar, Melchior, Balthazar bit.
GMB	Yes, except the Eskimo one I don't think ...
IM	No, no I'm sure the Eskimo is entirely yours. (L) It's interesting though—the Magi, I think, I suppose, is one of the few things that is still totally available, despite what we talked about (I think off the tape) before, the way in which Christian knowledge and so on no longer can be expected necessarily in young people. Most people know who the Magi were. There are other recurring things though in your work which are less perhaps familiar. You seem to get enormous nourishment from the notion of the Stations of the Cross.
GMB	Ah, yes.
IM	Is that something that means a lot to you?
GMB	No, I think it just stimulates the imagination, you know, and you can see the Stations of the Cross in so many situations—almost endless situations. But, I find it a very fruitful thing too—always have done!
IM	Yes, I was particularly interested in the poem, again, it must have been in the new book, *Voyages*, there's a poem called 'A Joyful Mystery'.
GMB	Ah, yes.
IM	Brackets—The Stations of the Cross. It's almost as if you are taking two different Catholic devotions and cross-breeding them. (L) I mean, Joyful Mystery I associated with the Rosary, is that not right?
GMB	That's right.
IM	So, on the one hand the Joyful Mysteries in the rosary include the finding of the child Jesus in the Temple, which is really the subject of this poem.
GMB	Yes, that's right.

IM   So, is you know, why is the 'Stations of the Cross' there in brac-
      kets?

GMB   Well, in the previous book *Winterfold* there was a whole group of
      seven or eight Stations of the Cross, and this one might have been
      included in that, but it didn't seem to be finished or satisfactory
      to me, so I kept it for two or three years and worked on it
      sporadically, and it seemed to work out all right in the end. But
      if I was doing collected poems I would put that one among the
      other ones and I would leave out one or two of the ones that are
      there already—or three or four! (L)

IM   Yes, I also particularly liked that poem. I don't know how you
      manage to keep on having *vivid*, fresh ways of imagining things
      which have been so handled by the collective imagination over
      the centuries as something like the finding in the Temple;
      something to do with the apple blossom in that poem was very
      sweet but ...

GMB   Well, you have to treat them in a fresh kind of original way, or
      right enough the images are pretty dead because they've been
      handled so often you know.

IM   But given this relative ignorance among the young of the Bible
      and obviously among non-Catholics of objects of Catholic devo-
      tion, is a poem called 'A Joyful Mystery (Stations of the Cross)'
      going to convey much?

GMB   It wouldn't convey anything to them at all unless they decided
      they liked it and would pursue it to its source somewhere.

IM   But, I can imagine giving that poem to students to read, and them
      doing better without the title—because the title would make
      them conscious that there were things here that they didn't
      understand or know about. Whereas the poem itself is fairly ...

GMB   Well, it's supposed to stand on its own feet, but it is tied to the
      original.

IM   But you can't deny the things you want to write about simply
      because ...

GMB   Because people might be ignorant.

IM   You said, also, about Christmas exciting you, that's another
      thing that I noticed, a sort of half-glimpsed or quarter-glimpsed
      nativity is a very important very potent sort of image isn't it,
      'The Winter's Tale'.

GMB   'The Winter's Tale', yes, that's right. It comes into that too.

IM   And 'The Box of Fish'.

GMB   'The Box of Fish'—oh yes—oh God!

IM   And there's a poem that goes back—I think it must be *Loaves
      and Fishes*, called 'The Lodging'?

GMB 'The Lodging'? Ah, that's right! True. No: it's before that—it's in a book called yes, *Loaves and Fishes*, that's right, you're quite right, Isobel.

IM   You're not *that* interested in money ...?

GMB Ach, well, so long as I get by.

IM   You gave up, for example, *The Scotsman* poetry reviewing?

GMB Yes, that's right. I got a bit tired of it in the end.

IM   Yes.

GMB I'm not a very good reviewer, so I ... Alan Bold does it now. Oh, he does it quite well.

IM   Do you get reasonable money for your things for the *Orcadian*?

GMB Oh, no, it's just peanuts really, but you just do it for the fun, you know.

IM   Just for the fun, yes.

GMB Yes, it's nice to be in touch with the community.

IM   What about Dr Johnson saying that no man but a fool ever wrote except for money?

GMB Ah, that was a very cynical thing. I think even if I didn't have anything published, I would still be writing stories, you know, occasionally.

IM   You think so.

GMB Oh, yes. I'm sure I would. Because I enjoy doing it so much. I was even doing it when I was a boy, you know. Ten or twelve, and that.

IM   Pity you hadn't kept them all in a drawer.

GMB I know.

IM   A few Ph.Ds in that lot.

GMB Ah well, they don't exist any longer. The only thing that does exist—I ran a little magazine when I was about ten or eleven, and it was all handwritten you see, and it was passed among just a little coterie of us. I think I charged them too, a caramel or something. (L) Or a couple of sweeties or maybe one caramel. Yes, yes.

IM   Ah, lovely!

GMB But that only had about five of a circulation, and I've got a fragment of it still upstairs. One of my friends resurrected it, you know.

BT   I love that.

THE SMA' PERFECT

JESSIE KESSON

Before her death in 1994, Jessie Kesson had lived in London for many years, and her visits to Scotland tended to have busy schedules. In 1985 she came to Edinburgh to take part in a morning Meet the Author session at the Book Festival. She and Iain Crichton Smith were discussing 'The Spirit of Place', with Isobel Murray as chair. Although she had an afternoon session agreed with Scottish Television, she agreed to be interviewed in the relatively brief space in between, and thanks to the help of Walter Cairns we were able to interview her in the library of the Scottish Arts Council, then still in Charlotte Square. She had found time to think about the interview, and had searched for things to say that she had not said on other interviews. Also, she was meticulous about turning off the tape if what she was saying was by any remote possibility likely to offend, hurt or embarass anyone.

In April 1988 Jessie was given a doctorate by the University of Aberdeen, at the installation of Sir Kenneth Alexander as Chancellor of the University. Isobel Murray was asked to interview her for student television, and as the interview was to some extent complementary to the first one, an edited account of it is given here after the first.

21 August 1985. Present: Jessie Kesson, Isobel Murray and Bob Tait.

IM   Jessie, we are anxious to talk to you for our archive because it seems to me that one of the things that future generations will simply not know about you is your voice, and I'd like them to hear it. Anybody who knows anything about you inevitably knows a wee bit about your life, but could you start just by giving us a few minutes about your upbringing—the kind of story that you tell in *The White Bird Passes* really. You were born in Inverness, yes?

JK   Yes, yes, I was born in Inverness. That was a bit o' an accident. I dinna think I was meant to be born in Inverness but you know, as you know, I was illegitimate and in Scotland in those days it was an awfa' thing for respectable folk like fit my grannie and the oe wis, so that my mother obviously took awa' fit they wid cry in those days her shame, and went to the nearest place and went to Inverness. But since this is for the Archives, this is something that winna maiter if I tell you it now, to be used maybe when I'm nae there to care aboot it. [This story is only included here because Kesson later published it: in *The Scots Magazine*, October 1989, pp. 11-22.] I knew I was born in Inverness, but, until I went to the orphanage you know, I was never known as Jessie. I was nine when I went to the orphanage but I was never called Jessie—because I was named for my grannie, and my grandfather objected very much to it being used and it never was used. And my mother—I was aye known as Ness and my mother said, 'You're Ness,' she said. 'Never mind about the Jessie, we'll nae bother aboot the Jessie.' Because obviously when I went to school I had tae hae the two names: she said to forget aboot the Jessie; we're niver to use it! She said, you see ... she told me that she couldnae use the name. She said, 'Eh, you see,' she said, 'You was born in Inverness,' and she said, 'We'll call you Ness because a town canna object!' So the name Ness was my name. In fact, now I'm beginning to feel a wee bit like Queen Victoria fin Prince Albert died—I don't know if you know what she said and I can well believe it. When he died she said, 'There's nobody left to call me Vicky now!' So I've just about two cousins, one in Erskine and another still up Morayshire and they're the only two that it's always 'My Dear Ness'.

Now, the funny thing about that, the other part of it, Inverness, which is not, never been in biographies or nothing, I really got the address of my birthplace when we went to sit the Eleven Plus, the Qualifying it was called in that days, at the Skene school that I went at, and wanted my birth certificate. And for the first time I saw exactly where I was born. 82-84 Old Edinburgh Road, Inverness. Now, Mrs Elrick, the Matron, her daughter lived in Inverness and every summer she would go there for her holidays. So this particular summer she wis gaun awa' for her holidays to Inverness and I said, 'Mrs Elrick, when you're up in Inverness will you look for my hoose?' Oh, she would look for my hoose. So, back she come, and she had looked for my hoose and she described it—a big house, with a big avenue leading up intil't, and trees and lots of geraniums and a' this—God I wis right set up, wisn't this something! I wis born—and I went aboot cocking up—I wis born in a big hoose, I'm telling the rest of the kids, and of course nobody could gainsay that

cos Mrs Elrick said it and she didna tell lees. It really set me up!
Well the thing is, I never *saw* that hoose till I was married, and I got
married in Inverness actually; and I thocht I'll hae a keek along and
see it, and I saw it. Everything she said was right—it was a big
hoose—and there was an avenue leading up till't. It wisna geraniums, it was in the autumn: I think it was chrysanthemums—that was
the only difference fae her story—*except* that she didna' tell me it
was the workhouse!

IM Wasn't that nice?

JK That says an awful lot for her, doesn't it? I realised she knew it was
the wrong time to tell me, and she probably realised that when I saw
it for mysel it widna maiter, and to be quite honest, it never did! But
the only reason that this little part of biography has niver come out
is because every time I hiv onything on, and *especially* wi' my last
television play—they emphasise 'prostitute's daughter' and the
orphanage, forever this orphanage, and I thought, my God if they
only got the ither bit I'd nae hae a life o't at a'. They'd be
workhouse—orphanage and everything else! And that is exactly,
nae that I'm getting dumpy about that, but I knew that this wid be
anither thing—'born in the workhouse'—that wid be a right added
thing. Because none of these things really maiter you know. Nae tae
me. It's nae that I've ever been the least ashamed of that. But I
thought, God it was bad enough with the orphanage withoot adding
a workhouse on top! (L) This is what I thought, and I jist thocht,
well I'm nae saying a word aboot it, but now when this ever goes on
it winna maiter!

IM And you've never been one for respectability and hiding things. I
think your writing is very remarkable for the confessional aspect of
it. The way you lay yourself open; you make yourself vulnerable to
your readers.

JK Aye, yes. But the ither thing ... There was anither thing that I've
never been able ... I wish I could dae this or think aboot it whin I'm
daeing my interviews—cos I think very deeply aboot things, you
know. You know how folk often say—reviewers and thesis writers
when they're analysing—(I read two theses on my work already)—
and I know that their folk had gane to a great lot o' bother obviously
and certainly daen their homework, everything—even my short
stories—but I do sit back efter they've come to a conclusion and
think God, was that really what I was writing aboot? (L)

IM Well, I have to tell you that Naomi Mitchison told us that there had
been a very learned American Ph.D. written about her *The Corn
King and the Spring Queen* and what she said to me was, 'I didn't

understand a word of it!' (L)

JK Well neither do I. I think: wis that what I was writing aboot? But I
realised myself what I was writing aboot. At long last. And I'll tell
you what it wis. You mightna' agree. But I actually put it in *The
Glitter o' Mica* in one line—wi' one of the characters! And I thocht
that's it, that's really what everything I've ever written is aboot—
queer fowk! Queer afore it had its current meaning. 'Queer fowk,
who are oot, and niver hiv ony desire to be in!' [not in *The Glitter
of Mica*, but *The White Bird Passes*, London, 1958, p. 118: 'Queer
folk who were "oot" and who, perversely enough, never had any
desire to be "in".'] Every work I've ever written contains ae
'ootlin'. Lovely Aberdeenshire word. Somebody that never really
fitted into the thing. And that is when I think o' it everything—*The
White Bird, The Glitter o' Mica*, Sue Tatt and Hugh Riddel himself,
and if you think on even my short stories it's always aboot people
who don't fit in! Now, I know mysel at last and it's just in one line
in that book where fowk were oot who never had ony desire to be in.
As ye ken maist writers really, really truly have only one book: the
rest's a' variations o' the theme, you know. At least I think!

IM The books that you talk about of course I know very well and I've
read and reread. There are also these plays that you've written for
the BBC which inevitably are not so real for me, either because I
haven't heard them at all or I've only heard them once. Do you feel
differently about the things you publish as books from things that
have gone out as plays, for example?

JK Well, not very much. First of a' as I've aye said, in the beginning
was the Word. I hinna said it, the Bible says it, but I repeat it. And
for me the words has always been the purest—the actual written—
the word! Always. Because, you see Isobel, whin you write a thing
it's in a way private, it's between you and the anonymous reader—
you're illuminating an experience for this person—you'll never see
them probably, you know: in the normal way o' things you'll never
know them. But when you're writing even a radio play, you write it,
and then it's somebody else's job to give their interpretation of it;
that is the director and she gives her interpretation and then the
actors give theirs. Now this applies to any form whether it's films or
television, but next to the printed word I love radio and I'll tell you
why. Because words mean so much to radio and words and the
sound and the meaning of them is *my* thing. I love radio. And I've
aye been very, very lucky in my producers; they did it very, very
brilliantly you know. But television and the films of course, that's
a different thing. There's their directors and you know *his* vision

and there's the actors and a' that, but the *finest* thing is the printed word; if it's wrang the onus is yours! You can accept it. But if say you've written a play as you know you might dae and by the time it comes oot wi' ither fowks' interpretation the onus is *again* on you and naebody thinks 'O it's Jessie Kesson, that play, it wisna awfa good, was it, ye ken', and this is the difference.

IM   But all the books that you've published contain a lot of Jessie, and actually very often they contain a lot of your actual life—your life circumstances and all the rest of it. But I know you've written more than a hundred plays for radio and I don't obviously know all about them, but do you take the subject matter for *those* as much from your own life, or perhaps from the List D schools that you've worked in or the old people's home, or whatever. Is it such personal experience?

JK   Oh, no, nae. But now, I have a play going on quite soon which is a Cockney play in Cockney dialect in which they say the dialect's excellent. I now *know* it, and I don't think it has anything to do with me, this play, at all. [A television play: *You've Never Slept in Mine*.] And indeed, *Glitter o' Mica* had nothing to do with me.

IM   Only very indirectly.

JK   Only in the landscape and the work. But it was not my story.

IM   Oh, no it wasn't your story at all!

JK   Though it had much of my feelings in it. I didna' ken whit to mak' o' it when a very, very good friend o' mine gave it, my work, a very good review, a very in-depth review, and describing said, and I quote, 'One of her many alter-egos'. (L) [Sue Tatt]

IM   It says that on the blurb! [See the Introduction to a 1982 edition of *Glitter of Mica* by William Donaldson, p. 2.]

JK   Well, I ken the friend that said it but I like him, so there's nae hairm deen. But of course he was quite right, you know. It is the possibility in all of us.

IM   It did strike me as an odd phrase to find on the blurb of the book, and I'm interested that it didn't originate from you, although you wouldn't on the other hand want to get rid of Sue Tatt. I think, *Glitter of Mica* is unique.

JK   Yes, it's my best book.

IM   Well you said that before, and I'm not sure about that!

JK   And the sad thing is, Isobel, I can understand it—it's never been very popular. And I'll tell you for why. Probably it was less, as you say, of a' the books less emotionally me. Mair clinical. Aye, that's...

IM   But what interests me is whether that's why you think it's your best book, because it's less easy to see Jessie in it!

JK   And it was a book that I wrote at white-hot speed. I really did. Far mair speedy and completely than *The White Bird Passes* itsel'. Which *is* very much concerned wi' me!

IM   Of course.

JK   And this one came white-hot you know. And, as I say, there's lots of things that have nothing tae dae wi' me at a'. But I think every creative writer, say Neil Gunn (and I love that man's work—I could go back and it's like drinking fae a fresh spring-well, I can go back again and again and again to read his work) but there's a lot o' him—we put a lot o' oorsels in oor characters. I'm maybe mair diverse than maist, you see, 'my name is legion'. [See Mark 5: 9.] The Bible tells you that, right? So I, I'm nae thinkin' o' the devil, (L) but I ken that's whit you two are thinkin' o', but I know the source and I wisna' thinkin' o' that. The same for angels—my name is legion. In fact very often in the main character there is a bit o' myself, and a bit o' myself in whit I call the good characters and the bad characters, or the nae-so-good characters. Because you know there's a bit of oorsels in a'body, and every character's a wee bit o' me, my attitude, but in the main character obviously my deepest feelings and that go in, if it's the big theme it's ma ain attitude to it what I use you see.

IM   Most of the things you write are short, they're pared down very much: and what you write tends to be a novella rather than a novel, a long short story. I wonder whether you were ever tempted to try for the other thing that might go over twenty years, and show you as it were Hugh Riddel at one stage in his life and then twenty years further on.

JK   No, do you know how that happened. I had a dominie, I dedicated *The White Bird* to him. But actually it was my mother, great credit to her, she was the one that had the poet in her—she really had—it wis her gave me my great love for all o' it, my mother.

IM   I'm glad you said that, because it hadn't come across to me.

JK   Yes, well, you have another read at telling the story of the cathedral and the singin' the ballads, and when the girl says 'Lisa in one of her rare, enchanting moods' [*The White Bird Passes*, p. 65]. It was my mother and in fact I say so in the actual book about the good times. So that really was it, which was added to by the dominie. But there was one thing he hated; it drove him berserk; he described it as *padding*! And if you used a little bit he would say to me at the top of my essays—he aye read them out you know, and he always said, 'One day I'll open a book and I'll know you've written it.' Sadly

enough he died before he knew it was dedicated to him. But if I—
and I'm still guilty of that today—(explanation in case somebody's
missed the point)—he would mark, 'This is Angela Brazil stuff!'
(L) I mean, you didn't dare, really, and this for all time was instilled
in me: condense! Never use two words when one will do—never
use a big word. There's no need for it. No journalese, no jargon,
nothing! And my dominie had a great influence, and I kept to that
and I suppose I aye will do!

BT   But how does this work? You speak of sometimes writing at really
white-hot speed. So at what point do you start cutting and editing?
Does it all come out in a rush and *then* you carefully go over
everything, or is it a process whereby the pages gradually accumu-
late because you're editing as you go along?

JK   Oh I edit as I go along. I edit as I go along. I never, never go back
and revise anything! There's certain words I'll say, Oh that's a
missed word, or some of these things, but I *never*—I do it at the
time. And sometimes like *Glitter o' Mica* it didna need a' that
much. That's whit I mean by white-hot.

BT   It is a less personal kind of book, and so it's kind of paradoxical that
that's the one which didn't require this editing process.

JK   Very, very little.

IM   Your dominie sounds a marvellous guy and I think what we owe to
him is a great deal, but the choice between writing long short stories
and writing novels is—it's not to do with whether you pad or not—
it's to do with whether you see the whole thing centring on one
image or one choice or one thing.

JK   Yes, yes.

IM   Or whether you actually want to portray twenty years in somebody's life. You never seem to want to do that.

JK   Oh, no, no.

IM   You focus on a turning-point and tell everything there?

JK   Yes. I've never felt I would write the great big novel. I've aye
wanted to write the sma' perfect! (L) I've aye wanted to dae that!
That's the only thing I ever wanted to dae was to write!

IM   *The White Bird* was televised, and *Another Time, Another Place*
came out, as it were, simultaneously, as a film and as a book—it
seems to indicate that you've got a very dramatic imagination?

JK   Well, I dinna ken if the word dramatic—obviously you've got to
hae a bit o' drama or it wid be a flat thing, but I'll tell you whit I *hiv*
got, and that's naething tae dae wi' boasting nor anything, a very
good visual sense. That is what I do naturally possess. I can see it
like paintings like you know. Yes, I do.

IM Well, it's certainly to me one of the amazing qualities of *Another Time, Another Place* which the film could never do as well as the book did, the way in which you get the feeling of the young woman looking out at these fields as the seasons change, and the feelings inside her warring with what she's seeing, and it's all done *so* economically.

JK Yes, and that's how I felt it. I've niver said to misel I'm gaen off to write a book about this—I've gaun off to write a *theme* rather, and then yes, this is writing, this is interesting—I can dee something wi' this, that's how I think, never beyond that!

BT Sorry to interrupt, but you talk about having an idea for a theme but is it after that that a crucial scene comes to your mind? Because there seem to be crucial scenes.

JK It's awfa difficult to explain that, you know. I used theme; the wrong word. It's something inside o' misel that I want to get oot and to write. I dinna start ... and as the thing continues so it forms its ain natural thing that's gaen to happen. That's mair like it! But in *Another Time, Another Place*, for once I really thought that this was what I want to show. And I think the reviewers missed it, *or* it could be that I didna dae it good enough. One or other. It was to show that the girl was as alien to the farm as the Italians.

IM Or more so!

JK And this, that was what was really meant. And what the film missed out obviously, and you couldna *get* this in the film. Because what they missed out was her relationships and her ootlinish outsiderness with the cottar wives. That's far a' that is shown. They couldna' get that.

BT Not as well. But actually to be quite honest with you I thought that the film did that surprisingly well. I mean, there was *something* about that there.

JK I'll always think that, despite as I'm saying the flaw's obviously there—it's very difficult ever to get your book exactly ever ...

BT Yes, but this ootlinish quality of the girl *was* there to some extent in my view in the film.

JK Never as it is in the book.

BT No, never as in the book, that's true.

JK There was this attrition between herself and them all the time in the book, and that didna really come oot. You saw the other one so seldom—shakin' her rag and very, very little. You never really got it or the relationship with Findlay; you never got any of that things. What you *did* get was wonderful photography and the sense of the faces of the countryfolk, and the parallel scene wi' the Italians and their culture and their faces and the scenes—Mike did that brilliantly. Oh gosh I'm nae condemning the film at a'! I think he made an awfa' good job o' it. But I'm only speakin' aboot the book; whit it wis meant wis a little bittie different. Mike obviously concentrated—and half the sex you know was fantasy! Half the sex wis in her heid!

IM   Well, in the book you can't tell where fantasy ends. But obviously in a film you have to decide. The director has to tell you what—

JK   You have to be specific!

IM   You have to be specific, yes.

JK   And I'll tell you something; it wis awfa funny. When Johnny and me went to the premiere Mike said (Mike comes up to the house very often because as I say we are we really get on pretty well together right enough), Mike says, 'What dae ye think o' the film, Johnny?' Johnny says, 'That winna win nae prizes!' (L) Now it's won aboot fourteen and a'thing else!

IM   As I recall, *Another Time, Another Place* came out simultaneously in film and in book but the way you've been talking makes it clear that it was a book first.

JK   I'll tell ye exactly.

IM   Out comes *Another Time, Another Place* both as a book and as a film, but it somehow seems clear to me that it's the book that is Jessie Kesson's; the film is somebody else's version and I'm quite interested in the process—you know—the difference.

JK   Yes, well what happened was *The White Bird Passes* was made into a television film, and after the preview in Glasgow Mike Radford who directed it, and Bill Forsyth who's a great friend of Mike's, and myself went off to a restaurant to hae a meal and a drink and a postmortem. And we got chatting and somehow we got on to the war, the conversation, and they said 'What did you dae in the war, Jessie?' (L) I often say just what I think but I don't aye think what I say! So off the top o' my heid, ach me, I said, I fratted with the Italians! (L) This set the lugs cocking! It was indeed true, this three Italians, prisoners, lived in the bothy next to me and I did little jobs for them, light their tilley lamps, and takin' in their milk and things like that, and I got to ken them obviously in a mair intimate wey than onybody else did, and I mean intimate in the pure sense of the word intimate.

IM   Of course.

JK   For a beginning that is onywey! (L) Eh, they were fascinated wi' this and they said oh, that would mak—baith being film men you see—that would make a marvellous film! 'Oh ye must dae that,

Jess,' Mike said, aye. And I remember we were looking on the wine when it wis red, when a'thing seems very possible, ye ken: aye it's a *fait accompli* that nicht anyway. So I gaed hame to London and I forgot a' aboot it, I mean, in the clear light o' day. I forgot a' aboot it. And aboot three days efter that up pops Mike: 'Jess, we *must* dae that! Now,' he says, 'I'll tell ye fit we'll dae!' He said, you write this novel and I'll pit it to the Arts Council, this here Arts Council. So I wrote the synopsis. So the Arts Council decided to pass the synopsis. Now, we got, fit wis it? £400—£4000—we must be honest: £2000 for me to write the book and £2000 for Mike to dae the film.

IM   Oh so it was as even as that?

JK   It was as even as that! And so, as I was writing the book Mike was taking bits I'd written and daein' the film. And it was made to come oot thegither—Chattos raced it oot to get it oot wi' the film, you see.

BT   So they were starting to do the film as the thing was in process of writing?

JK   Aye, we were writing together, simultaneously! It is a *wonderful* partnership, as ye can see! And remember Mike was as often in Paris as not, awa' in Paris with the thing, Jess, have ye got ony mair written? It's a wonder that it ever became so good, God only knows! But that is exactly if ye really want to ken that is *exactly* how that film started and Chattos in panic to get it oot in time for the film. (L)

IM   Of course. Were you not tempted at all yourself to write the film scenario as well as the book?

JK   Well, we worked very closely thegither on't. I'll put it as simply as that! I mean I wrote it and I was consulted.

IM   It wasn't really like just leaving somebody else to get on with the thing?

JK   Oh no, no. We discussed it. Really discussed it!

IM   It seems to me a great pity if nobody has got round to dramatising *Glitter of Mica*.

JK   I think that! I've told Mike, I've said, Mike listen, there's more in *Glitter of Mica*, and there's the three generations—there is everything! Lasting things, I think, and one day I'll maybe dae it. I can now write a filmscript and I've always thought, oh, *Glitter of Mica* wi' the father and the son and the lady and the frigid wife you know, just everything! And it's completely modern because the Social Service that the girl went into you know Helen Riddel ... They're a' things, aye again, there's where biography comes in. I know exactly how it was to work in that place and how she felt. I can never understand, it was never popular, *Glitter of Mica*. But I still think it contained far mair, that's why I like it best! It's because there's so much mair *to* it really than to *The White Bird* or *Another Time*.

IM   Well, not necessarily agreeing with you but I know what you mean!

JK   Well you're speaking aboot a longer book. In a way, *in context* it's a much longer book.

IM   Yes, instead of covering sixty years in time, you give us Hugh Riddel's father, you give us Hugh and you give us Helen.

JK   Yes. And he's a little boy and he's up and he has his own daughter and things like that.

IM   And in a sense that telescopes it all.

JK   Yes, the whole lot. That's why I *think*, that is exactly why I think it's my best book.

IM   And it's why I don't understand why Jessie Kesson hasn't written a film script of *Glitter of Mica*.

JK   I will dae it one day, I promise ye. I've always wanted tae dae it. Naething to dae with *Another Time, Another Place*. I've always know this is ... you see ... that is a record, a time that'll never—you know, that is worth holding on to.

IM   Absolutely!

JK   Isn't it? It's worth holding on to the changes that came over the farmwork, the changes that happened to their families; the girl at the university; a hundred things—the nearly uncivilised way we lived in those days. I mean, you never got the sack. If you weren't asked to bide on—it was ridiculous—if you weren't asked to bide on by the month of late March or the beginning of April, you jist went doon the road. The farmer either asked you to bide on or he didna say a word! I mean it was absolutely amazing. The term days were the only days you had off—because you see the cows had to be milked Saturday, Sunday, Monday, Tuesday, we'd no days off or nothing. Our first fee, Johnny and mine, we worked at this farm Wester Rothienorman, was £72 a year. And I worked in the byres as well, and that was the first fee. And the apprehension, as we come along the cottars' row when the late Spring wis comin' in—his the fairmer seekit ye? Oh dear. I mean this was absolutely primitive! It's worth recording; these are the kind of things that are forgotten, you know.

IM   It's not just *recorded* in *Glitter of Mica*: that is one of the places in your books where most there is something that amounts to comment on politics and comment on religion. In *Glitter of Mica* you talk about how the farm servants are expected to vote like the farmer, go to church with the farmer.

JK   And nae only that. They're parallel; they're in the toon. They're haein' a drink and they're at the market, and there's the farmers, 'never once, not even in trust amongst each other confessed to profit!' [See *Glitter of Mica*, p. 28.] (L) And there is the servants, fit *they* wid dae wi' the land: 'that's no mixed fairming, it's kye for ever up on yon place, that's no mixed fairming'. And they're telling aboot the land, because they do ken an awfa lot. Oh aye, tenanting their farms, daein their farms, rotating their crops 'by right of deed' and that's a sort of pun—you know, right of the action. The whole thing, the farming life's in there, and I aye think that was the book, that really was the book.

IM   Here's a question that separates the Ian Macphersons, the Lewis Grassic Gibbons from the David Toulmins if you like. Did you *like* the cottar life? On balance, did you like it?

JK   No.

IM   Good lady! I'm glad you came out with that this time!

JK   No, no!

IM   That's what Toulmin said. Whereas Macpherson liked it, and as Toulmin said to me, Macpherson was an owner's son. He wasn't a—

JK   A tenant farmer! Ah! Now, a good man, David Toulmin. If you remember again in *Glitter of Mica* when Hugh Riddel gave the Immortal Memory, he said it was easily seen it was written by a tenant farmer, not by a ploughman. [See *Glitter of Mica*, pp. 34-35.] So you see we're baith agreed on that. That's how I didna like the cottar. It was absolutely feudal! I liked my neighbours, we always got on, my cottar neighbours still come doon to London and bide a week wi' me.

IM   The job, the life, the neighbours, even the children, must have been difficulties to you in the way of trying to become a writer?

JK   I don't know, you know. You see, writing made my spiritual life that things easier. Supplementing me, I had my writing. It was like a dark secret and fit ever else wis wrang I knew.

IM   Was it always there?

JK   Always. I niver mind when I didna want to write. And then I started seeing the light when I used to write little bits for the *People's Journal*, the woman's page. The editor, editress—they cried theirsel editress in those days—by name of Flora Scrimgeour, asked should I write margin notes, and accepted mine. I think I got two guineas or something at a time, keep it cosy, keep it cosy! And I really wis getting nae only used to writing kailyard but beginning to believe it. I found it easy, a half-hour play, a couthy, nice little play.

BT   Do you reckon you were always aware that there was a difference between the Jessie Kesson who could really write things that were true and honest about the situation, and this other kind of thing. Were you always aware of that?

JK No, no, I'd be dishonest if I said that. I only became aware o' it when a critic, and his name was Alistair Reevie, long ago, and I mind his name even; he wrote this, I canna mind the full crit but I always remember the implication o't. 'I wish we had a man writer that could write wi' the charm' and that that I could write. 'She has the same charm of her words as Barrie'—*but* he meant I had the same faults as Barrie an' a'. And it was only then that I had a look at it and I thocht, he's right! He is right! In a way I wis aware o't— this is nae the real me, nae the real me at a'. I've got mysel couthie doon. That's why I hate that photograph but I kent it wisna me. Couthie mole! [Off tape, Jessie had criticised the photograph of herself on the jacket of *Another Time, Another Place* (1983), on the grounds that it was too 'sweet': she called it 'a couthie mole'.] That's why I hate the couthie moles so much, because it's an awfa' danger. And obviously a bit of the rotten couthie mole stuck, or it couldna come oot in the photograph, but I didna like it.

IM How did you find having your own family came into the whole business of being a writing lady and all the rest of it? Was it easy to cope?

JK No, I *hiv* one regret really, but I've spoken to other mothers and they have the same regret, nae because they're writers. I think their childhood passed awfa quickly, and I would be writing a lot, and also, remember, I wis aye workin' full-time, up until I was 60 as well as daein my writing. Oh mercy yes. Always! Full-time job, from the day I went to London till I retired, and had tae for my age wi' the mentally handicapped: hard jobs, I've done!

IM And how old were your children then when you went to London?

JK Oh, they were young, Kenny was about four and Avie was about eleven or something. And as I said as I wis working, I'd got to work, and I wis wantin' tae write tae, and very often I used tae come hame frae *my* work tired and wanting to get on with a bit of writing, and maybe they wid be wantin' tae tell me fit happened at school, and I wid sort o' dismiss it, I wis that busy. Their childhood passed very quickly and I thocht, Oh, I didna enjoy yer childhood, but I have spoken to many mothers who found the same thing and they are *not* writers. I had my children young you see; the sad thing aboot that is you're still young yersel'; you still feel you have a bit o' life left; *that* is fit causes that, and you've aye the regret; I wid like tae hae their childhood ower again far I hidna tae work or dae naething and

I could have—put it that wey!

I've had more pleasure from my grandchildren. Ah but no quite because of that. You see when you're a young mother, ye're aye worried; ye're aye nagging them, don't do this, don't do that, but when you become a grandmother you're much more tolerant, ye're nae near so feart, ye ken there's nay near so much to be feart o', but fin ye're young and you're you know watch, watch, watch and that sort o' thing. Another thing it's great, ye've the best o' them, them playing and that, and then when they start their grumbling because o' their teething, 'Mam' you know ... (L) Oh but I, oh we always were very very—always got on. We are a very, very close family. Always great affection, great love for each other. What I wis saying to you was what I felt sometimes.

IM Oh yes, oh indeed.

JK What *I* felt. But oh Avril and Kenny—that's my son—really, they live not far from me and it's funny, I was very proud two years ago, Avril studied for two years for Cordon Bleu and I went to her prize-giving, and she got it with distinction and she got the only prize in the class, and I wis as proud o' that as I wis o' anything. Cos I feel now you are something in your own right. That's how fond we are of each other—oh I was delighted! The only thing was I've got to cut down weight a bit.

IM We all have this problem.

JK And while Avril was daein' this course she used to give me these getees and a' the things and oh, God, for two years and I said, Avie I know you'll get this, you'll get your degree or your diploma or whatever, but I says my God you're gaen to kill me in the gettin' o't. (L)

IM Oh, that's a lovely way to go! (L)

JK I really meant it, I wis gaen to pass away before ... (L)

IM Now can we fill in very briefly? We know that *you* were a cottar wife and that *you* at some stage later on lived in East Lothian, was it? Near Tantallon, anyway, I remember that, and then you went to London.

JK Oh no, no no! Shall I tell you the right wey?

IM Yes, please, that's the whole point.

JK I wis a cottar wife. I'd aye been wantin' to leave the cottars and that, always, and I think this is maybe the bravest thing I ever did; I think, I'm nae sure but I think it wis. The Elgin Townswomen's Guild were daen a pageant, and they asked me if I'd dae Marie Curie— well anything, but my favourite was Marie Curie and I did that, and I got £20. I thought it was a big sum of money. And I thocht right—

I'm off to London, so I'm off and I said to Johnny, if I get on, I'll get ye a' doon. If I dinna get on, I'll be back. So off I go in the bus wi' my £20. I winna tell you a' the details o' that, and remember I'm from a cottar house, and I didna' know a living soul, I widna dae't now. Anyhow, I am sitting and my money's jist aboot gone and I thocht oh, I'll hae to go hame, I've enough. I'd enough for the train and I hidna got onything you see, an' it was a spring day, it wis April or March, because it was the night o' the Welsh International comin' doon to play and it was awfa funny in a wey. I think it was Waterloo Station. Onywey, there wis a' the fowk that hid nae wey to go; there was an auld, auld wifie wi' a' her bundles and her chamber-pot and her tea-pot and a'thing sitting there, and they knew the time the police came round the station you see, they were habitués, but I didna, but they kent, so fit wid I attempt to dae but to lift this auld body, because I wis young and strong and a' her bits! She'd run awa from this old folk's home because she wis a bit incontinent and she wisna happy, and so she took a' her wee bits and shot off doon to Waterloo Station. So I wis stuck wi' a' the auld wifies. (L) Anyhow, before the train comes in, this woman wi' a black scarf roun' her heid, nae stockings on, I aye remember, ye ken the wifie that might have had pee-marks doon her legs; ye know what I mean.

IM Indeed!

JK A homely wifie; she hidna, I'm sure, but she could have been. So she sat doon, and we were speakin'. They're very hamely, a Welsh wifie, her brother or somebody wis coming down to see the match, and she, well you ken how ye start chattin'. I said well I come fae Scotland and I was looking for somewey to bide, and I couldna' get naewey to bide so I'm gaen off back. She invited me hame to Muswell Hill tae her place. I got a job within a week. I sat doon and I wrote a play. Also I got a job cleaning oot the Nurses' Home in the Colney Hatch, you've heard of it, the great mental hospital. I was cleaning the Nurses' Home straight away: it wisna far fae far I bade so I'm off, but I also did my writing. And I wrote. *Virgin Soil Upturned*: dae ye ken the Russian who wrote that. Oh ye ken,

IM Turgenev, was it?

JK No: Sholokov. Aye so I thocht, my word, again back to the country, back to the landscape, back to the spirit o't. I thocht, *this* putten into the Doric. So I wrote this and sent it up to Elizabeth Adair; she accepted it, peyed me for it, and I sent the money to Johnny. By this time I'd gotten a room for us. Jist till we'd get a hoose. And doon comes Johnny! But he'd an awfa, awfa trauchle. He's nae awfa big, ye ken, (L) and he's a friend Ernest, a great friend, his wife wis my freen tae ye see, and he was in the Air Force, and he'd a privilege ticket. Johnny had a' my blankets and God knows fit a' humphin' and he's only wee, and Ernest selt Johnny ane o' his privilege tickets so's Johnny wid get for a wee bit less. And Johnny hid an awfa time: he said when the ticket inspector came he wis frightened that he wis lookin' for the mannie wi' the dark grey country blankets. And I think that wis the most anxious moment in Johnny's hale life! (L) Anyhow, that's how we came to London.

IM Except that I think it was very brave of *Johnny* to come to London.

JK I thocht a'body blamed me. When I say blamed—oh, it wis her, and Johnny he said no way. But no. You see I'd come back to Scotland and Johnny winna. He wanted to come to London. He hated it. Johnny wis mair keen to come to London. Mind you, I wis aye the strong ane. I canna see Johnny ever havin' been able to come—he wid niver—he's too quiet a man and a'thing, and wandering aroon' London wi' his wee bonnet and nae kennin' naebody. Whereas I could, you see. Anyhow, the thing aboot East Linton is, so we're in London for a long time and that's where I'm going the nicht to stay, [i.e. on 21.8.85] at East Linton, and an old, old friend of mine. I wis up daein' a reading at Haddington, the Literary Circle, and the Secretary was a very old friend of mine who's a very big farm, Smeaton, in East Linton, and I'd known her fin I wis cottared: we always kept friends and they really are I mean, very, very, very, very ... So that's where I'm going to bide. So when I went up to dae the thing at Haddington—this is aboot twelve years ago—Ann said, 'When does Johnny retire, Jessie?' I said, next year. So Ann said, 'I'd like ye to come and see something.' So next morning we set off down, to ah, the most beautiful cottage you have ever seen, beautiful cottage. Wi' a lake and the deer there, oh, a lovely cottage. And this wis to be mine, and the rent it wis pepper-corn. It wis £3:1:10, oh! So Johnny was dancin' and up we shoots—marvellous—and I got a job in Tynepark, psycho-drama: I loved that really. And I loved my job and a'thing else. But roon' aboot that time, you may remember fin a' the councils changed and other things changed—

IM The regionalisation?

JK That's right. Now they're big landowners faur I wis, you see. And the husband George he got put on to the district council, this sort o' thing. And of course he wis getting on too, you see, and they needed ... The eldest son was in New Zealand doing agricultural research and jist got married and that ye ken, and Ann came doon one day and George wid be nae longer able to look efter the estate and

Duncan wis comin' hame tae, and my cottage—he needed! It wis as simple as that. So, I kent fit I was gaen to dae, I wis gaen to gang back to London, apart fae which, my family were a' there.

IM Well you must have been missing London a lot, however idyllic it was.

JK Aye, I—exactly, my family wis there. I wanted to get back. I kent now, ye see, comin' fae London, how terribly hard it wis to get places, and I thocht, and I didna' really hae enough money to tak a' my furniture, nae that it wis worth an awfa lot onywey. I thocht, fit'll I dae? But I had worked and I had saved my thing, so I get *The Lady*—oh my God, if you're ever in trouble you get *The Lady*—I get *The Lady* and in *The Lady* I see: cook-housekeeper wanted for Abbeyfield, for New Abbeyfield, you know, for the auld fowk, so I apply. A' the wey fae East Linton. I get a letter back; I get an interview; at Osterley, it's a very lovely part of London, down beside Richmond. So I gae doon, I get the job, I come back. I have a friend that worked in Tynepark, she's one of the house-mothers, and I hired a nice van and I had my Labrador dog and my cat and Johnny and a'thing (L) and Eileen my good friend who was having a week's holidays onywey fae Tynepark, and a good driver, she drove us a' doon. I arrive at this Abbeyfield, it wis aboot six at night, a lang journey, and then there's eight auld wifies and there's the committee lady, 'I am so pleased you've come. Now,' she said, 'you'll easily find your way around here.' Here's me wi' eight fowk that I've niver seen afore in my life to cook for, (L) and nae kennin' faur the meat wis, and there's a big major comin' through lookin' for his supper and I haed to dae it. Anyhow, niver mind, I set up the Abbeyfield and I worked there, and I saved and I was still writing little bits o' plays and that, and still saving up till I could get a placie o' my ain, and you know, help me God, I got it. That wis fit happened. That wis exactly ...

IM And most of these jobs you had when you were in London were something to do with some kind of an institution? Do you think that your own experience of being brought up partly in that orphanage helped you to know about it? ... It seemed to me certainly from the recent play we saw on television—alas I can't remember the name—

JK *You've Never Slept in Mine.*

IM *You've Never Slept in Mine*, about the lassie whose father had made incestuous advances to her and she was sent off to an approved school. It caught at my heart in the way that an awful lot of the other things you've written caught at my heart because you just seem to

understand the feelings, the utterly lonely feelings of people who
get, you know, into these situations.

JK   Well, in a way, you know, Isobel, to me, that was a different job.
But as you say my other jobs were all about, you know, the sort of
have-nots or whatever, but I would like to say, 'Ah yes, I had a great
feeling for them and a' that.' Actually I did the job very well and I
did hae a feeling for them. But that was *not* the reason I took the job.
The reason was, it was one of the few unskilled as they call it jobs
that paid reasonably well. It was as simple as that. And I did take the
job. I did it well, and I had an aptitude for people and interested in
people, but it wasna altruistic at a'; it wis better than working in
Woolworth's or anything, or ony ither thing that I could dae
because it wis mair money, you see. And much harder than ever
working in Woolworth's would have been. It aye *is*, when you're
dealing wi' human beings wi' disabilities. You're much mair tired,
and I mean you're shattered. The two jobs that I loved was I was six
years wi' mentally handicapped teenagers. That I loved! And I
taught them their little plays and a'thing, that's what I mean, I get
on well with the young. And at Tynepark, but wi' the ither jobs, like
wi' the old age and a' that, really, it wis just because they paid well.
They paid the kind of money I needed at the time.

IM   But they were not intolerable jobs. They were jobs at which you
were at least as good as anybody else was going to be?

JK   Oh, yes, and there was satisfaction because I knew I did my job
well. Yes. I did do a good job. But I always worked the nitty-gritty
you know. It's really the nitty-gritty.

IM   Well, in a way, everything you write seems to be about some kind
of combination of the nitty-gritty and the glamourie, the magic, the
possibilities: the movement between those of any human soul:
that's what you write about.

JK   I wis aye observant, speaking about human souls. Unconsciously.
There was somebody once said to me, 'Oh do you tak jobs tae get
material?' It's the last thing in the world I've ever done in my life!
Ah'm nae Monica Dickens, that's nae me at a'. But anyhow, I
observed almost against my will, and speaking aboot the auld fowk
again, it's a strange life. I had sixty-seven old folks, but I did mainly
night duty, because it helped me wi' the children you see. I could
get hame. I mean I wis hame in the morning for the school, and I wis
hame at night. And that was the hardest job I ever did. I was on my
own wi' sixty-seven men and woman. But I'll tell you fit killed me
then. At night they are at their most vulnerable. That is fin ye really
ken fit like it is for them. Really, truthfully. And I wis there five

years. And fit killed me wis, we had rich and poor, there was a mixture: I mean, the ones who couldn't pay, Social paid, but there was quite a few well-off anes and ye ken there's something awfa queer aboot fowk. It's queer (I hate using that word now) because it's something so wrang sometimes aboot fowk. I thought that then. There was me and daein the *real* nitty-gritty, pitten up wi' them and they dinna sleep even wi' their sleeping pills and they're aye needin', and that's when they *die*, at night, and I had that kind of thing. I mean on the early morning. And when anyone would die, the relatives—*Matron* would get a bottle of brandy and a bottle of gin, a box of chocolates and a' that. It wis niver—and *Matron* niver wiped their bums or washed them in the morning or did naething else! It wis never, never me, or soulies like me that did the day, it wis niver us that got it. Anything good or nice—present for Matron. How does fowk like that—surely they must ken that apart fae Matron saying good mawning, how are you? She didna dae their sores or nothing else, you know. Nothing for us. And nae that one wis greedy, but you couldna help noticing these things, you see.

Oh, the greatest compliment. Again, you see the children barring me from taking real full-time jobs when I first went there. So I got a job at the Queen's Cinema, Palmer's Green. I was a cleaner there. I'm the lowest cleaner because there was a hierarchy there. I'm cleaning the ootside steps. (L) The Broadway and the men's dirty lavvies, and they *were* filthy! And my 'Ladies' I worked wi', there was ane on the ground floor and that wis a bittie promotion, but my God, the anes in the Gallery! But I'll never forget the Manager, one day he said to me (and the word scrubber hasna the connotation it has now) he said, 'You know, you're the best scrubber I ever hid.' And you know that was a week I had a Third Programme play gaen on, and I'll tell you I thocht I was mair complimented wi' *that*, than I wis wi' a' my Third Programme, because you see the play wis something I could dae and rather enjoy daein', and this was something I hated daein' and yet I still did it. And I thought, there, isn't that funny. That was a proud moment, I'm the best scrubber! I'll maybe get a promotion. My God. But it was the wifies that made me laugh—human beings—you see, the junior—if onybody leaves, they said, you'll get on to a hoover—and there wis a Third play gaen on! Fortunately my humour never deserted me.

IM   It really is one of the constants in your life: in all the bits of your life that you talk about you have one foot in two different worlds, at *least* two different worlds, all the time.

JK   Yes, that's how the theme of my books is really the ootlin. That's
     what I mean. Whatever I've done apart from my writing I've been
     an ootlin' in a funny wey. I shouldnae hae been. And you know the
     sad—I'm sure if they'd gaen me the education I should have got—
     the dominie wanted me to get it, you know, and bought my books
     for me, but the Trustees said no. Maybe again if I had been a boy ...
IM   You might not have had so much to say.
JK   Ah, but my life would have been on different lines.
IM   Aye, but you don't really regret it.
JK   Yes, I do. I've regretted it, that's why I was so pleased with the LLD.
IM   Hold on, I'm precisely coming to that.
JK   That was why—it was something I should have had, I would have
     loved every—Oh, I canna explain, not even to you, I know my life
     would have been awfa different. Cos although I can laugh and say
     all this things no, no, it widna ...
IM   It might have been bland and boring.
JK   Never! because my nature's nae bland and boring.
IM   Some of life imposes itself.
JK   No, I dinna agree wi' that ever, so we'll—
IM   Some people get stuck in some pretty bland situations and there's
     not a lot they can do—
JK   Well I'll tell you, Isobel, I could have daen something that wouldn't
     have been bland and boring! (L) I'd hae gaen off ...
IM   But what interests me here is this wonderful world of contrasts.
     There you are in London having to take some of the more amazing
     hard-working drudgery jobs because you're not qualified for jobs,
     and you're writing plays for the Third Programme and in the end
     you know, this final wonderful paradox, you get an LLD. Tell me
     about the LLD.
JK   There's something before I tell ye aboot that. The one job I got
     towards the end, but when I was a good bit younger, was the job I
     loved best of all. It was the only job ever I got paid for in my life for
     standin' or sittin' and thinkin' my ain thochts. (L) I became a life
     model at the Art School.
IM   You didn't?
JK   I did! For aboot ten years and a very good model was I! In the sense
     of reliable, could always stand in poses, I could, and very few could.
     I went all over, I know London inside out and a' the suburbs, and
     again you see it was well paid. You'd no tax, you got your bus fares
     and a'thing. And, it was the kind of job when you went home at
     nicht ye didna take it wi ye, and ye didna' worry aboot it. I could
     concentrate on my writing, because I had no worry, I could pose

very well and a' that. But there wis little things that went wrong
now and again. I wis daein' this six weeks sitting for a painting in
Guildford. Because as ye ken I like a smoke, I would get undressed
and into my cubicle as quick as onything afore onybody comes and
hae a nice smoke, and the same at nicht: I was aye the last to gae into
my cubicle to get myself and my bags and my bits thegither and get
awa hame. Now, there was a French tutor, a nice man he was, a
tutor, and I went by train you see, an early morning train and ye ken
fit like they are in the train, a' ahin' their papers and I wis haen' a
look—I've aye been a bit short-sighted and I thought, that's my
tutor: I said, 'Good Morning,' and being a polite mannie he looked
up, slightly vaguely, smiled at me and turned his heid and went tae
his paper, and I wondered fit on earth's wrang wi' him. And
suddenly he popped his heid—ah, he said, it's you, I did not know
you with your clothes on! The carriage—oh! (L)
IM   That's wonderful!
JK   And I really was a very good model.
BT   And you did that for ten years?
JK   Oh, at least. Off and on. When I wis a bit hard up I'd tak a—you see
I could tak a space tae dae my writing, my mannie, and then go back
and it was a lovely atmosphere, and if I had been an artist instead o'
a writer what a lot I could have learned, you know. And then there
wis anither wifie come in aboot. There was two models often used,
and that was why when I said I was a good model, (a) I could hold
my poses and (b) I could be utterly relied on, you know, if I took my
booking, but this ane hidna turned up, the ither ane that wis workin'
wi' me, and sometimes casual anes would come in you know
wanting a bookin', and in come this wifie one day—mind I wis
younger then, and rather critical of a'thing—and she'd on a mangy
auld fur coat, and she was a bit lame, and her hair was really dyed
a terrible shade o' reid and in she cam, but they were desperate for
two models and it didna maitter much what she looked like, they'd
to get their two models. Although the students didna like it, they
niver liked onything like that. An' we were sitting haein' our
coffee. She said you know, she cam frae New Zealand she said,
originally like, she said, 'You know, we should have a Union.' I
said, 'We dinna need a Union.' Anyway we should hae a Union, but
as I said we dinna need a Union: we'd nae tax or nothing to dae you
know. Oh she said it's not that, it's the students! But I said God aye,
which I did! I said young fowk, I get on fine wi' the students, and I
did. And well, she said, you know this, she said, when I sit up on the
throne, she said, they get so excited, she said, they pass out. I said

you're bloody lucky, they've never passed out at me! (L)

BT   You obviously feel that if you'd had more of a chance of an education that things would have been different. The LLD has meant quite a lot to you?

JK   Well it meant it because of that you know, it really did.

BT   How did it come about?

JK   Well I didna ken. I got quite a surprise. But I'll tell ye something; it was sorcery. Oh, I wis awfa pleased! Dear Professors, they were, you know.

IM   Professor what?

JK   Professor John Norton-Smith; a dear man! And the St Andrews ane was as good. I've daen talks there in St Andrews and I think that's fit did it. But onywey, it was a very moving experience and I wish I could remember the ones who got it but they were very tall men by me; I'm nae very big. And when ye got it; you know, yer blue and gold goon ...

IM   A beautiful gown.

JK   Lovely gown. You send yer measurements right enough. But fin I gaein into my goon jist the same I could have gone oot and in at the sleeve o't. You understand?

IM   Let's have it clear though. Which university was it?

JK   Dundee.

IM   Dundee, right.

JK   Fin ye come in, and the Chancellor and a' the graduands are called, a' them and they're all, and the Lord Provost you know, marching in this long aisle and the Caird Hall packed, with everything, and they a' stand as you process doon the narrow and up in the top the organ's playin' the Gaudeamus: and the most ridiculous thought came into my heid, and yet in a funny wey it's in context; this tall chap was behind me and it cam into my heid and I thocht Alice in Wonderland right enough and it wis richt I thocht there's a porpoise right behind me!

IM   Treading on my tail.

JK   But any minute this lang man is going to catch his fit on the tail o' my lang goon and I am gaen to bring this serious lovely procession to a right abrupt close. But it didna happen. But can ye see it?

IM   What year was this, Jessie?

JK   1984. 13th July: it's written on my heart, like Calais on Mary's. Oh, I wis awfa pleased.

IM   Well, I think all we have to say at this stage is that Bob and I would both like to continue this conversation at some other time, at some other place. But meanwhile we are enormously grateful to Jessie for sparing us time on a really hectic visit to Edinburgh and that we know you'll be grateful too.

JK   Thank you!

[An interview for Aberdeen student television. April 1988]

IM   Jessie Kesson has just been given a doctorate by the University of Aberdeen, a Doctorate of Literature, and she is the author of three novels, one book of short stories and ninety plays, but because these plays are written for radio the novels are what we tend to know most about. Jessie, are the novels the most important thing?

JK   Yes, I said to you afore Isobel, it sounds like a cliché to me, in the beginning was the Word and that's the book—so that comes first. Secondly comes—but still in the beginning was the Word, because as you ken radio uses words a' the time, gies words their full meaning, and I far prefer it to television or the theatre or onything else. I think even mair than the book, I like radio better, because of the sound of the words. If you've listened to the plays—maybe ye haena I dinna ken—ye'll find that the words are awfa important. They can transcend time and place and a'thing else, I mean you can go to Africa if you want till in a minute, and then your words will evoke that in a wey that a book would tak a chapter to describe even the scenery there. Am I right?

IM   No, not as regards your own books, you don't take a chapter to describe the scenery ... (L)

JK   No, no, but then I've niver described Africa in a book! Bit if I wis to dae a travel book it would tak me an awfa lot to describe Africa. But wi' this background sounds and jist an African accent if you like, twa or three African accents in maybe ten minutes you'd hae your African scene in Africa. Nae that I'm wanting to dae Africa, I dinna ken about it but you know ...

IM   No, but does that mean that in a sense you feel uncomfortable to be best known by *The White Bird Passes, Glitter of Mica, Another Time, Another Place* and *Where the Apple Ripens*, than you know— people count them rather than read them—the radio plays ...?

JK   No, no, the only ane I really feel sadly a bit uncomfortable about is *The White Bird Passes*. I know it's the maist popular book. I know that it is.

IM   This is the one that is mainly autobiographical?

JK   Aye. It's now been reprinted for the fourth time by Hogarth Press. Chatto and Windus did it the first time while I was there and I know it's the maist popular book and I feel it aye will be; you know without being conceited or anything, it's a classic book, but it wis niver my favourite. For the simple reason is—it was the easiest book I ever wrote! (L) You know, because, you know, it wis mainly autobiographical. My ain favourite was *Glitter of Mica*. And a freen' o' yours it's his favourite and that's Douglas Gifford. Strangely enough he's aye said that. It's my ain favourite because it was a much harder book to write.

IM Mainly because it's not about you.

JK The only direct sentence in it aboot me is I know its background absolutely. I've got to know that and you've got to know that—

IM That is the background of rural Aberdeenshire.

JK Aye, that's right. So therefore I know it and if onything in my experience has come oot o't it is the background. But the characters—I think I telt you how I got the character—

IM Tell me again.

JK Well I wis at Charing Cross Road, I wis looking—oh nae the same like as 84 Charing Cross Road, but I prowl aroun' the bookshops and I found this book—an auld book of Irish ballads and things, and I came across this and I'll quote it for ye—just a verse—and it said: it was called 'To Cashel I'm Going': and that was actually the first title I chose for the book, *To Cashel I'm Going* and it said this,

> Tis pity I came where my name was unknown in the town
> Where no-one could tell how so well I had earned renown,
> Where the young ones I sought should have thought them-
>   selves honoured in knowing
> A man of my name and good fame—So—to Cashel I'm
>   going.

And all of a sudden I saw that man! Hugh Riddel. I thought, ah! I see him in the cottar's eyes. This is him—'To Cashel I'm Going'. This proud, bitter man and I knew why he was bitter. And I've always felt very deeply for that book.

IM In a sense it's interesting that Hugh Riddel *is* the central character of *Glitter of Mica*: it's like Lewis Grassic Gibbon choosing somebody of the opposite sex as the main character in *A Scots Quair*. It's almost as if because you're offering it to the other sex you feel more free to create the character.

JK I'll tell you a compliment I felt was paid to me about *Glitter of Mica*. The critics a' said that this book must have been written by a man. Div you ken 'at?

IM (L) I don't think that's a compliment!

JK I do! Because you ken I'm no *transvestite*! (L) Nothing like that! But I could write a strong book that could have been written by a man.

IM   But I just think that's a *sad* comment on your male critics.

JK   Yes, aye, well but that wis true. And hiv you ever really read *Glitter of Mica* yersel truly?

IM   Indeed I hope so!

JK   Aye, well dae ye nae see that, that hardness I got—and mind you, I wis jist as sorry for his wife and his mistress.

IM   I see the quality of hardness: I absolutely refuse to believe that it's to do with being male or female.

JK   I don't think a wifie could have written it!

IM   Away you go! (L) A wifie in your understanding is a very special thing. What do you mean by a 'wifie'?

JK   A female. No. Maybe George Sand might have written it. Aye, she might have written it, but I canna think o' mony. I canna see Jane Austen, she's 'at busy among the cornhills down in Bath, she widna've touched them.

IM   (L) So what do you think makes *Glitter of Mica* particularly good? Is it most of all just the fact that it's not about you, and that you ...?

JK   No, no, it's also the thing that in a wey I got it oot o' mysel, what I really felt about how it wis to be a cottar in by, and a lot, you know, and the snobbery, the hardness of the work.

IM   Now, tell me exactly what a cottar was. I think a lot of the folk who are watching this won't know.

JK   Well a cottar is—mind they're nearly like the dodo, they're nearly—is it extant?

IM   Extinct. And that's not a bad thing in some ways.

JK   Aye, they're nearly extinct. A pity in other weys though, you know really, it's a mixture thing. A cottar was in the older days farm workers who lived in a row—usually a' shoved thegither in a row o' wee cottages. Funny, I aye thocht about it, the cottar used to hae lots o' bairns you know, and they had this wee, wee hoose we hid, and the fairmer who might only hae two had the biggest hoose you'd ever seen! So that's off for a start. He didna need so sair as we needed for lots o' bairns. Bit onyway the cottar, the farm-worker, but the cottar was the word—Burns used it ye ken 'The Cottar's Saturday Nicht', it's an old word, he lived in a—his cottages were tied.

IM   Tied to the job, so that if you lost your job you lost your cottage?

JK   Aye, if you lost yer job you lost yer cottage. Two days off in the year: nae days off, naething, and when the cows were calving we'd be up a' nicht. That was the cottar's life *but*—and the rest had the same ye see, the same kind o' thing—we had oor cottar-hoose, we didna pey rent. We got mind you this is what we got, we got about two gallons o' milk a day, we hidna to pey for that, we got aboot ten bags o' tatties, we hidna to pey for that, and we got the meal you know six bales, ye ca' six bags o' meal.

IM   Coal?

JK   No, sometimes you waud get a farmer to gie—but that wis nae-thing—we used to pinch the sticks roun' the steading. (L) And so we got that. The—what we called perquisites, right? Ye niver got the sack but fit would happen was in March every year if the farmer didna ask ye to bide on for anither year, if he didna speak tae ye at a' aboot it, ye knew ye had tae leave in the May. The fairmer used to come roun' and seek workers that he wanted to bide on, but if he didna want ye to bide on he said nothing. You know: it really is incredible, isn't it?

IM   Barbarous, absolutely barbarous.

JK   Yes and we left. And this, I got a lot o' t oot o' my system in *Glitter of Mica*.

Now, I must tell you. *Glitter of Mica* the title, it's fae G. S. Fraser the poet, he's a great international poet although he's an Aberdeen man, ye ken he is. [The poem is titled 'Home Town Elegy (for Aberdeen in Spring)', and begins: 'Glitter of mica at the windy corners'. See *Poems of G. S. Fraser*, edited by Ian Fletcher and John Lucas, Leicester, 1981, p. 51.]

IM   And literary critic.

JK   Aye, oh yes, he's dead now. But his 'Glitter of Mica' was a marvellous poem I wish I could say it a', but that's where I took the title for the granite—

IM   Is this about the wee shine that you get on the granite in Aberdeen everywhere when the sun comes out?

JK   Aye, you know, the glitter of mica, the hard shine, the 'glitter of mica at the windy corners', he writes, and dae ye ken how he ends it? This poem ends on Aberdeen—it's a' aboot the wind, and the fishing and a'thing—and it ends: 'Where Byron is not the whatever, the poet, that fool but just a tall, proud statue at the Grammar School.'

So *Glitter of Mica* was written: that's what I felt so much when *Glitter of Mica* was written, get this oot o' my system.

IM   Later two things happened almost together, and you had a big hand in both of them—you wrote the whole of the book, and you wrote most of the film: *Another Time, Another Place*, about a young woman who was working in the Black Isle?

JK   Aye, Ross-shire. A farm again.

IM   Ross-shire. During the war, and found herself envying the Italian prisoners of war who came as workers on the land because of the breadth of their experience and because of how trapped she felt. Is there an autobiographical element in this?

JK   Oh yes, very much, Isobel. They were exotic compared to the reid-handed phlegmatic country men, you know, and remember the girl was very young, and ye ken fit all Latin countries are, they fuss a woman you know, and it was a' that wis autobiographical: the sex was overemphasised! That was in the mind, it wis *there* a richt, but it was maistly in the mind, as you'd ken if you read the book.

IM   As I recall the *Press and Journal* got quite excited about that.

JK   No sex in Scotland! A' the auld wifies were gaen mad! Little did they ken it wis an auld-age pensioner—too much sex, it was an old-age pensioner who complained. (L)

IM   Or remembered as the case may be! Right so the first book, *The White Bird Passes*, was about your own personal experiences; the second book, *Glitter of Mica*, is about the *situation* that you know so well. And then the third one was this one about the young woman with the Italian prisoners of war and the affairs of all kinds that were involved.

JK   Here and there and a'wye.

IM   And then last year you were short-listed for book of the year with *Where the Apple Ripens*.

JK   It's short stories.

IM   Well, yes, except that the actual title story *Where the Apple Ripens* is a novella rather than a story, and it's very important. Now, is *that* autobiographical?

JK   No, a bit was autobiographical—obviously no, it wisna, if you remember it, it's aboot a young girl wi' her father a sma fairmer, and proper parents which I niver haed, and the relation I think between the parents is awfa good, I'm sure it is: instinctively I know that's how it would be. I didn't experience any of that, except I experienced the adolescent thing, a desperate need for love, a desperate, you know ...

IM   That's very important.

JK   That certainly has nothing to do with me, except in my *emotions* as a young teenager.

IM   Precisely, that is so important, I mean I think you are one of the authors who has best *ever* got what it's like to be a young girl at the—on the edge of everything—just about to have things happen.

JK   Knowing everything aboot sex and yet at the same time knowing nothing about it. That puts it in a nutshell.

IM   Exactly. And this lassie is extraordinarily anxious to experience it all, and the whole story is given in the context of a senior girl not many years older who has gone into service in the town, and had an illegitimate baby and died, and there's a funeral going on and so the heroine of this novel or novella is on the threshold, with all the awful things shown, but I think—

JK   I'll tell ye what I think a'body's missed, Isobel, and you're a fair reviewer, you've been kind to me, a good reviewer, even Douglas Gifford ... but I'll tell ye fit I think, a'body missed the point, and I ken you'll see it instantly; there's this girl so affected by the sudden death through an illegitimate baby o' a classmate who remember, she had a great admiration for because o her poetry and a'thing, because she came fae a mair exotic world, a sort of hero worship if you like, or heroine worship it wad be. Now at the same time despite the fact that her feeling is deep and genuine, in a way horrified, she's jist going off to dae the same thing.

IM   Without even noticing.

JK   She's nae aware of it, but she's desperate to be seduced herself. And that is, I think, a'body missed that.

IM   Saved not by the bell but the postman. I didn't miss it, but I thought it was so obvious you didn't have to actually spell it out.

JK   But you ken fit I mean—naebody's pointed that oot. It was a parallel thing. Despite her genuine grief—actually again that was a real incident, and it affected me so much. It really did hurt me and I was awfa affected, although as I said I only knew the quine was a different species athegither fae me, well-off, beautifully dressed, nice-spoken, and my God, how it affected me. But a' the time at the same time actually, I could dae the character wi' her proper Mam and that. At the same time, at that period o' my life, I was desperately lookin' roon for somebody to sleep wi' me, (L) and there's the irony o' the whole thing. Indeed it could have happened to me, it could have happened, bit it didna happen because I make it interrupted by the postie. Actually it didna happen at all, it's a bit like *Another Time*, it niver happened, but it *could* have happened and that's it, you know.

IM   It almost inevitably happens, yes.

JK   That's the whole thing aboot *Where the Apple Ripens*.

IM   Would you like to tell us a wee bit about why you started: what started you actually writing radio plays?

JK   The very first radio thing I ever did in my life wis a poem called 'The Scarlet Goun'. Right? The reason it happened wis, the BBC rang and gave me an audition; actually thought I'd make an actress, and my gosh I acted a lot, in fact ane of the critics says I acted the rest o' the actors off the air!

IM Mm. How about that!

JK But I niver wanted to be an actress, I wis a writer and I'd nae ambitions of acting. Bit onywey, they rang and said they were daein' a poem Aberdeen, Town and Gown, university; hid I onything that I felt aboot the University. Now it's nae a poem. If it were a poem I'd remember every word o' it. It would be memorable, *but* I remember a bit o' it, and this is the first thing I ever wrote and I must have been aboot maybe twenty-five at the time, and I'm seventy-one now on this day. So the poem was this:

> Gin I'd worn a scarlet goun,
> Fit wad I ken? Mair or less than I ken noo,
> Workin' 'mong men wha niver heard o' Aristotle,
> Or Boyle that made a law,
> Or Pythagoras, and sic like chiels
> Wha's wisdom's gey heich up and far awa?
> My Alma Mater's jist the size o' other fowk,
> And jist the colour o' their thochts,
> Grey whiles wi' grief, and green, for jealousy torments
> Even lads wi' nae letters ahint their name.
> But still, I'd hae liket a scarlet goun
> And a desk o' my ain neath the auld grey crown,
> Instead o' howkin' tatties in mornings blared and cauld
> O the regret as a bodie grows auld.

I was in my twenties but I *foresaw* in a way what I'd missed.

IM That's a lovely poem to quote on the day when you get your second scarlet gown. Your second doctoral gown.

JK No, this was the first *scarlet* gown. What did ye think o' that? That wis written when I was in my twenties. The very first thing I ever wrote.

A METAPHORICAL WAY OF SEEING THINGS

NORMAN MacCAIG

These conversations between Norman MacCaig, Isobel Murray and Bob Tait took place in February 1986 in Devanha Terrace, Aberdeen.

IM Norman, perhaps I could invite you to tell us a little about your famous three-quarters Gaelic and one quarter Borders ancestry. Just a little to place you in time and place.

NM Yes, well people—not just Scots—are fearfully proud if they can get some Celtic blood corpuscles waving shillelaghs and claymores through their veins, and I suppose I have the same ambition. But I don't need to, because my mother was born in a little island, Scalpay, Harris, came to Edinburgh at the age of 16, she didn't have a word of English in her mouth. She made up for it. My father came from Dumfries, a little place near Castle Douglas. They collided in Edinburgh, with this happy result!

IM Were you the only result?

NM No, I had three sisters. Quite nice sisters. So go to my grandparents—three were total Gaels. Gaelic speakers. One was not a Gaelic speaker, she was born in Galloway, Dumfries really, called Currie. So that I used to boast that I was three out of four grandparents, three-quarters Gael and I mentioned this to a learned scholar and he said what was the name of the Border grannie? And I said Currie and he says but that's MacMhuirich. So I now say I'm a seven-eighths Gael.

IM Well, could we start with what you remember about your grandparents in your childhood?

NM Well I had a misfortune. Three of my grandparents were dead before I was born, and the fourth one, who was my Grannie Currie, died when I was about seven or eight, which meant ... I think it's an awful loss if you don't know your grandparents because they are the carriers of tradition, and I used not to be interested in the past at all—I am more now—and I've often wondered if it was because this link of grandparents is missing in my case.

IM Where did your Grannie Currie live when you were very small?

NM In Dumfries.

IM So you did visit the Borders?

NM Yes, oh yes.

IM Do you remember that?

NM Very clearly, yes.

IM Could you tell us a wee bit about it?

NM Well my father of course took me there holidays, and we stayed with relations of his, cousins, and we, *he*, hired a car and we went all over the place—we went through so many places that I had heard him *name*—and some of the names—oh!—I don't know that I envy my father—he had a hard, hard life! But I do envy him the fact that he went to school at a place called the Haugh of Urr—straight out of a ballad! (L)

IM What did his father do for a living?

NM His father was a grieve on a farm in—across the river from Dumfries.

IM And your father went on to—?

NM He became a chemist. He was a bright boy at school I believe. He got a bursary to go to the university, it would be a very *tiny* bursary; and his parents couldn't afford it, so he became a pharmaceutical chemist.

IM So your father was a chemist. In Edinburgh?

NM Yes, in Edinburgh and a wage-slave, in those days. We were very poor. Of course, being a pharmaceutical chemist, it was a white-collar job you know, lowest of the middle class, and he wore fly away stiff collars all his life you know, very, very, very 'boorjoysie' but he had a lot of interests. One of my regrets is that I didn't get to know him better—filled with questions that I hadn't bothered to ask until it's too late. He was interested in many things outside his job but the hours he worked were just appalling, terrible!

IM He had his own business?

NM No, he hadn't *then*. It became his own and in those days there was no chemist open all night; and desperate people hunting for one asked a policeman. They always came to my father and about two or three times a week he was pulling his trousers o'er his pyjamas and going down to the shop. (L) On top of the huge hours he worked. He was a good man.

IM So he eventually got his own business, or inherited—the business he'd been working in?

NM Yes, partly that.

IM I'm not entirely clear about your father's background.

NM Well I don't know about his background—I don't know about his boyhood background—except one or two odd stories he told. It's only since he came to Edinburgh and met my mother that I really know much about. You see I wasn't interested in the past, as I say, and now I'm *devoured* with curiosity and nobody to ask!

IM Yes. So how old were you when your father died approx.?

NM Oh I don't know dates. Well he died when I was round about sixty I suppose. Both he and my mother lived to a reasonable age, sort of eightyish. Then both of them, thank God, died like pressing a switch and putting a light out. No agonies.

BT You had a long time in which to talk to your father.

NM A long time? Yes, in span of years, but as I said his working hours were so awful. When he came home he was exhausted. Oh, we talked, I mean we had a 'good relationship'. He had TB at one period, and I remember sitting on his knee while he read me *Tarzan of the Apes* and being overwhelmed with the smell of creosote that came out of his breath, which was some medicine he was taking. (L) He recovered.

IM What do you know about your mother's coming to the Mainland?

NM Well, it was a common, common thing, remember this was *nearly* the beginning of the century, it was a very common thing in the Hebrides in those days for the girls, seeking work, they either went round with the herring fleet, or they came to the big cities and got a job as servants or nurses. And my mother got a job as a servant in some big house and how she met my father, this douce 'boorjoysie', I do not know!

IM And they must have conversed almost in their minds ...?

NM Well she had no English when she *came*, I don't know how old she was when she met my father, but by that time she had accumulated more than enough English for several people. (L)

IM You never got the impression, nobody meeting her in English, would have thought she was inadequate in the language at all?

NM Well I don't know about *then*, cos I wasn't here, but in her life as I knew her, oh, she could run circles round Professors of Sanskrit and leave them gasping!

IM So if somebody was going to try to find the springs of your intense interest in words and all that they convey, do you think they'd be looking at her side of the family rather than your father's?

NM Oh on her, definitely her! If there's any poetry in me it's from her.

She thought on images as metaphors. Sometimes so hilarious that when she was giving us a row, which she frequently did because she was a volatile lady, she would say, use some image or metaphor that was so funny we burst out laughing and of course so did she, because she was an extremely, is it riseible or risible?

IM I think it rhymes with Isobel.

NM She loved laughing, she laughed seismically—she was a big woman, not in height, and hardly any sound came out of her mouth and tears rolled down her cheeks—helpless with mirth! She was a marvellous lady! But this thinking in images and metaphors which she did, obviously I inherited that from her, because that's the way I *still* think really, and it must be one of the reasons why I write the way I write.

IM And as you came, growing up, to trace her roots back to Scalpay, you went to Scalpay often on holiday and met uncles and aunts and so on whom you've written about; could you detect there as well the kind of interest in language or metaphor or whatever that you see in your mother ...?

NM Well I don't know about that. They spoke Gaelic of course. I mean the older people didn't have any English. I had two of my mother's sisters and one brother still alive when I started going there in my teens, aged 12, and the brother was very literate, he wrote two or three novels in Gaelic, and at least one in English, and yet his two sisters had no English *whatever*, absolutely none. So conversation was limited, it was limited on my part just to gesticulations and opening and shutting my pores and looking helpless. (L)

IM I imagine that went down all right?

NM Och yes, yes. I loved them and they loved me, and my sisters. They're very affectionate people.

IM And were they themselves centres of other families, or were you supplying something very important when you went back?

NM Auntie Julia didn't have any children, I don't know why. Auntie Stinag did, she had three, cousins, cousins of mine. Girls. All of whom I liked very much, and still do. Still alive.

IM Good, good. That's nice. So Scalpay was obviously *enormously* important to you as a child. When gradually you came to the part when family holidays changed did you stop going back to Scalpay?

NM Well, yes. I'll tell you two things about this. These teenage visits to Scalpay, I didn't realise how important they were to me at the time but looking back it's the first time I began to realise that I had ancestors, not just my father and mother. They gave me a connection. It was meeting my aunts and my cousins *there* that made me realise that I was a miniscule and unimportant part of history. No, that's putting it too portentously. I felt I *belonged* to people in a way that I hadn't before, except to my parents. Your other question was?

IM   About why you stopped going back to Scalpay?

NM   Well, it's not a nice reason. The Scalpay people I think are absolutely marvellous and it's not just my view: even the other people in Harris say so. (L) But they have a breed of religion which I cannot tolerate—Free Presbyterianism—and I know—I got to know fine—that if I were to go back there, oh, if they knew I was coming they'd be at the pier, and before we'd walked a quarter of a mile they would say, and what church do you go to in Edinburgh, Norman? And I would have to say I don't share these filthy, spurious and murderous superstitions. (L)

BT   So you don't go?

NM   So I don't go, right.

IM   Did your mother share these filthy—murderous superstitions?

NM   My mother was a very sensible woman!

IM   Go on!

NM   Of course she didn't! Nor did my father, of course!

BT   Were they church-going people?

NM   My mother went to a church in Edinburgh because in the evening there was a Gaelic service, and it was just to hear the language. They didn't force any form of religious belief on the children so that I ...

BT   Have you always been an agnostic?

NM   No. Always been an atheist!

IM   Have your sisters always been atheists, if you know?

NM   Two were. One of them lapsed.

BT   Well, can I return to my question. You have always been an atheist. Did you *decide* to be an atheist? Or ...?

NM   No, no, I was born an atheist. The first thing I said when I sprang out of my mother's womb was, 'Down with Popery!' I said it in Gaelic of course! (L)

BT   You've had no inclination ever to hold any religious beliefs?

NM   Absolutely none! And my schoolboy friend right from the age of infant class right through university, the lot, knew he was going to be a minister, as I knew I was going to be a teacher, I just knew it and he did. And he became a minister! In the Church of Scotland.

IM   And it didn't cause any problem in the relationship between the two of you?

NM   Not a bit.

IM   Oh that's nice. Do you have, as far as you know, friendships and ongoing relationships with people who are, now, practising Christians?

NM Oh yes.

IM That doesn't seem to occur as part of the fabric of the friendship at all?

NM No, no. I mean everybody's got handicaps. (L)

IM But these people on Scalpay were concentrating on one area in which you couldn't please them?

NM Oh yes, yes! And I would hate to offend them you see. They would be hurt. They wouldn't reject me but they would be hurt.

IM So, have you been back to Scalpay in living memory?

NM Yes, infrequently and briefly. I went up with my mother and one of my sisters, and I've only been back about twice, three times, since. And of course most of the people I knew these years ago were not there, or I'd forgotten them: but my cousin Seonag she was there and the first time I went nobody knew I was coming. They thought I was in Edinburgh. And I decided to go, and I went over on the boat to Scalpay and I knew fine I could find Seonag's house but I wasn't too certain, so I went into the butcher's shop, MacSween, whose sons I had known. And a girl was—I got cigarettes or something—and she'd a look on her face—she was a bonny lassie—and she had a look on her face, and I said 'Do you know who I am?' and she said 'Oh, yes, yes.' Nobody knew I was coming. And of course in two minutes flat everybody in Scalpay knew I was coming.

IM Do you think that Scalpay has been important in the kind of basic pool of images and memories?

NM Oh yes. It's *profoundly* important to me. Even though I've been back so few times. For the reason that I gave. And also, I loved the place and I loved the people, except their religion.

IM So is—you'll excuse my ignorance of geography—is Luskentyre for example—

NM Luskentyre is on the mainland of Harris, Scalpay is a ...

IM But when you talk about the graveyard at Luskentyre?

NM That's where my mother's people are, well, that's *the* graveyard for that big part of Harris. Very beautiful place! Very beautiful people buried in it, in spite of their religious beliefs! (L)

IM Meantime, getting back to Edinburgh, to this immensely pure and non-religified childhood, what part of Edinburgh did you live in when you were a wee boy?

NM I was born in London Street, and when I was very, very young, I think an infant, we flitted to Dundas Street, to a house which was just beside my father's shop.

IM So the centre of all your Edinburgh life for a long time would be Dundas Street, if you lived there and your father's business was there also. Where did you go to school?

NM Royal High School.

IM From age five?

NM From age five or so, yes. I know I went into the Infant Department.

BT Was that a fee-paying school at the time?

NM Well it did, it was a fee-paying school but it was an Edinburgh control school all the same, it wasn't a private school.

BT So it was grant-aided?

NM I don't know where they got their money from. I know that if you went before you were five or something you paid £4 a term. And I went before I was five.

IM Which only goes to show that you were in the ascendant middle-classes! Right.

NM Unlike so many people, I enjoyed school very much.

IM Ah, you took the next question out of my mouth. Right. Do you remember a lot about it?

NM Oh, yes. Oh, yes. A great deal.

IM Even the primary?

NM Yes, yes.

IM And you liked it from the start?

NM I did, I enjoyed school. I was sorry to leave.

IM It was an all boys school, wasn't it then?

NM Yes, it was, yes.

IM Did you miss your sisters?

NM Och, I had enough of them when I got home! (L)

IM So the single sex school didn't affect you, didn't worry you at all?

NM I didn't know any other. And my sisters had female friends you know, I wasn't without feminine company.

IM Not like being a boarder.

NM No, I would hate that.

IM And is it too crude to ask if your sisters went to the same kind of Edinburgh school, or whether there was a preference for the boy?

NM There was a preference for the boy! Because they had very little money! And any money was for the boy.

IM Did you find that weighed on you at all?

NM Not a bit! No, no! I was so used to being pampered! (L) I just took it for granted.

IM Never looked back since! (L) So when you were at school if you thought about what you would do when you left, what kind of thing did you imagine yourself doing in the future?

NM   Oh I—from the age of twelve, fourteen, I just knew I was going to
     be a teacher. Just as my chum knew he was going to be a minister.
     I never thought I would be anything else. So I became a teacher.

IM   You decided on your career before you decided on what subject you
     might teach; you knew that you wanted to teach.

NM   Yes.

IM   Yes, and then when you went to university it was Classics you took
     there. Did you have trouble deciding that?

NM   No I hadn't. And I don't understand this. I wasn't thinking about
     being a poet, never, never, not for one minute! I didn't start *writing*
     poetry till I was in the fifth, sixth, fifth form. And it was nothing to
     do with that. But I knew that I didn't want to teach English. So I
     didn't take English. Which was of course my best subject!

IM   Of course.

NM   So I took my second best subject, and I'm very glad I did!

IM   So, do you think that your Classics at school was fed by having just
     a natural interest, or did you have a very good teacher?

NM   A very good teacher! An excellent teacher. A man called Mr
     Young. Who fortunately I had all the way through secondary
     school, six years. A marvellous man and a marvellous teacher who
     understood bairns. And I enjoyed the languages. I'm a terrible bad
     linguist, very, very bad linguist. I depend on translations. And
     fortunately the last half century has been a marvellous fifty years of
     translations.

IM   Do you depend upon translations these days, if it's a matter of Latin
     or Greek?

NM   Some. There are some I still occasionally pick up. I love some of
     Plato's dialogues, imagine that. Because they're so beautifully
     written. He's one of my big men, Socrates—not Plato, Socrates.
     And some of the dialogues I still occasionally read especially the
     Crito, where he's about to take the hemlock. It's beautiful prose,
     it's beautiful prose! And of course, Mr Socrates and his lamenting
     friends, it's just a marvellous piece of writing.

IM   You've certainly come back to Socrates, and Socrates either about
     to drink or having drunk a couple of times at least in your poetry,
     haven't you?

BT   Oh, more than a couple of times. I mean one of the things that
     strikes me about your poetry is that it is very Socratic, it's about
     know thyself, and also about ...

NM   Yes, that's true.

BT   ... values which through Socrates Plato gave to the Western World.

NM   That's right..

BT   Against himself.

NM   Yes.

BT   Plato was a man who wanted social order to be regulated by
     certainly *philosopher* kings but undoubtedly kings, who'd be much
     superior to the people. Socrates seemed to be another kind of
     person.

NM   Yes.

BT   Who was always questioning the authority of those in power. And
     he made a fool of people by leading them on with questions.

NM   He had a method of arguing which we all know, question/answer,
     question/answer/question. And he leads people on until they're
     saying something absolutely ridiculous. I call it the Socratic side-
     step. (L) Because he asks them a question and he pretends to agree
     and he asks ... and before they know where they are, they are saying
     something absolutely idiotic. (L)

BT   That forensic mind, that ability to show the absurdity of positions
     seems to be part and parcel of your entire poetry. We've already hit
     upon something which is fundamental.

NM   Yes. That's true. I don't like to say this but three days ago I think it
     was, I wrote a poem and it was exactly about this. It was exactly
     about what we are talking about—Socrates comes into it. I don't
     want to tell you about the poem. Except to say that it's this man
     Socrates and his way of thinking has been a huge influence on me,
     right up till three days ago. [IM hazards that the poem in question is
     'Backward Look', in *Voice-Over*, 1988, pp. 45-46.]

BT   Isn't it astonishing that Plato, the author, is remembered for Socra-
     tes, because the two couldn't be more different.

NM   I think that's one of the reasons I'm so fond of Socrates. Plato was
     just an up-market journalist. (L)

IM   So, you liked the languages, but obviously the values that you were
     coming across studying, finding, in the Classics when you were a
     student, were making far more than a simple superficial effect on
     you.

NM   Yes.

IM   Do any of the other authors of the ancient world seem very im-
     portant?

NM   Not in the way I'm talking about except this general one which
     might be interesting.
          Gaelic art is all very formal, I'm meaning the times when Gaelic
     art was marvellous in poetry, for example, and you've got to go
     back a century and a half, and in song, too, where there are
     thousands of *absolutely* beautiful songs. An awful lot of them

written by women, oddly, and everything, even their carving of which there isn't much, Celtic crosses, the decorations are absolutely formal, abstract. Pibroch, the most formal sort of music ever written. Bach would have loved them, and this rubbish of Celtic twilight you know, golden-haired boys lamenting, twanging on a harp in the mist, while their lassie's away marrying a seal, you know. (L) That's Matthew Arnold rubbish, Celtic twilight. It's absolutely opposite to reality—they're the most practical, formal people. And maybe that's why I took to Latin and Greek, because it's formal and I am a very formal writer.

IM   So apart from Plato-oblique-stroke-Socrates, who was a special case, do you think any of these writers have affected the way you think or have often come up in the way you express things?

NM   I think they established the way I was likely to think, because of this formalism. They strengthened something that was already there.

IM   So, when you left the Royal High School in Edinburgh, did you go to *Edinburgh University*?

NM   Yes.

IM   Did you think of going anywhere else to university, or was it just financially obvious that you would stay at home?

NM   Ach, it was just up the road. And I'm a bit sorry about that, because I missed a lot of university life: it was just an extension of school to me. I went up to the lectures and came home, just as I had gone to school and come home. And therefore I missed a lot of valuable things at the university. Just because I just came home. Sorley Maclean was at the university: I didn't meet him.

BT   Then you taught in primary school?

NM   Yes, when I came out the teaching profession was overloaded.

BT   Let us get the date more or less right.

NM   Well I went to the Training College in 1932.

IM   Moray House? Still in Edinburgh?

NM   Moray House, still in Edinburgh! There for a year. This is therefore 1932-33, and I was not going to take jobs abroad. I mean by abroad, of course, England! (L) The adjacent kingdom. And I think I applied for four or five Classics jobs in Scotland between there and the outbreak of war, and I didn't get any of them. And so I started teaching primary. The war broke out, six years pass, and I thought well, I quite like it in primary school, and you don't have to take cricket and rugby and photograph societies, Eng. Lit. societies and stretching your arm another six inches every day taking home homework, so I decided to stay in primary school.

IM   There were some positive reasons for that as well, no doubt. Like that you liked the young children?

NM Oh yes, I liked teaching primary school.

IM And you liked teaching quite a wide range of things to them?

NM Yes.

IM Imphm. So that it wasn't just laziness!

NM No, no. And also the difference in salaries between primary and secondary *then* was nothing like as wide as it became. And a *third* reason was I thought, in my innocent vainglory that with an Honours degree I would get promotion quite quickly. Ha, ha, ha, I didn't! Do you know why?

IM Well I know why Chris Grieve said!

NM Oh well, it's true! It is true!

BT Well, come on, for the tape!

NM Well I was a conscientious objector in the war, for pagan reasons, and had a little visit, you know, to prison.

IM A little visit?

NM Yes.

IM Was it quite brief?

NM No, it was a little visit. When I was brought before the Tribunal, or if you like, when the Tribunal was brought before me, (L) I said I was perfectly willing to join the RAMC, or the Quakers, or the Red Cross, but I wasn't going to kill anybody. And for people like me they formed a corps called the Non-Combatant Corps—which consisted of people like myself, who wouldn't kill but were willing to try and save. The NCC non-combatant, and I was in it—I stayed in it for quite a while, because I couldn't see we were furthering the war effort in any possible—they didn't know what to do with us! These odd persons! The officers and sergeants and corporals were all regular army, Pioneer Corps, and when they came to us oh, they hated us, yellow bellies, but they weren't with us a month or two before they got to like us! In fact there was an Irishman, oh he used to excoriate us with hydrochloric adjectives, you know, and he kept coming back to camp at the weekend, you know on Sundays, with plaster: he was fighting in bars because they were insulting the conscientious objectors. (L) Thank God I was in Britain: it's an awful country in many ways but they treated people like conchies in a way no other country in the world did. Most other countries we would have been shot of course. In America like Robert Lowell, three years in prison.

IM But they did put you in prison for a while.

NM Yes, but gently. You see I stood this job, Non-Combatant Corps, och it was hilarious—one of the most hilarious spells in my life—

because not *one* of us had any respect of course for military
authorities! (L) None whatever! (L)

BT   That's why you were there!

NM   Then came a time when we were put on a job which meant working
in a tank depot and I said I'm not doing that! Might as well drive a
tank! So I got the sergeant who was in charge of arrangements for
the following day's work and I said I'm not going to go there! I said
do you want me to refuse orders here in camp or will I wait till we
get there? And he said, better do it here. But it was all like this, it
was a farce! (L) In the morning I couldn't find him! He was hiding!
(L) He didn't want to put me on a charge! He told me later, I've
been a sergeant for twenty-five years and I never put a man on
charge yet, and I'm not starting wi' you! (L) So I had to go, I had to
refuse orders the next day. Now the routine was that you were court-
martialled. Now it happened at the time we were very near Alder-
shot, the place was *polluted* with Grenadier Guards, and Scots
Guards, oh, oh! So you were court-martialled and if they accepted
that your refusal was honest, that it was on conscientious grounds,
you got 93 days in a civvy prison, and then you were brought before
a Tribunal again. If they didn't accept your honesty, you were put
for at least six months in a military prison, which was hell, and then
sent back to your unit. And of course if you *were* honest you refused
again. And I met a man who had been three times. Anyway, they
believed me because in those days I could put on an expression of
ultimate purity, innocence and honesty! (L) I can only do it sometimes now! (L) So I was sent to prison for 93 days, brought before
a Tribunal; they accepted I was honest, and there were always two
options—work in a hospital or work on the land! So I was dismissed
with contumely. My army career was cut short.

IM   But you were sent to do one of these?

NM   Yes, that's right!

IM   Hospital or the land, which one?

NM   I came to Edinburgh, and I ...

BT   Oddly enough!

NM   Oddly enough! And I applied to several hospitals and they wouldn't
have me! (L) Because I was a Conchie! And I was strolling around
Corstorphine and I saw a nursery garden and I went in and I said I'm
looking for a job. He said, oh, aye! I better tell you I'm a Conchie—
and he said that doesn't matter as long as you can dig! (L) So I
worked with him for two years. I didn't know a daffodil from an
albuminous bullfoot. (L)

BT   I can see why you were an atheist from birth, but it doesn't follow

that that would mean you had a Quakerish disposition to your
fellowmen; that you wouldn't recognise the threat of Hitler ...

NM Of course I recognised the threat and I have no answer to this except
that I was born a pacifist, absolute 100% pacifist. I didn't need
reasons, I didn't need to wave the Bible in people's faces, and say
I am a pacifist: or wave books of philosophy or ethics or morals, I
just knew there were some things I won't do, and that is drop bombs
on Hamburg and such things, which were then going on. I saw a
photograph of a bishop blessing a bomb that was going to be
dropped on Hamburg, and I knew that I was having nothing to do
with this. And when I'm asked the question, but if Hitler came in, I
have no answer, I don't know! But I knew that I wasn't having
anything. Do you know at the Tribunal I was actually asked that
First World War question—what would you do if a German broke
into your house and raped your wife? I said, I'd tear his jugular out
with my teeth! (L) I mean there are some things ... (L) but I'm not
going to put myself into a position of being in a room where a
German ... (L)

BT But you *were* in that room, that was the point!

NM Yes. I don't know, and nobody does, by the way, even people that
supported the war. They don't know what the results of wars are. In
my view every war brings more horrors into the world than are
solved by them. I know you could quote one war or two, say on
Muckle Flugga, which resulted in a few seagulls getting bed and
breakfast ...

BT Well, what do you feel about the American War of Independence?

NM I tell you—I'm a pacifist—I'm against all wars. I approve of the
liberation of the slaves in America, of course I do, but wars are
different. I disapprove of all wars. But in the old-fashioned war
professionals fought against professionals. Civilians suffered, but
this last war civilians suffered far more than the boys in the army.
Women and children, I won't have anything to do with it.

IM Were tribunals not harder on people like you than on people with
clear religious backing?

NM Generally so. If you were a Quaker, for example, practically always
they accepted that. But you see I wasn't—I offered to join the
RAMC you see—Quakers wouldn't do that—except in their own
organisation, which I offered to join as well. I have no answer to
what would have happened if Hitler *had*—I don't like pseudo-
questions. Questions that begin with if—because nobody knows. I
only know that I'd be shot against a wall before I'd drop bombs on
Hamburg, Cologne or anywhere else.

IM But you didn't get too badly treated by these Tribunals?

NM I quite expected to go into Military Prison and out and back again and out again you know. But no, no, they were very fair!

IM And did the experience of being in—it was Wormwood Scrubs—wasn't it?

NM I was first of all in Winchester, and then in Wormwood Scrubs, yes. Nothing but the best for me! (L)

IM Was it an important thing in your life or is it something you just put behind you?

NM No, it wasn't important. If I'd been guilty—to be in prison must be hell—if you're guilty—it must be absolute hell—locked in for nearly all the hours, but I wasn't guilty at all. I walked up and down six steps, six back. I inscribed jigs that I invented and hung them behind the mirror. (L) No, no, it was all—it was all interesting!

IM So after these 93 days which didn't make too bad an impression on you, you were back digging in Edinburgh for a while. Now, do I take it that you were by this time married?

NM Yes

IM Did your wife agree with you?

NM Oh yes, yes.

IM No question?

NM Thank goodness! Because she's a woman of independent mind! (L) But she did agree.

IM When did you get married? Approximately, Norman.

NM It was the year the war broke out—1939.

IM So you hadn't really had time to have a family before all this happened?

NM We managed, yes. We had one. And I got home on leave, so we had another!

IM Good, excellent.

NM But my wife with her *impeccable* good taste, bred one—I didn't know it was born till she told me! And the other one—I was working as a jobbing-gardener, and so I knew this one was coming. (L)

IM Is that the total?

NM Yes.

IM And can we know the sex of these two?

NM We got the girl first you see to help with washing the nappies. (L)

IM Excellent.

NM Very organised!

IM So, with the end of the war and your return to teaching the impact of the more dramatic elements of history in your life ceases and you become more a decider of where your life is going for yourself?

NM   Well, in a way. I was never a terrible man for deciding. I just did what I wanted.

BT   There are deep principles of conscience involved in the decision about the war.

NM   Oh yes. Sure. That was an absolute deep—absolute *final* one. But I don't like the word *decision*. I didn't decide it. I had refused to do what they wanted me to do because I am a pacifist, that's my *nature*, there was no decision about it.

BT   Can we hear a bit more about Mrs MacCaig? About whom little has been heard for quite a long time.

NM   Mrs MacCaig? Yes, my wife? Isabel?

BT   Isabel, yes. You married her in 1939, and you met her at the university?

NM   At the university!

IM   What did she study?

NM   She got a First in English, and did hardly any work because we were aye going to the jigging. (L)

IM   Was she a teacher too?

NM   Yes, she taught for a few years. In fact, until the first child was born, yes. And, I don't like to talk about her because it would seem so improbable—she's just an extraordinary woman! Everybody who knows her—most people meeting her for the first time are put off, so was I, and then they meet her and they discover that she's just an extraordinary woman! Energetic, kind, clever,

IM   A super cook!

NM   She's a very good cook, no, no, she's too extraordinary: if I told the real truth you wouldn't believe it. [Sadly, Isabel MacCaig died in 1987.]

IM   Oh, that sounds all right. So, by the time the digging was finishing and the teaching was starting again you got a job in Edinburgh?

NM   Yes. I did a number of jobs in primary schools and then I eventually got a permanent one. But I taught for a year and a half in Portobello High School, teaching Latin. All these incidents are so farcical. The headmaster was a terrified geographer. And there had been no Classics, Latin teacher for years; it had been extremely badly taught by the French teacher, so that every term the kids were lined up, every session, outside the Headmaster's room saying they didn't want to take Latin. So the numbers had dwindled, and when I took over first year and third year pupils at the back of the room doing exercises, none of which had been corrected for *ages*. So they knew nothing. They were just repeating their own mistakes. So that at the

end of the term, I gave them an exam, the sort of Dux mark in the
third year was something like 17%, and the terrified geographer
cockroached through the school, could I have a word with you—
you cannot put these marks on the report cards. And I said why not?
It's all they're worth. The parents! The parents! Add twenty on to
each mark! (L) And I said, you can do that: I won't! And the text
books they were using were printed about 1880, so I demanded new
text books. And he said well, he grudgingly agreed, he said, if the
inspectors disapprove it's you're to take the responsibility, etc.! It
was all farcical! Well, after a year and a half the job was advertised
and this man—who hated me—obviously, I was the one to step in
but he wouldn't have it; so I was thrown out into the cold world and
took up primary school teaching again—quite gladly!

IM   Still in Edinburgh?

NM   Yes, still in Edinburgh.

IM   Right.

BT   What kind of range of things did you teach? I mean what do you
     think primary teaching was all about in that time?

NM   Well, ha, ha, ha, well it was about bairns and I'm not being funny.

BT   No.

NM   Cos most teachers treated them as if they were infants and I talked
     to them as if they were human beings. And I taught *everything*
     except sewing. (L) And I was a good teacher—I really was. And it
     was mostly because I treated the kids as if they could think. And, I
     don't know that there's anything more to say. The wives of two
     headmasters under whom I worked in two schools told me that I had
     cured their husband's ulcers and I remember very well, one of them
     who was so nervous of authority he'd come addling into my room
     and say look at this—it's from the office—what are we going to do
     about this, Mr MacCaig? And I would say—put it in the basket!
     And I cured his bloody ulcers! (L)

BT   Obviously you relished teaching?

NM   I enjoyed it!

BT   And you liked bairns.

NM   Yes.

BT   Yes. You were conscious were you at the time that on the whole
     primary teachers didn't treat bairns as bairns?

NM   The commonest fault was that they talked down to them. And the
     other commonest fault was to suppose that discipline meant sit up!
     fold your arms! you know, that sort of thing. The letters you read in
     the paper about teachers walloping kids are grossly exaggerated!
     Grossly! But their idea of discipline was not mine, it was dead

silence. March out two by two, left, right. You know—all Fascist stuff. Of course, I didn't agree with this at all.

IM Yes. Did you teach different age groups in the primary over these various different jobs?

NM It was mostly primary six and seven.

IM So it was the older children in primary?

NM Yes. In one school I went to I got a class at primary four and I had them for four years, every day, the same kids. Fortunately, it was a nice, good class. I mean to be faced with a row of 36 turnips for four years ... but these were nice bright kids, it was no bother.

BT What was it that made you start writing poetry—I mean to what end? What was it all about?

NM Well, I remember the occasion. The English teacher at the High School when I was in the fifth form—this is absolutely true—said that by next Wednesday he wanted us to write either a composition on something or other or a poem. And honestly, I thought, well, a poem's shorter. (L) So I wrote—that's absolutely true!

IM Do you remember what it was about?

NM Yes. But I'm not going to tell you! I wrote it to a tune of a Gaelic song in fact, and it was awful sentimental. The teacher, Puggie Grant, gave me 17 out of 20 for it. But I think it was more for effrontery than effect! (L) And I got interested and started scribbling away!

BT When did you start to think of yourself as a poet?

NM I don't think of myself as a poet to this day! I don't. I don't like people being sliced up into compartments. I am a man who fishes, who listens to music, who has good friends, we sit and blether, I do this, I do that and I write poetry—or try to. I never say I write poetry.

BT OK. There is a truth that I recognise in what you are saying. There is also a sense in which you are, and consciously are, a poet. You spend more of your energy, you value what those little things say, more than anything else in your life.

NM Oh yes. I like catching seven-pound trout too!

IM You'd rather have a good trout or a good poem?

NM Ah, a good poem! Oh yes. I love poetry!

BT You became *so* interested in poetry that it really took over, didn't it?

NM Oh yes. I got interested—I'd never thought of writing poetry till that happened. Everybody likes creating something that never existed in the world before, even if it's a beautiful table! Even if it's a baby. And I found an extraordinary interest in making poems, because that poem had never existed. Something totally new. Now, mind you, I'm thinking back, I don't think I was aware of this at the time, and also being this formalist, as I said partly genetics, partly Latin and Greek, it was just a marvellous game making an object out of words that sounded nice and the rhythms and the assonances ... That makes it seem perhaps a wee bit more of a game than I *intend* that to mean, but to write a thing with a strict formal structure, and keep to it all the way through is an absolutely fascinating thing to do. I'd like to go on—I'm still answering your question.

BT Yes you are.

NM I went on writing after that first one and I got fascinated. This lasted right into University age and I got interested in Surrealism. I used to buy—well, I bought that long defunct *Transition* magazine and I got a magazine which was called *The London Bulletin* (what a name!) and it was concerned with Surrealism in all the arts including writing, there were even poems by Picasso.

IM Really?

NM Not worth a docken! (L) And part of my genetic thing from my mother, apart from images and metaphors, was a kind of grass-hopperish-nature in her mind and mine. So I was ruined for years by this interest in Surrealism. I used to blah ... an awful lot of them, almost every evening, I thought, writing poetry's easy! What a fool I was! And they became more and more surrealistic and therefore more and more incomprehensible! And when I was in the NCC in my jokey part of the army, Isabel gathered some of these abomina-tions and posted them to Routledge and Kegan Paul who printed them, because they printed *anything* during the war, on bad paper. And, in fact, two of these books came out. I was pleased. I was so *stupid*, I didn't realise how awful they were! Oh formally, they were ok, oh, yes. Oh boy! But rubbish—incomprehensible rubbish! And the story that I know you know—a friend asked to see one of the two, I forget which, and when he gave me them back he said-the only critical remark *ever* spoken or written about me that was of any help—he said—there's your book, Norman, when are you publish-ing the answers? (L) And I immediately saw what he was up to and started on the long haul to lucidity, which is a rocky road because to be obscure is easy, but to be lucid is hellish difficult. And I owe that man that debt.

IM Is it an idea to put his name into the records since he did so much?

NM Och, he was called Dickie Knock! He was in the NCC, as I was, an Englishman; awful nice chap!

BT   So what were you trying to be lucid about?

NM   First, I love poetry. I love all kinds of poetry, not all, a great many
     kinds! And I love the world, I'm a very affectionate man. I love
     animals and landscapes and people and differences and likenesses.
     And to write a poem or try to, is really a kind of—Dylan Thomas
     said this—but if he meant it? I'm quoting him, and meaning it—
     every poem is a kind of celebration, of whatever the subject of the
     poem was—and of the art of poetry, and I've had an extraordinarily
     lucky life, and you'll look a long time in the earlier poems to find
     very many sad ones. And I don't believe even the sad ones are
     rejective. And the sad ones started coming in, which was noticed by
     some perceptive reviewers, fairly recently, in my long life, the last
     two books ...

BT   The last six years or so ...

NM   About that. He said there are more sad poems than there used to be.
     And I know fine the reasons, cos people are terribly important—
     friends—far more important than poetry! And I've been lucky; and
     I'm not talking about acquaintances, right friends. And in the last
     eight years not six of my closest, but my six closest have died; and
     you can forget the deaths of acquaintances but you never forget the
     deaths of friends; so there are more shadows in the last two books
     (not talking about the *Collected*) [All references to the *Collected
     Poems* are to the first collected edition of 1985]. And all the same,
     my closest friend, outside of my wife and one of my sisters, I was
     closest to them—apart from them, was a man up in Lochinver way,
     Angus MacLeod, now he died and I was there, and I wrote a dozen
     poems or so.

BT   Some of your best.

NM   And I recognised—well I recognised the easy thing—I wasn't
     grieving for him—he's dead—I was grieving for me. And the other
     thing I recognised was that writing about my grief was in a way a
     celebration of Angus.

BT   Your grief was his celebration.

NM   Yes, yes. But it comforted me to recognise that.

IM   And when you were reading for John McGrath on television you
     still said, and we can see why it's true, that Angus' death was
     something from which you would *never ever* recover.

BT   Mortality is there throughout the *Collected Poems* and it increas-
     ingly becomes more obvious. As your poetry goes on, you're
     interested in the crucial and drastic factor of death; it doesn't just
     happen in the last six years.

NM   Oh, sure. Until these friends started dying, I told you, I've had such a lucky life, lived through two world wars and never saw a corpse, until my parents died. As you said, they had done their eighty years and they died like that. And death to me was only a concept. I didn't know what death *meant*! It was a concept up here! Only. And it wasn't till my friends started dying that—Christ! that's what it means! You know.

BT But you'd been writing about it all these years.

NM Oh yes. But only as a concept. I love life, and death to me was just something ends, and I wasn't taking into account *really* the sufferings. So when I wrote about death it was generally about animals or plants, and flowers and the grasses in the canal, rotting and rotting and—but they're only going to come up in some other form, etc.—we all know that! Matter is indestructible! Unfortunately, people are not! Except they rot, like everything, anything else, of course, and breed daisies and—other things.

IM But you don't give in to the modern, the fashionable heresy, which goes in for animal rights, and animal liberation, and says that Man has no rights and values that are not there also. He who would not kill must not kill a fish, must not shoot a rabbit, or whatever ...

NM OK. Ha, ha, women always have one of these *disgusting* forefingers that put their point plonk on a polestar! (L)

BT She's very good!

NM Ah, well. I told you, pacifist by nature, I never killed anything in my life except once or twice of necessity.

BT Apart from the trout.

NM Wait a minute, wait a minute! Except fish. And I have killed fish ... I don't *know* the reason. I catch trout and salmon and sea-fish. And I always kill them, I don't leave them flapping in the boat. But I never killed an animal—I've killed a mouse because it was in the house—and you don't like mice in the house—and I don't kill things. I mean, if a wasp comes into the house I catch it in a clout and put it out. You know, even a wasp. And I don't understand why I don't have these feelings about fish. I don't mind killing fish. And I know they don't enjoy being caught. I'm not very sure how much pain they feel. But even if they don't feel any pain you play them till they're exhausted, and that's not funny. And I really don't understand why I don't feel compassion. I'm beginning to!

IM Well, I asked about it because I am supported by your inconsistency in this matter. I share it. And I don't know whether it's just a hangover from religious belief, that I do see people still as more important than animals.

NM Oh yes, oh yes! More important than *anything*, poetry included!

BT   Right, let's start with the poems that you now don't like so much, the so-called Apocalyptic ones!

NM I wish you would use words accurately! Don't like so much—I *hate* them! (L)

BT   Well, yes, I prefer *you* to say that! (L) And you published your first book.

IM   Because your wife went behind your back with the poems to the publisher.

NM Yes, I was away from home, or I wouldn't—yes, I would—I was so stupid I would have let her do it! (L) Well, when I started writing, I never thought of—it never entered my head to try to get them printed anywhere, didn't even send magazines—right up University age and all—I just wrote for my own pleasure. And each poem was a vomitorium of unrelated images which nobody could understand, including me. Until I came to what was left of my senses, and began to realise that what's the use of a poem if nobody understands it, and began to struggle on my hands and knees towards clarity, lucidity, cos any fool can be obscure: in fact the bigger fool you are, the easier it is! But to be lucid is terribly difficult! And that is the way I started. I wasted years writing rubbish like that!

IM   And there was quite a long gap of time between those first two books and then *Riding Lights*.

NM Yes, that's when I was on my hands and knees crawling towards clarity!

IM   And do the poems in *Riding Lights* now seem very far away, or do they feel recognisably by *you*?

NM Oh yes, they still feel like—I feel they are mine! In spite of some changes since then, but I recognise my voice when I—I never *read* the things of course, unless I have to.

IM´ But you would still sometimes read poems from there at a public reading?

NM Not often, not often. There aren't very many—there are *some*: but a lot of them are not all that easy to grasp at a hearing. They're easy enough off the page *I hope*, but not easy to grasp at a hearing, and it's stupid to read poems at a reading that aren't comprehensible at one hearing, so I don't read many of them. Anyway one's apt to read the later ones, you know.

IM   Do you think the very fact that reading poetry has become such an accepted activity has had any effect on the kind of poems you write?

NM I don't think so. When I write a poem, I never *ever* think, would this do for a reading? Never, ever. Thank goodness because I was once speaking with Roger McGough, who makes his living by troubadouring round the poetry dens, and I said to him, it must be rather difficult when you sit to write a poem—it must be impossible for you not to be biased to make it a poem suitable for a reading. And the way to get clap-clap handies at a reading is to write jokey poems. They love jokey poems! Even if they're not poems! And he agreed, he agreed that it was; you couldn't any more sit down and accept a poem of complexity, because it would be no use for a reading. Well that doesn't bother me.

BT It doesn't have to.

NM No.

BT Because your search for clarity and lucidity was very successful in fact.

NM Well one hopes it was. Of course.

BT But there are some poems which obviously would work pretty well at readings and which you do come back to for reading purposes don't you? Like 'Wild Oats'?

NM Well, yes. Well that's a nice jokey one you see. They think—och, he's quite nice—he makes me laugh! He's just like us! (L) He's got one nose and two eyes and he's not dead! (L)

IM But you don't choose just a selection of jokey poems.

NM No, no, never, never!

IM Do you spend some time choosing the menu, balancing what you're going to read?

NM Not enough—if you choose a selection and it seems to work—you're *very* apt to keep to it, and you wonder have I read to this lot before? (L) And there are some poems, like that one you mentioned, 'Wild Oats,' which I read over and over and over because it took a trick, and I'm certain I read it more than once to ...

BT Oh dear—I've heard it more than once!

NM There you are! (L) Well I haven't read it for *years*! I decided, no more! I retired it!

IM Do you actually enjoy reading?

NM I do, I think, yes. I quite enjoy it. You get this odd thing that actors know about well, a reading's an act, you know, it's all acting, teaching's an act as well. Once you stand up and give utterance to your vaguenesses you're being an actor. And you get the feeling, giving a reading, that of rapprochement between you and the audience and it's a nice feeling.

IM So that, having discovered the benefits of communication in writing the poetry, you go on, right on, through to communicating that much more immediately when you read it?

NM Yes.

IM Do you get tired of it? You know, faced with a programme of so many readings, does it sometimes make you quail?

NM I always look forward with mournfulness and foreboding, oh, another reading! God help us! But once I get into the place, and meet the people, and curiously the people that go to poetry readings always seem to be awful nice people! And then you get up in front of them you know, and the adrenalin starts trickling through your veins and I quite enjoy it! It would be *terrible* if you got a bad response! Or no response! That would be awful. The worst audience I ever spoke to was the fifth or sixth form in Jedforest School. It was like addressing six rows of turnips. They sat there rows of neeps! And the hour seemed to last about four hours and oh, I was glad to get out.

BT There was no response?

NM No response at all!

IM You told us before a story I'd love you to tell again, about an Australian audience that was very different from that.

NM Och, yes, yes. Adelaide Festival, there were poets there from literally all round the world. And I performed on the Thursday—it had been going on all week—and I never got such a reception in my life. Clap, clap, clap, clap. More, more, more, more, you know. I had to go back up and do some more. I wasn't deceived, I wasn't deceived! One reason was a lot of the other poets were very dull, and a lot of the poets who weren't very dull were very inaudible! And with my brazen Scottish voice they heard *me*! That was one reason. And the other was that three out of four Australians whom I met had a Granny in Kirkintilloch! And were proud of it. And after the reading, I was talking with some of them, the audience, and a lady said in her Australian accent, which thank God I can't imitate!—Mr MacCaig, you hadn't said three sentences when my eyes filled with tears; you reminded me of my Grandpa sitting at the piano playing 'Roaming in the Gloaming!' (L)

BT Thank you madam! (L)

NM A story about readings. I always ask questions—ask *for* questions after. And I was invited by telephone to talk to a school in Polmont—a primary school—I didn't know it was a primary school or else I would have said no; adapt my own stuff to primary kids! I went, terrified, and was ushered in to a room, the Gymnasium, where there were *200* primary school kids sitting on the floor! (L) And I thought—wow ... —so I read three easy ones, you know, and I said would any of you like to ask any questions? Two hundred arms went up! (L) Well I picked a few branches from this Dunsinane wood and a boy said—a very common question—when did you write your first poem? So I told him. Then I went groping through this forest and accidentally landed on the same boy, who asked me a marvellous question—he said, 'When you wrote your first poem, why did you bother to go on and write any more?' (L)

IM You've often said that you tend to know whether your poem's a hit or a miss, more or less as soon as they're there. That you enjoy throwing the misses in the waste-paper basket.

NM Yes.

IM But with the publication of your *Collected Poems* it does become clear that there has been a later process as well; that what, at the time, you put in the slim volume, say *Riding Lights*, isn't exactly the same as what you have kept for the *Collected Poems*. You've left some poems out that you now don't like so much; you've put some poems in that you've kind of allowed yourself second thoughts on.

NM Yes, well, *Riding Lights* was the first one after that gap that you mentioned, and I had far too many for a slim volume, so I just sent out a slim volume's worth. (L) By the time I was ready for the second book, the one after *Riding Lights*, I had enough for it, you see, and I just left these behind. It wasn't that I didn't like them! If I didn't like them I wouldn't have them in the *Collected Poems*, for a start. I just had too many for a slim volume.

IM And when you're choosing a slim volume, is it a question of choosing what you think are the *best* so many, or again is there any thought of the volume itself having a kind of shape or ...?

NM No, I don't think of shape or anything. I put them in an order where one leads to another—either because it's similar or because it's totally different, just for variety for the reader. Which is a waste of time, because they don't read from the first beginning of the book to the end of the book anyway. (L)

IM About ten years, after *Riding Lights*, was it?—you began to write, quite unexpectedly, free verse?

NM Yes, I think it was more than ten years, maybe not. It doesn't matter. Up till then I'd always written, in formal stanzas, with rhymes, sometimes what people consider, not very solid rhymes, you know, there are so many different kinds of rhymes. People think that it has to be June-soon, sorrow-tomorrow, hum-drum. (L) But there are dozens of kinds of rhymes which have been used, rhymes like: looks rhyming with backs, where just the final consonants ... or God rhyming with dog, where the consonants are the same but they're in the opposite order and the vowels the same, you know. All kinds of tricky little nonsenses like that which of course fascinated me. And in those earlier poems, strict form poems, very, very often they're written with half-rhymes and assonances—but always formal. I used to wonder why I wasn't attracted to free verse because so many poets were using free verse, and one night I sat down feeling like writing and a thing came out in free verse.

It just came out in free verse. And then of course I got fascinated with the techniques of free verse. Where do you end a line?—that sort of thing. How is it since there's no metre the rhythms, the verbal rhythms are different from prose rhythms? Things of that sort, and I mean the fundamental unit in a formal poem is the foot— five feet in a line—the foot is the fundamental unit—but you cannae have that in a free verse poem where the unit, it seems to *me*, is the phrase, and by a judicious, but quite unconscious, manipulation of the lengths of the phrases, the poem is a form. If you don't do that, it's chopped-up prose. And the first word in any line, formal or not, and the last word in a line, are in the strongest place, so you have to make sure that the last word in a line is a word that you want to have slightly emphasised. It's a kind of punctuation really, because by the time your eyes goes from that to the first word in the next line, there's a wee pause, and an awful lot of free verse I read are honestly chopped-up prose, and the manipulation of the words at the end of the line sometimes are fearful! 'So I went to the'—next line—'shop'—I ask you? Ha! (L)

IM   Is there mileage to be got out of starting lines in different places on the page?

NM   Not for me! Not for me!

BT   You don't go in for that sort of stuff.

NM   No, I don't at all, because what people are attempting to convey by doing this, insetting lines in various places, I think that should be implicit in the rhythm, in the verbal rhythm *already*, without the author sticking his elbow up from the page saying, nudge! nudge! nudge! (L) The same way you'll look all through an awful lot of my poems before you see an exclamation mark! It ought to be implicit in the ...

BT   I think that's true, and I think there's an effect which you often get and play with in your free-verse poems which I might call the cantilever effect, that the thing, the line stretches out into space and you're talking about the importance of the final word, and it just balances there nicely. You very often do that—the thing is just out there in space and then you come swinging back to the pillar of the bridge and you take off again.

NM Fair enough.

BT It's all to do with weights and balance and all sorts ...

NM Yes, I agree. But this isn't a matter of calculation, you do it—I do it—I can only speak for me—I do that just subconsciously. I don't calculate it. Sometimes when I've written a poem I actually force myself to read it, because I am a bit of a masochist. (L) And occasionally, I might make a wee change in a line length because it's interrupting the through-flow of the rhythm, the verbal rhythm, not often, but I see what you mean, but it's not calculated.

BT It works. You get the distinct feeling—I suppose I'm so familiar with your voice that I tend to hear your voice quite a lot, when I'm just reading off the page. But even allowing for that effect, the very distinct feeling of the thing being very finely tuned and balanced, so that I often read what you would call free verse poems, and don't really feel them as particularly free verse, the structure's so clear.

NM That's right. Yes, fair enough.

BT I take your point that it's an unconscious or non-conscious sort of thing. But it works.

NM Oh it was quite, quite, quite unconscious. I think the only thing I would say boastingly, I'm not giving to boastingly, the only thing I would defend if I were accused of the opposite, is that I think I have a very good sense of verbal rhythms. I think I have, and maybe that's related to my love of music. Cos I love music, more than poetry, I respond to music more than poetry. Music to me is *the* great art, partly because it's liberated from dictionaries of course, but maybe this feeling I have that I'm not bad at verbal rhythms comes from the same part of me that responds to music.

IM Yes. You don't just respond to music either do you, at least you did, you used to play the fiddle.

NM I used to play the fiddle, yes, but I'm illiterate about music. I don't understand the grammar and syntax of music. I just respond to it. I have a son who's mad on music, and he knows all about the grammar and syntax, and when people talk say on programme notes—oh programme notes!—oh, programme notes!—they're either romantic waffle about the hunter's horn sounding through the trees; I'm listening: where's the hunter? Where's the horn? (L) And there's not a tree in sight. (L) Even inside my skull. What was I going to say?

BT You were saying that you were musically illiterate.

NM Oh yes. I mean when they say 'the second subject enters in the forty-fifth bar', I'd say, oh, does it?—to a piece of music I know and love—I don't notice the grammar and syntax. Modulated from key this to key that—I never noticed it. I noticed the *effect*, but I didn't know it was modulated from key this to key that.

IM Interestingly though, in the art that you do most obviously and most permanently practise, you *are* very acutely aware of grammar and syntax, and you love dictionaries, and you know, sometimes a whole poem is leading up to one very unusual word. I seem to recall for example the one about Mary Queen of Scots that ends up with her spaniel looking at her with exophthalmic eyes. (L) ['Queen of Scots', *Collected Poems*, pp. 381-82]

NM Oh yes. that's right. That's what I wrote and I thought oh, oh, stop showing off, and I was going to put in another word, I forget what it was, it might be bulging, you know, it wasn't actually bulging and I scored out exophthalmic and I put in this other word and then I said 'Damn it! If they don't know the meaning of exophthalmic, it's high time they did!' So I put back exophthalmic. I can't even say it! (L)

IM On the one hand people say that you're a very private man, but on the other hand they notice that your poems are very, very often spoken by an 'I'—an individual person. This 'I' is very honestly looked at, but I'm reminded of Ruskin talking about his autobiography, and he said it was 'the natural me, only peeled carefully'. I think you are very there in the poems where you say 'I', but it's only a segment of you, is that fair?

NM Yeah. I think that everybody has his rights to have his reticences. You could never ever call me a confessional poet.

IM No, I wouldn't dare! (L)

NM No, no. I don't hit women often! (L) But if one reads the *Collected Poems* with interest I think you'd know an awful lot about me: indirectly, you know. Even verbal rhythms give shows away, never mind choice of subject matter and treatment. I think that that's my autobiography really.

IM Yes. Again the critics say that you don't go in for writing much about politics and things like that. The night before you came up Bob and I were sort of just paddling round among some of the poems, and we found one much more outspoken about things political than most of them, and interestingly we found it was written almost—here I'm really risking smacking—very unusually for you it was written as a kind of dramatic monologue, it was written from the point of view of a 'we' who had been grateful that, for example, when 'they' killed the Pope they didn't gouge his eyes out first ...

NM Oh, that one.

IM And when they killed the women they didn't kill the babies first. I was just looking for it and I couldn't remember the title so I can't find it. Do you remember the title?

NM No. ['A New Age', *Collected Poems*, 1985, pp. 367-68]

IM No? It was interesting to me, though, that it's a very direct poem. It perhaps allows more emotion than a lot of the poems, but there isn't an 'I' in it.

NM No. Well, people are very very important to me, and I know I am not unusual in that. Friends are tremendously important, and yet I think that man as a whole are monsters. Think what's happening all round the world, from Ulster to Thailand. The things, the brutalities, so I *hate* mankind, I think man is on a suicide course. On the other hand I like people, you know. Individual people, but I don't like Man with a capital M at all. That's why I hate—that poem is about Burns's 'man's inhumanity to man' which makes me sick when I think about it.

IM I think on the whole so sick that you don't often write about it.

NM No, I don't. I don't directly at all.

IM No and in that poem when you are writing very clearly about that you don't intrude the MacCaig 'I' ...

NM No.

IM that perceives landscapes and animals and that sort of thing.

NM Yes, that's so.

IM So it was really quite interesting. It's almost that the subject of the awfulness of Mankind just releases such a strong bad emotion, fear and foreboding and all the rest of it that it's not much use for your poetry usually?

NM No. I don't think there are a great many political poems which are successful. I don't mean of mine, of anybody's. MacDiarmid, who claimed of course to be a carnivorously political animal (L) attempted of course to write political poems, and hardly one of them works as poems. They're just versified propaganda—no poetry in them. And a really successful political poem I think is a very rare thing. You can deal with politics indirectly, you know, by implication, but a direct political poem is a very rare thing, almost impossible to write.

IM Do you think at all you were reacting against the kind of poetry that was being published when you were beginning to read poetry? People like Auden and the other Thirties poets who did for a while believe in writing the political poetry, actually writing poems that were trying to get people to do things, like going to fight in Spain?

NM The same man of course said that no poem ever induced anybody to any action. He's wrong.

IM And was Yeats wrong then when he says, 'did that play of mine send out / Certain men the English shot?'

NM Yes. Oh, I don't know whether he was right but he was right to wonder about that, certainly. It's a poem about his guilt and fear, that he had actually stimulated people to go out and shoot people. ['The Man and the Echo']

IM Yes. It implies a belief that poetry somehow can do that.

NM Yes. And I think it can, of course.

BT On the whole your poems do quieter things. They don't send people out to revolutions, but they do seem to be about how people's view of things might change, Isobel's mentioned the 'I' of Norman MacCaig, you know, capital I as opposed to the one in your head. (L)

IM Though it's a very seeing 'I'.

BT One of the themes that comes up, again and again is the change-ability, the transience of the self, and one of the things that often your poems do for me is that there *is* a touch of Surrealism in that.

NM Oh yes.

BT You find yourself in a slightly displaced position, and you find yourself in a landscape that is familiar and unfamiliar at once; and that's an effect that you work for a lot isn't it?

NM Well, I think so.

BT And self, you talk about the self sometimes in the plural—you have selves—

NM Oh well, yes, we all have. There are three faggots of selves sitting at this table. (L) May I tell this about this faggot of selves thing? A person whom I have known who was a collection of contradictions to a ridiculous extent was of course Hugh MacDiarmid. I remember I was introducing him to an audience and I said, I don't really know what to call this man. Is he Hugh, is he Mr MacDiarmid, is he Chris, is he Mr Grieve, is he Christopher Murray Grieve? I said he's not really a man, he's a committee. (L) And all the members disagree with the chairman. (L)

IM I was going to ask you about Chris Grieve, Hugh MacDiarmid, anyway, obviously. So why don't we just stop on him a little while. And you said a moment or two ago that you didn't think his political poetry really worked, that it was more chopped-up propaganda. Which of his poetry do you see as particularly fine?

NM Political or not?

IM   Any.

NM   Any! Och the whole of the *Drunk Man.*

IM   Right.

NM   Straight off; which to me is an absolute masterpiece. It's certainly
     one of the greatest poems *ever* written in Scots, because of reasons
     it would take too long. And some of the lyrics; and some poems
     actually in English like 'On a Raised Beach', 'The Glass of Pure
     Water', a handful of English poems in English, but really, if he had
     written nothing but *A Drunk Man* ... I think that Iain Crichton Smith
     was all wrong in that pamphlet he wrote, *Golden Lyric*, where he
     claimed that the lyrics were far, far, far greater than *A Drunk Man.*
     I think that's quite wrong, utterly wrong. The *Drunk Man* has got all
     the kinds of poetry that he was capable of writing in one consecu-
     tive piece. With such variety of styles, manners, feelings, vulgarity,
     sublimity, philosophy, wit, it's just an extraordinary poem. That
     would do me. You could almost put all of his work in the fire as long
     as you rescued that one, almost, almost!

IM   But you're not going to say the opposite of Iain, that these lyrics are
     not particularly fine.

NM   They are. Some of them are absolute masterpieces, of course they
     are. But to say that they are superior to *A Drunk Man*—oh, control
     myself! (L)

IM   Now, when you and MacDiarmid/Grieve were friendly would you
     tell him that you didn't like this or that poem? Did you discuss them
     in that way?

NM   Well, he and I were very, very close friends as everybody knows,
     and we didn't often talk about his poetry, and when we did, it was
     usually myself talking about a poem which I had read recently or re-
     read probably, and from which I had got great pleasure. Oh, I
     argued with him about political poetry of course. We argued about
     everything, savagely. We both believed that vituperation is an art
     form. Often to the bamboozlement and discombombulation of any
     innocent bystander, who thinks we're going to punch each other on
     the nose. We're just enjoying ourselves.

IM   (L) Do you ever remember truly losing your temper with him ?

NM   Oh no, no.

IM   Or him with you?

NM   Yes, he did, twice. It was very strange. It was, with other people in
     the room, he suddenly launched on a tirade—none of your flyting—
     twice. Once it was in New York and our hosts—the husband and
     wife went out of the house, and walked up and down the street (L)
     till I went down and said, it's all over, it's all over. Now I didn't care

a ha'penny because I knew it was all wrong. It didn't bother me, I just let him go on, agreeing with every word. You know, yes. Quite right, Chris. No, our friendship was so solid, it didn't matter tuppence.

IM   And did you know how you had somehow tripwired that or it was just something inside ...?

NM   No, it just suddenly came out bang! I don't know why, but it didn't matter.

IM   And did he tend to discuss your poetry?

NM   No. Except he praised it, but he had no judgement of other people's poetry. He wasn't interested, by the time I knew him, I met him only in 1946, just the other day. And he always praised me in public, you know in an article, or something. Best poet writing in English and so on that Scotland ever had, you know, always goes to extremes. (L) But that didn't bother me either! (L) I knew he was just saying that because he liked me. Nothing to do with the poetry.

IM   It is obvious, he thought of himself as very qualified to judge other people's poetry.

NM   The man couldn't judge his own! I mustn't be unfair. He obviously had read voluminously in the first half of his life; poetry, the lot. By the time I got to know him he was only really interested in reading a book which would excite him to write more poetry. That's really what it meant. I'm beginning to find myself the same. I read books, I don't read anything like I used to. I used to buy every possible slim volume. Not now. And when I read them, unconsciously but not altogether, I'm really doing what Chris did in his time, looking for a book that would prime the pump inside this skull of mine. And he was like that: he really was looking for a stimulus, because he was stuck as a poet. He hadn't written for years. And he was reading, reading for something that would start him off again.

BT   You were saying to me yesterday that for almost forty years he suspected that he was stuck in an irretrievable kind of way.

NM   Yes, he was. His—he'd dried up about the early, the middle forties, nineteen-forty something, and he would never admit it, even to himself. He often spoke about his next poem, which was to be about the East-West syzygy, and was to be the longest poem in any language. (L) And he said, 'I'm too busy just now, Norman, but February, I'll be freer after that.' He never put a pen to paper. But in private, sitting at the fire by himself, he was a very sad man. A tragic figure. His muse was off with another fella. And it made me very, very, very sorry for him.

BT   It was a long time to carry that around inside.

NM Wasn't it. Forty years! Terrible.

BT Astonishing, yes. In itself it helps to account for his lurches into extremism, one way or another, doesn't it? He'd be trying to hype himself up.

NM Yes, that's right. Writing poetry; you write a poem and it might well be the last one you'll ever write. I mean, if you're writing a novel, you write so many pages, and then you sit down and you've got these pages to start off and build up on. But if you write wee poems, as I do, it's a fresh start every time. And you've got to have, not an arrogance, but a simple faith that the well isn't yet dry! (L)

IM Right. Have you ever even contemplated writing a novel?

NM Now you've known me long enough to know that I am a very sensible fellow! And couldn't write a novel if I was offered a million pounds a word. For this reason. One reason, a big one, is that when I was a baby my bump of mimicry was sawn off (L) which means I can't mimic people. I could never write dialogue. impossible. Take it to an extreme, a play! If I wrote a play with five characters on the stage, they'd all speak exactly like me, regardless of age or sex. Couldn't do it! No, I have no gift of invention or of mimicry: the poems are all about things which are immediately in my experience. I never invented the situation or whatever. Never, I couldn't.

IM Never once?

NM No. The poems really are sort of upmarket reporting. (L) Organised verbal juice. And also, therefore, an extension of that, another reason why I couldn't write a novel or a play is that I couldn't invent anything that could be called a plot. So, if I can't invent a plot and I can't write dialogue I just better stick humbly to trifling little versifications! (L)

IM That could be another reason why we keep seeing an 'I' in the poems: it isn't necessarily as it were a tremendous egotism, it's because of this feeling that you can't invent, or you don't want to invent, and so you stick to your own experience.

NM Although what we've been saying seems very solipsistic, narcissistic, my hope of course is that I'm just like anybody else, I have certain, many, experiences, but my hope and belief is that other people have them too. So that although I'm talking about me, I'm talking about something which everybody knows about. You know, it's not so fearfully narcissistic as it might seem. I hope!

BT Well that brings us back to the self. And the self in the MacCaig poems is continually surprising itself by discovering a new form.

NM Yes.

BT   Isn't it? I mean that's why it's not narcissistic, it is a continual
     delight in surprise and discovering new things.

NM   Mind you I must enter what is a lawyer's term but I forget it ... a
     waiver! (L) It's a dangerous mistake to suppose that if a poem is 'I',
     'I', 'I', 'I' that is strictly about me. Very dangerous assumption.

IM   It might just be a man in your position.

NM   It might indeed be a man in my position.

BT   Which is the name of a collection and a poem in which you
     complain about this intrusive other self who keeps elbowing you
     out of the way and uses your eyes for windows, so you've got an
     ambivalent relationship to this 'I' that sees things and surprises you
     with them.

NM   Yes. Well it's what we've said so often—we're a bunch of different
     persons and there's an ugly person inside me just as there is inside
     everybody, and sometimes it's he that's speaking not the real, nice,
     me! (L) So I have to lock him up!

BT   But the 'I' in its various guises connects also with this central thing
     that you have about metaphor? That things rise from the dead,
     phoenix-like, in a new, transformed shape and the poems are often,
     it seems to me, celebration and taking a delight in the diversity of
     creation ...

NM   Oh, yes, yes indeed.

BT   There's a poem about death in which you say that you're not going
     to make friends with death yet, you're not going to be reconciled to
     it, and you will cheat death in the end if either or both of the
     following things happen. Either you go into an absolute nothing-
     ness which is grand—or the grave can't get you anyway, the bogey
     man can't get you or you live on through the ideas, the poems.
     ['Two Skulls', *Collected Poems*, p. 356]

NM   I remember that poem, yes, and that's the way it finishes. I say I hate
     death: of course, I hate death! Because it's a full-stop to life, that's
     why. And it takes your friends from you as well. And I said never
     mind death, this isn't a quote, I've got ideas in my head that you
     never thought of! And when I die, either these ideas will continue to
     live in other people's minds or else I shall be restored to that
     wonderful absolute, nothingness. (I nearly said 'Bugger-all'!) (L)

IM   I'm glad you didn't say that on the tape! (L)

BT   Yes, there is a conviction there that one way or another death can be
     defeated, in the sense that you get round it by the absolute nothing-
     ness of the nothingness. Or, and/or, and the real confidence is in that
     possibility that you can continue to live.

NM   You continue to live!

BT Through these celebrations of delight.

NM Yes. I wrote a wee poem about Angus, one of the twelve, I believe
    I might quote it, I'll try.

BT We could find it for you.

NM All right, find it. It's called, it's got a very simple, simple, simple
    name. 'In Memoriam'. It's exactly about what you've been saying.

BT I've got this one. Very fond of those poems, actually.

NM Thank you. Oh, decrepitude!

IM (Puts his glasses on.)

BT The specs come out!

NM It's just what you've been saying, Bob. It's called 'In Memoriam',
    corny, corny!

In Memoriam

On that stormy night
a top branch broke off
on the biggest tree in my garden.

It's still up there. Though its leaves
are withered black among the green
the living branches
won't let it fall.

BT That's brilliant! Just exactly what we were saying.

IM You had begun to talk about how you can be tempted to go too far
    with metaphor. Can you just explain why one can have too much
    metaphor?

NM I don't think I mean too much, I mean too extravagant. Too far-
    fetched, which is very apt to become sheer whimsy, you know. And
    is out of tone with the rest of the poem, you know. I sometimes write
    poems which are, deliberately, extravagantly metaphorical or
    imagistic. Just for the hell of it, playing, playing. People seem to
    expect poets to go around with their eyes rolling in a frenzy. (L)
    And their feet three inches off the floor. They confuse, of course,
    the old confusion, they confuse solemnity with seriousness. And
    they expect poets to be solemn. What a ridiculous idea! And if
    every man has his right to reticence he's got his right to playfulness
    as well. Why not? And I still occasionally write jokey wee poems,
    you know, because I like reading jokey, wee poems. What's wrong
    with that?

IM Nothing.

NM And also people say why do you write all these poems about toads, blackbirds and weasels and stags, cows, dogs, you know? Tut-tut-tut! That's another thing that enrages me (I have to borrow a rage because I don't have one myself). The subject of any work of art doesn't matter all that much, it's what you do with it. You go into the National Gallery in Edinburgh and there's a painting a quarter of an acre in size on a huge subject—the Ascension of Jesus Christ by an Old Master, Titian. And people stare at it in awe, marvellous, a masterpiece, and they toddle into the next gallery and there's a painting four feet by three of a guitar, two lemons and a kipper; and they stare at it and say marvellous, a masterpiece. And they're right both times. Art is most amazing.

IM But you were off-tape agreeing with Bob that there is a certain tendency as your poems go on, to suspect metaphor a wee bit more?

NM Oh yes. I do.

IM And to be more careful in restraining it.

NM Yes, yes, I do. If you've got a metaphorical way of seeing things, which I have, for good or ill, the temptation to exploit that knack of metaphor and image is very strong, and if you don't control it, I've said it before, it's very apt just to develop into silly whimsies, you know. Or else it sticks out like a sore thumb in the middle of a poem which *isn't* using metaphors so extreme. It's to be watched. It's too seductive!

IM You go up to Sutherland every year and you stoke up with what you see there and what you experience there and then you come back to the city, to Edinburgh, but you're writing really about the things that were there.

NM Or if I'm not I'm using metaphors and images which obviously come from there. Yes. The way I put it is I fatten my camel's hump up there; I never write when I'm up there—too busy doing nothing! And then I feed on that hump the rest of the year.

IM One wouldn't want to make pompous utterances about how interesting it is that MacCaig doesn't write much about television, and railway trains and things in the city.

NM Well, two extraordinary things of that kind. I taught kids for—och while empires rose and fell (L) and I hardly ever write about them, hardly ever. And I've lived in Edinburgh all my life and I love it, and I *hardly* ever write about Edinburgh.

BT That's true.

NM Very strange.

BT There's also, pertinently to this, that set of poems about New York, which you wrote—after your trip to New York?

NM Yes, immediately after.

BT And both in form and content they're unusual.

NM Yes.

BT Because they express your exasperation at how you can't catch all this in a very formal structure, and they go off at all sorts of tangents and it's very deliberately played that way.

NM Yes.

BT They're very different from most of the rest of your poems?

NM Yes, they are. Yes, well, it was a different experience from anything I'd ever experienced. But about the Edinburgh thing there are poems, lots of poems, which are actually situated in Edinburgh although Edinburgh isn't mentioned. Lots and lots and lots. So I've written more poems about Edinburgh than people suppose. For an example, there's one little poem called 'By the canal'; well, the canal's two hundred yards from the house, but Edinburgh isn't mentioned. ['By the Canal, Early March', *Collected Poems*,1985, p. 61]

IM And is it significant when you do mention Edinburgh, like 'November Night, Edinburgh'?

NM Well that one, yes because of Edinburgh's situation, with the Firth of Forth down there and in mists, haar creeping up and foghorns lamenting into the mist. There aren't awfully many cities like that, and Edinburgh's hills and crags and stuff, so naming Edinburgh was necessary there. I mean if I'd called it 'November Night, Kilmarnock' it wouldnae work! It *has* to be Edinburgh.

IM Do you ever consciously get inspiration from things that other people have written?

NM Ah, sometimes. Sometimes to prime the pump, I pick up a book of poems which I've been recently reading and liking, and I read three or four and suddenly a phrase is up my street—I don't use the phrase—but it starts me off.

IM Do you actually find yourself consciously influenced, whether it's by Wallace Stevens or whichever other poets you particularly admire?

NM I said I'd no powers of mimicry, which in a way is a good thing, because of the poets that I've loved and still love, you'd have a job looking for an influence except for two. In one book, there are some poems and any sharp-witted person would say ha, ha, ha, MacCaig's been re-reading John Donne. And in another book there are a few poems, where people would say ha, MacCaig's discovered Wallace Stevens!

BT Would you like to identify these books?

NM Oh, I can't remember which ones they were. They were a good few years ago. Outside of that I don't think there's a very obvious influence, although if a man isn't influenced he's a fool! (L) So I am influenced, but I don't think it comes out in any direct way.

IM You don't recall ever, for example, *answering* somebody or *arguing* with somebody in one of your poems what they've said in another poem?

NM Don't remember.

IM I ask because there is one that occurred to me that is very possibly just the concatenation of poems in my head. It's 'Old Edinburgh', your poem, in which instead of talking about the Kings and Queens you go on to, for example, the picture of the 'lice on the march / tar on the amputated stump ...'.

NM Oh yes.

IM Your picture of the past, and it ends up 'And history leans by a dark entry / with words from his mouth / that say *Pity me, pity me / but never forgive*'. I have an inextricable connection in my mind with a poem of Auden's, 'Spain 1937'— the one that keeps coming back to 'today the struggle' and it ends up more or less you've got to go now because 'History to the defeated / May say alas but cannot help or pardon.'

NM Well, it's obviously a connection because of course I know that poem. But it wasn't in my conscious mind at all. Ah, damn it, I'll remove that poem from the next edition.

IM Not at all! We'd begun to talk again off the tape about the third member of the triumvirate that you're often described as being part of in your personal life; not just Hugh MacDiarmid, Chris Grieve and however many of him there were, but also Sidney Goodsir Smith?

NM Ah yes. Sidney Good God Sir Smith! (L) Oh yes, I was very, very close to Sidney and he had some resemblances to Dylan Thomas. One striking one was that he had an extraordinary comic gift. As Dylan Thomas had. But Sidney's comic gift appears in his poetry, some of it, in *Under the Eildon Tree* and Dylan Thomas's comic gift never appears in his poetry, it appears in his short stories. But Sidney's is often and often in his stories. Now it was a comic gift, it wasn't wit. It's very difficult to quote him. Because it was just *comic*; not brief epigrams that you remember. He had me sore laughing—hundreds of times, and there was nothing to tell anybody. (L) Terrible! It's like my disbelief in God. It's a terrible frustration to me that He doesn't exist, because I want to spit in His face. And He doesn't exist. It's a terrible frustration. The only quotable thing I recall of Sidney's was, one day we were walking in the afternoon, and there's a long flight of steps in Edinburgh, steps, landing, steps, landing, beside the National Gallery, and he started telling me that he had been walking with another friend who managed to fall down the whole flight. Now you see I told that in five seconds, he took about three minutes. And I was doubled up with mirth: as I was just recovering he said thoughtfully, of course he was a Catholic! (L) But generally he wasn't quotable. I said once to my wife that I was going down to Rose Street to listen at the pub doors for Sidney, because wherever he was people were laughing. And he louder and uglier than any of them.

IM   When you knew him he was writing?

NM   Oh yes. His history is, as you know, extraordinary. He was a New Zealander. His father was a New Zealander. His mother was from Fife. He was born in New Zealand, came to Britain, to an English public school, and a couple of holidays in Scotland at that age, that's all. And he was writing, this lasted right through his university years—Oxford, not a Scottish one—he was writing of course in English, very poor stuff. His father was posted to Edinburgh University and they came to live in Edinburgh, and he immediately met the Boys, that's to say, MacDiarmid, and Sorley Maclean, and was converted to Scots, a language he had hardly ever heard! And he is one of the few writers in Scots who never ever after that wrote in English. It was a total conversion. The first attempts were pretty rough and ready, you know! I told him he took to the language like a duck to glue. (L) But it wasn't long before he formed his own kind of vocabulary, what he found instinctively to be his, and he wrote particularly *Under the Eildon Tree* which I have large admirations for. And another thing about him: I never ever heard him once uttering a malicious word about anybody. On the other hand I knew him awful well. There were sides to him that the general—his other friends even—didn't know about; he had great depressions, worries about his poetry and financial worries. But he was far more complex than people thought. Good old Sid! is the cry.

BT   He was such a humorous man.

NM   He was so comical, so humorous. But he had his sufferings. He had his sufferings, about which he told me a number of things, but it was his extraordinary psychological energy, and I think energy is the life blood of all the arts. A delicate watercolour of a beautiful wee bowl with delicate flowers in it—it's got energy or else it's no bloody good! Energy isn't violence, you see, it's nothing to do with

violence—Ted Hughes is violent; but energy, now *he* had it. Any
company he was in was uplifted, they became nicer, better, and
funnier.

IM   That's a wonderful thing to be able to say that about somebody.

NM   Yes. Well, he was like that. He juiced-up your batteries, an excellent man!

IM   I have felt guilty because I have found his novel hard or shall I say
impossible to read.

NM   *Carotid Cornucopius*, so do I. I gave him rows about that! It was an
alleged part of a novel, and it was a sort of—it was modelled
obviously on *Finnegans Wake*, where Joyce made innumerable
puns and invented words you know, but the difference is that all
Sidney's inventions, and they're mostly inventions of course, they
all had a secondary meaning, but the meanings were either sexual or
lavatorial, whereas Joyce's other meanings were helping on the
story. They were functional. Sidney's weren't, in that book. So I
think it's a lot of rubbish.

IM   And did he *mind* when you told him such things?

NM   I don't suppose he did. You see, a lot of people loved it: Sorley
Maclean loved it. He can actually quote it. Imagine quoting *Carotid*
... I suppose he was sorry, but he wasn't offended.

BT   We have mentioned Sorley Maclean and he is another friend.

NM   Oh yes.

BT   How much Gaelic do you have?

NM   Less than I had. My mother came as I've said from Hebrides
without any English, but my father had no Gaelic and this so often
happens—a Gaelic speaker marries a non-Gaelic speaker so the
children don't learn it. On top of that my mother was illiterate. She
never learned to read or write. She could sign her name. It looked
like a four-year-old's first attempt. And this gave her a wonderful
freedom with the English language. But I started trying to learn
Gaelic in my teens, latish teens, and she was no help at all. I mean
I'd say, what's the Gaelic for yes and she couldn't tell me. Now
there's a very good reason for that; there is no Gaelic for yes. But
she couldn't explain why, and I would say coming back from
Scalpay I had some noises stuck in my head parrot-wise, and I'd say
what's ... and she would say that means certainly and I'd say, is it
one word? She couldn't tell me [*gu dearbh*]. She was absolutely no
use to me in that respect, so I went on learning Gaelic, and I became
fairly proficient at reading it, never spoke it, and then I met Gaels
including one in particular, John MacInnes who of course was a
Gael—passionate Gael—who loved Sorley's poetry. And he'd

come to my house and we'd sit and he'd think of a poem and he'd
say 'Sorley: bring down *Dain do Eimhir*'. That was Sorley's first
book, and he'd translate a poem of Sorley's into English, better
translations than I've ever seen in print! Marvellous! I'd be following it, you see, so I owe John MacInnes that huge debt that I saw
further through the opacity of the language than I ever would have,
and began to see just what an extraordinary poet the man is. And of
course I had met Sorley, and—I've been awful lucky with my
friends. You would have to give him a throat operation before he
could tell a lie. (L) He's 100% honest! He's very proud, he's a Gael:
a terrific friend, but boy, I wouldn't like to have him for an enemy.
Passionate man, more than emotional, passionate, the way Yeats
was. And I think one of the reasons his poetry is so impressive is that
this passionate man writes in strict traditional forms, and the strict
forms and the passion are at each other's throats. Every line feels as
if it's going to explode in your face. Only it doesn't, because the
form won't let it, and this gives an extraordinary concentration of
feeling to his writing, more than any poet I know of, alive!

BT Even in translation this comes across ...

NM You've no idea how much is lost.

BT Is that so?

NM This that I'm talking about isn't in any translation. Every verse is
like a clenched fist, you know. Even the translations by Crichton
Smith, a Gael, and a good poet, they don't get this, that quality is
just not there.

BT How does it get lost? Has it got something to do with the structure
and syntax of the language itself?

NM Yes it has, but it's mostly the passionate feeling and the rigid forms;
the strict forms.

BT Using rhetoric in a non-pejorative sense: it's specific to the rhetoric
of that language that you get this intensity?

NM I think so, yes, yes, I think so. Oh there are whole sorts of things, the
sounds, the noises that Gaelic can make are quite extraordinary.
They've more sounds than in any language I know anything about.
Actual noises so that a poet say, or a speaker, have got more things
to use for their effects, so it's very much the nature of the Gaelic
language. But I think the main thing is this passionate fella, who is
still miserable because he didn't go to the Spanish War, he's still
guilty, all these years later. And the quarrel between that and the
forms, the strictness of the forms. If he didn't have that he would
have written sprawling things that would have lost this particular
quality.

IM He's using the old forms in Gaelic?

NM Well, I wouldn't want to exaggerate that. He does use old forms, but I don't mean in any sort of pedantic or even scholarly way, cos some of the old forms had extraordinary complicated rhyme-schemes, extraordinarily complicated, but strict form. In later years, he started writing free verse poems. By this time he was so experienced in writing that he still manages to give this effect that I've been describing, but I don't think so powerfully as in the poems in strict form. Oh, they're still marvellous! But this particular ... you've got a hand-grenade in every verse and somebody's pulled the pin.

IM I've heard two Gaelic poets, Donald MacAulay and Iain Crichton Smith, complaining quite a lot that the poetics of the language are set so far back in time that it's very difficult in some ways to write a twentieth-century poem ...

NM Exactly.

IM But that's the strength, yes?

NM Exactly. May I add? He did to Gaelic poetry a very parallel thing to what MacDiarmid did to Scots poetry. The last time there were good poems written in Gaelic was about the time of Burns. The last time good poems were written in Scots was about the time of Burns. And each of them dragged these two languages into the twentieth century, so that it was capable of dealing in a contemporary way with contemporary matters and all that. An extraordinary achievement, and they both did it in these two languages.

IM I have a mental picture of MacCaig and Grieve and Sidney Goodsir Smith—the bit I can't work out, is when they talk about whether you write in English or in Scots or whether it's such a sore subject that they don't.

NM Edwin Muir said that no Scot could possibly write good poetry in English because it's not his blood language, his ancestral language. In the first place I don't believe it, and in the second place my ancestral language is one I don't speak, and that's Gaelic. It's a ridiculous notion. Now Sidney and Chris, and also Alex Scott, this was no problem to them either. Sidney's the funny one of course, because he was writing in what was to him at first a foreign language really. And Alex has said in print, sometimes I write in Scots and sometimes I write in English. If the subject happens to suit English I write in English, and if it suits Scots I write in Scots, and I don't see why not. Now, that is a common sense view and Edwin Muir's rubbish was rubbish, insanitary rubbish, Chanel No. 1 bilge. (L)

IM   But MacDiarmid is a complicated case here, because when he was writing in Scots he more or less thought that people *should* be writing in Scots.

NM   Oh yes.

IM   Was he not annoyed with Muir indeed for writing in English?

NM   Of course he was. He hated Muir. He had several irrational hatreds, and that was one of them. And he claimed that in one of Muir's prose books he had stabbed the Scottish movement in the back because Muir had said what I just quoted [*Scott and Scotland*, 1936]. But Muir had also said that Scots was a dying language—he was pessimistic about its future, which annoyed Chris, and he said nevertheless there is a man called Hugh MacDiarmid who is writing the most remarkable poems in Scots. So you never can tell if a language is dead or not, its death-rattle might be marvellous art. And Chris ignored that praise and chose, being Chris, to pick on the other side and hated Muir the rest of his life. And Muir was very sad about this. When Muir was in Prague, British Council job, he wrote to Chris, Chris told me he was offering an olive branch, look, come on, that was in the past; he showed me the letter, I read it, and I said good for him, I hope you gave him a nice answer—he said—did I hell! (L) Wouldn't budge, wouldn't budge.

IM   And did he, MacDiarmid, find any difficulty facing his different selves when he himself started writing in English?

NM   He started at the very beginning writing in English, and he printed in a magazine written almost entirely by himself, that Scots was finished—it's a back-water in European languages, and the future of Scottish poetry is obviously a development of this wonderful language, English. (L) Then he told me, this was when he was in Montrose, the early twenties, just when he came back from the war. He said, you know in Montrose I came to three important decisions. I decided I was a Communist, and Communism was practically unknown in Scotland then: and I decided I was a Scottish National-ist, which then was just a parcel of freaks:—in fact he founded the Scottish Nationalist Party along with four others, Monty, Compton MacKenzie and others. So these were two of his big decisions, and the third one was that he had decided that he was going to be a great Scottish poet. Now contrary to the general ideas of things, poets are extremely practical. So he said, how do you become a great Scottish poet? Think what the English do, and do the opposite! (L) And one of the things the English do is that they write in English so he decided to write in Scots. He had plenty Scots. He was born in Langholm in 1891 or something, where Scots was still rich but, extremist, he decided to enrich his vocabulary so he bought the *Etymological Dictionary of the Scottish Tongue* and C. M. Grieve dived in one end and Hugh MacDiarmid splashed ashore at the other, shaking off beautiful little masterpieces of lyrics. And after that of course it was Scots, Scots, Scots till to the dumbfounderment of his fans in the thirties he reverted to English—Traitor! Traitor! Lick-spittle of the English Ascendancy! Etc. ... cultural quisling! That's what they used to call me!

The final tape was a four-way conversation: Iain Crichton Smith arrived after dinner.

ICS Was MacDiarmid ever interested in drama? Did he ever go to the theatre, no? I know he didn't like the novel, he never read novels.

NM No, because like myself he read plays, but he never went to the theatre and he never went to concerts. Because he was tone-deaf to both of them. He did go to an occasional concert, when wild horses on bended knees—what I mean is the Scottish USSR Society! (L) And he'd sit in the front seat, tortured. He told me music—it's not that I don't like it, Norman, it's a physical assault. (L) And he'd sit in the front seat and when he was quite sure the piece was over he jumped up—Bravo! Bravo! Bravo! (L) And took his tortured—

BT Was this general? Did it also apply to things like pibroch?

NM It did. He was tone-deaf. There's a passage—

BT I mean he writes very movingly about it.

NM Ah, come off it! There's a passage in a poem of his describing a piper playing a pibroch which has more gross errors in it than a lesser man would have managed to stuff into what? twelve lines, for example, 'the pipes play louder and louder'—impossible! 'Modulations from one key to another'; and there are others: the punch one is 'the improvisations become wilder and wilder'—improvisations—in a pibroch?! Ever heard—'he fluffed the G grace note in the *crunluath*'? No prize! (L) G grace note?

ICS But Norman, music means a lot to you doesn't it?

NM Yes.

ICS And you've often talked about Mozart and Bach especially?

NM Oh I love music. More than poetry.

ICS And pibroch?

NM Oh very much, yes yes, yes, yes, yes.

ICS Do you think that music has had any influence—listening to music has had any influence on the way you *write*, I mean your timing—your form?

NM I don't care but I think so. I think so, but I don't know. But I suppose so. Because verbal rhythms matter, not just in metrical poems but in free verse where you get no help; in strict form poems you're given assistance, you're given a form. Iambic pentameter. Stanzas, four lines, AB AB AB AB, but in free verse you're not given that assistance at all.

ICS No, no and it's very tricky isn't it? It's very tricky writing free verse.

NM In strict form metrics, verses, stanzas you're given a strict form. Of course, you mustn't be too strict or else—one of the extraordinary things about Alexander Pope's couplets is that they don't become boring, and to write iambic pentameters—couplets, couplets, couplets, couplets—without them becoming boring is hellish difficult, because you have to, they go ... May I quote three lines of Mac-Diarmid? They are marvellous, beautiful lines and I—the third line in particular I think ah, ah, ah, ah, phone a prosodist and ask him to scan that one! It's the first three lines of 'Cwa'een like milk-wort'. ['Milk-Wort and Bog-Cotton']

ICS Ah yes.

NM And the first one is nearly metronomically Di-da-di-da-di-da-di-da-di-da. The second one is—no the first one's the second one is nearer a strict di-da-di-da-di-da and third one takes such liberties! But behind it there is a ghost, a paradigm of di-da-di-da-di-da-di-da-di-da.

    Cwa'een like milk-wort and bog-cotton hair!
    I love you, earth, in this mood best o' a'
    When the shy spirit like a laich wind moves

Scan that, chum! And yet that ghost of a strict one, it's there, or else that line would be rubbish.

ICS Yes.

NM And to do that is a—certified sign that the writer is a genius.

[Norman proceeded to quote Horace in Latin, stressing the importance of the metrics.]

NM Isn't that beautiful? Even if you don't understand a word of it. And it's this quarrel between di-da-di-da and speech rhythm. But that third line, oh! Can I say it for my own relish? Please.

IM Yes.

NM   I love you, earth, in this mood best of a'
      While the shy spirit like a laich wind moves
    It's like playing the notes between the keys in a piano.

ICS Yes. You said something very interesting there Norman. You said that you could actually relish that without understanding it even.

NM Oh when I quoted that in Latin I don't know if any of you know any Latin, but suppose you don't.

BT Not enough to follow ...

NM No, but there is an aesthetic pleasure, purely aesthetic. Nothing to do with meaning.

BT It's got to do with music.

NM It's got to do with music. It's got to do with rhythm. It's an aesthetic pleasure.

ICS With rhythm, yes, with rhythm.

NM And an awful lot of people these days don't seem to realise that the Arts give you an aesthetic pleasure. For instance, the Till is a tributary of the Tweed, and it's very different, because the Tweed is a bustling little floozy, flouncing her skirts, swallowing men, and the Till is slow, deep pools, and somebody wrote, Anon, Mr Anon—

> Said Tweed to Till—
> 'What gars ye rin sae still?'
> Said Till to Tweed—
> 'Though ye rin fast
> And I rin slaw,
> For ae man that ye droon
> I droon twa.'

(L) Isn't that marvellous? Now some academic oaf corrected the rhyme scheme to

> Said Tweed to Till
> 'What gars ye rin sae still?'
> Said Till tae Tweed—
> 'Though ye rin wi' speed
> And I rin slaw' ...

Isn't that awful? This aesthetic thing, which I can't explain, nobody can, as far as I know, he just pulled the plug out of that wee dinghy of a poem and it sank tae the bottom.

BT It's a smashing wee poem.

NM Ah, beautiful.

ICS In Sorley's new book, a book of criticism [*Ris a'Bhruthaich: Criticism and Prose Writings*, 1985]—where he's talking about sixteenth and seventeenth-century Gaelic songs he says that he can't appreciate any poem at all which hasn't got music in it. Do you agree with that? I mean, when you ...

NM I'd like a definition of music.

ICS Well put it like this way, like for instance, Auden said poetry is something that is made of words only.

NM Well, he was a fool. Anyway he wasn't the fellow that said that, he stole it from Mallarmé.

ICS But do you feel that you need some kind of musical quality in your poetry before you can appreciate it? Not in your own poetry but when you're reading poetry?

NM That stupid question which used to be asked (things are getting better) they've stopped asking it. The most beautiful line of poetry that you know. 'The moan of doves in immemorial elms'—that kind of thing—

IM 'Bare ruined choirs, where once the sweet birds sang.'

ICS That is beautiful, yes.

NM I would add, 'Grate on their scrannel pipes of wretched straw.' Isn't that musical?

ICS Yes, yes, yes.

BT So it doesn't have to be mellifluous?

NM No.

ICS Not mellifluous.

NM That's why I said I would like to know what you mean by music.

BT I'm interested in the composers that you like, Bach, let me guess, Bach obviously, Mozart, obviously, Scarlatti, you've mentioned Scarlatti so I know that, in recent times I'm willing to bet you like Bartok?

NM Yes. I do.

BT And you like sharp edgey music?

NM That's right. I don't like most nineteenth-century music.

BT That's what I suspected.

NM I don't like men who I know must be great composers because people whose judgements I respect find them so, the big one with me the difficult one with me is Brahms. Now when Brahms is just writing wee tunes, oh, they're lovely! And then the silly fella tries to write a thing that lasts forty-five minutes and he doesn't know what to do with his beautiful wee tunes.

BT I bet you don't much like French music.

NM No. Why do you suppose that?

BT Because French music relies so much on colour, tone, rather than structure.

NM Quite right, quite right. I'm a linear man. And painting, what appeals to me most is the shapes, rather than the colours. O.K.? Right! what appeals to me most, *most*, I'm only saying most, is melody rather than harmony, this is very Celtic ... linear people in their music, pibroch, their poetry, in as far as I know it, sculpture, crosses, line, rather than colour or harmony. In music I don't mind two lines, counter-contrapuntal music, where there are two lines sinuously insinuating themselves.

ICS You said something about Brahms. Now, I was going to ask you, do you feel that within your own work that you don't want to go on to write long poems? You're quite happy to ...

NM I don't want to go on to write long poems. I am one of the most kind persons, especially to myself. I don't like reading long poems. (L) So why should I write them?

ICS But you must like reading—*A Drunk Man Looks at the Thistle*.

NM Oh yes, I do, yes.

ICS But that is not a long poem in the sense you mean. It's more a collection of short poems—

NM No, no, no, no, you're quite right. There are *some* long poems I have loved, and love, well Homer, for a start. And ...

BT Homer's very episodic.

NM Yes and so is the *Drunk Man*.

BT That's right. Just exactly Iain's point.

NM But it's a whole poem, though.

BT Oh, sure.

ICS Do you think it's more—do you think it's more difficult to write long poems now, than in perhaps Homer's time? (L)

NM You don't need to go as far back as that. The epic, the long poem, the function, I'm talking as if I knew something. (L)

ICS Do carry on!

NM A good number of the things that poetry did for many many centuries have been taken over by other arts.

ICS Oh yes, yes.

NM Long epics, which I think *must* have a narrative—exit Mr Inflated Pound and his shabby portentous and ridiculous cantos! The narrative has been taken over by the short story, the novel, the film, etc. Tell me something to say, I'm running out of verbs.

ICS No you're not. (L)

NM And the administering of ideas, I say because there's a philosopher in the room, the administering of ideas which poetry used to pretend to do.

ICS Lack of communal symbolism people immediately understand.

NM Yes. That's true. Communal beliefs. Poets used to be able to make references with the certainty that they would be understood, and two things happened. The interest in Classical literature vanished— that stimulated the Renaissance so much, and the influence of Christianity diminished until it is a—ho, ho, ho, farce! And there were references writers could make to classical things and religious things, Christian religion.

ICS That you can't do any more! Because people don't know them.

NM So the area in which poetry operates now, has shrunk and shrunk and shrunk. They can't any longer tell stories; they can tell anecdotes. Many is the anecdote I've told myself! (L) But not a huge long thing: that's been taken over by the novels, short stories etc. etc. And I therefore don't think that it's possible to write a long poem. People cheat. They write sequences. Thirty-four poems. One-two—all the way up. And they call it a long poem, it's nothing of the kind! It's thirty-four wee poems, waving and saying, Hallo, I hope you're my cousin. (L)

ICS So do you actually think that poetry has diminished in some sense over the years? I mean nowadays that there are things that poetry can no longer do?

NM Oh, yes. I think there are these things.

ICS What are the sort of things that you think poetry should be doing now? If it has lost ...

NM Poetry can still do what poetry always did and that is, amongst other things, it's a psychological Optrex, it clears your eyes and you see things. (L)

PLATO IN A BOILER SUIT

WILLIAM McILVANNEY

We interviewed William McIlvanney when he visited us in Aberdeen on 11 March 1984.

IM The purpose of the interview is to get Willie to tell us something about what he's writing for and what he's writing about, and it should be explained to the audience that Bob and Isobel know Willie really quite well because he spent a year as a Writer in Residence in Aberdeen in, I think, 1980. Well, could you try to say what, at the moment, you feel you're trying to do, writing your books?

WM Ah, just as the question is fairly wide, the answer would have to be multiple. You know, one thing I'm trying to do I think is to engage—one of the things that has always struck me in trying to write—is that I have a particular problem because of the kind of background that I came from.

IM Would you tell us just a wee bit about that background?

WM Well, it was a working-class background in the west of Scotland, in Kilmarnock and the relevance of that to what I was saying, is that books were not a popular commodity where I come from. The fact that from the age of fourteen really onwards I was trying to write was not a fact I broadcast in the streets. (L) Since people had suspicions of what you were up to doing that! And so, the general background from which I came was not one, in fact, I think you could say that the whole of the west of Scotland is not one which is kind to the more aesthetic pretensions, you know. To try to be a writer there is a bit like trying to be an orchid in the Arctic. It's a wee bit sore. On your pretensions. But the thing that I had that supported me was the family within the house. That was another

case. There was always books in the house and we, all of us except
my father, loved reading. Because the truth is, my father read little
and when he read it was fact. He used to say when I was reading
fiction, 'But somebody just made that up oot o' their ain heid! And
why are you spending your time with that?' (L) But my mother was
a very keen reader and my two brothers Neil and Hugh and my sister
Betty—all of them. In fact when you look back on it it seems a bit
bizarre, but in that wee house in a housing scheme in Kilmarnock
we used to have spontaneous poetry nights where we just—we'd all
found poems that we liked and we sat round reading them *at* one
another. (L) Because there was a definite element of performance
about the whole thing. And at the time they seemed—they *were*
absolutely natural: they didn't happen with any deliberation. But I
suppose that engendered in all of us an interest and a liking for
words, so that say from the time I was fourteen I was *trying* to write,
but I was aware all the time of a kind of dichotomy in what I was
doing, because the people I wanted to write about and therefore as
far as possible to write *for*, in the hope that they would read it, were
people who you know did not have a lot of immediate love of books.
So I've always had the dilemma when I write of justifying what I do
as I go along. I've never had the feeling that some people have
that—isn't it a wonderful thing to write books—to be a poet—to be
a novelist. I've always had the problem is it worthwhile? And on
what terms is it worthwhile for me to do?

IM And you started when you were fourteen? Can one ask just in
parenthesis whether your brother Hughie—the well-known sports
writer—is he older than you, and did he start writing before you or
was there an element of competition?

WM I think there always has been. Most of the time benign. It has struck
malignant episodes (L) in our lives, but I think it's mostly benign.
Yes, Hugh's a significant two years and nine months older than I
am—you know I think the parents must have been working things
out fairly carefully! (L) But, as I say, I started about fourteen, and
I know that when he was about sixteen to seventeen, he was
certainly writing. He would never admit it now in public, but he
actually wrote poetry. I use the term loosely—as I use it very
loosely about what I wrote as well, but yes, we were both interested
from an early age, and he went into journalism at the age of sixteen,
I think sixteen and a half. He's an interesting example of the kind of
thing I was talking about from another angle. Both of us went to a
wee primary school in Kilmarnock called Hillhead Primary School,
and Hughie had the chance to go to Kilmarnock Academy, and in

fact, without informing my parents—and that's how vague things were in those days—he decided to go to Junior Secondary School, because that's where his friends were going. And because there was a certain stigma (L) among some people where we lived about going to that school [the Academy]. And when I came along I just knew that I was going to do it and I wanted to go and I would take all the opprobrium of going to a Senior Secondary School. And I think that's had an interesting effect, you know, on both our lives. Because I think what happened with Hugh was that he always had to prove—he had to go into journalism to do it—he had I suppose a need to prove to himself that the intelligence and the ability was there. Some graduates achieve a degree and then go to sleep on it for the rest of their lives you know, like a Dunlopillow! (L) Well, he could never do that. He had to scuffle all the time to prove to himself that the talent was there. I think it's given him energy, you know. Frequently a very painful energy. In other words—it's meant that there's not been a lot of rest in his mind about his own talent. He doesn't carry around a wallet of self-esteem. He has to earn it anew every day.

IM   Yes, but you're not suggesting that you carry around a wallet of self-esteem either?

WM Not at all, no. Maybe that's why I set off trying to write novels rather than doing journalism, I suppose is what I mean. Through the university process I became very interested in novels, and so I had, I suppose, a set of criteria to try to measure myself against. I think what a degree has done for me is a very simple thing—it has meant that having gone there—gone through the process, entered the fortress of academe—I was not intimidated by it. I hope I've no arrogance in relation to it, but I don't feel intimidated by it, and I think if I had *not* gone there, I would have had a kind of inferiority complex, as a lot of working-class people do, who have not gone into that area.

IM   Yes, I totally see the point about the psychological difference it's made to both yours and your brother Hugh's lives what kind of education you had, and it helps to define the chips on the various shoulders.

WM That's right; that's right.

IM   But one of the fascinating things is that there are ways in which the two of you write so similarly. One of the things you both do is— these *wonderful* metaphors: you both have a gift for that. You've been chastised for it from time to time ...

WM Oh, many times! many times! (L)

IM   For indulging it too much, and perhaps a journalist is in a better position to over-indulge without fear because of the daily wastage. So it's almost as if whatever it is that is making you write is prior to all the education, and something you've got in common—something almost in common with the ideal of the west of Scotland patter itself!

WM   Yes. The business of metaphor is, as you say, Isobel, one with which I have been flagellated many times, (L) and I'd made a decision at some stage, maybe after the first novel, that there were two ways for me to approach it. I could self-consciously whittle away and purify, and try to burn off some of that, or I could just keep writing and hopefully in the end the style would achieve its own balance. And I chose the latter, whether that's wise or not. It's certainly what I did. Because the metaphor is sometimes central to what I do. The use of images. And I think it's a valid point to say it may relate to where I come from. Because I think that certainly Ayrshire speech, which is the Scottish speech I know best, Ayrshire speech is full of metaphor. I had an uncle who worked in the pits who spoke in metaphors all the time. I mean, I remember him describing a fellow going to the dancing who had dancing pumps on, and he said, 'He had shoes that narrow you could kick the ee' oot o' a robin wi' them.' And those are narrow shoes! (L) And his favourite threat if he was angry with somebody was 'I'll make a new road oot o' you!' That was without planning permission! (L) He just spoke in metaphors all the time! This for me exemplifies that kind of—the directness of the imagery in Scottish and certainly in Ayrshire speech. There was a woman in a village in Ayrshire, in Crosshouse, who was a bit fond of the drink; this was maybe in the thirties—and her husband had a special tool for the pits called a ratchet. And like a lot of these ladies she would go on the batter for maybe a fortnight, and then she was more perjink, more douce than anybody else: the character reformation, however brief, was amazing. And she had taken her husband's ratchet and sold it and gone on the bevy with the proceeds. So she had a week or two in which she was careless of all things domestic, but when she sorted herself out again she was really—she cleaned the house, and she was walking down the main street in Crosshouse like a galleon in full sail, and one of the guys at the corner looked at her and he said 'Aye, Maggie's walking very straight: you wouldna' think she'd swallowed a ratchet!' (L) There's a whole—the implications here are epic, yet it's put very succinctly.

IM   Yes, it's all summed up in that wonderful scene in *Docherty* where young Conn is made finally aware of the implications of which language he talks, because he gets punished for speaking Scots and he's offered the chance to change his mind and speak English and he doesn't do it, and he gets belted. And he sits down—one of the things he does afterwards—he sits down and he lists the—what seemed to him the powerful Scots words on the one side of the page and the weaker English words on the other and then he stops and he makes a list (*I'm* telling *you*!) of the things for which there is *no* English equivalent that he knows. Do you think really the Scots speech and this kind of gift of language and so on *is* untranslatable...?

WM Yes, I think, it's not so much the specific semantic content of the word, I think there is a whole tone, there's a whole stance, there's a whole implied philosophy in Scottish speech: and that is what I love about it. But for one thing it just will not tolerate pomposity. I don't think you can be pompous in Scots—you try it. I mean, you get words like sheugh, and speug and .... And at the same time in the best of MacDiarmid's early lyrics I think you see it illustrated, that you *can* talk about *very* large issues without, you know, ballooning into the empyrean. You can stay with your feet on the ground: it's like seeing Plato in a boiler suit or something, (L) you can talk philosophically and still stay very firmly attached to the ground. What I love about Scots words is that they love to dismantle attitudes you know, to their roots. Take a simple word, it always struck me that the Scots word for a pimple is *plook*, and that is it, that is what it is, a plook is a plook is a plook!—a rose is a rose is a rose—and a plook *is definitely* a plook. It's like the sound of illusions bursting, you know. (L) And I think Scots words have that quality: that's what I love about them.

IM So you get to a problem then when you're writing fiction, you don't obviously write fiction in Scots—not many people do—it tends to be ineffective. But perhaps you think you can take some of this tone you're talking about.

WM That's right.

IM This spirit, and using English words and English orthography which is very important—because it's very off-putting—when you see large chunks of a book actually phonetically described.

WM Exactly. It's like a verbal acne.

IM Verbal plooks!

WM That's right—you've got verbal plooks there immediately, my dear. Yes, that's right! I think what for me is important about the Scottishness is that it's got special rhythms, and I think the rhythms

themselves have the same effect as I was suggesting about the
vocabulary. Now again, you could say, as people have said to me,
why don't you write entirely in Scots? The answer is simple. I
mean, I remember speaking at a St Andrew's Night, and I made the
point of how strange it was that I was doing this, I hope, non-
jingoistic celebration of Scottishness in English words, except for
the quotations which were in Scots, naturally. And somebody
shouted from the audience—you know, it being a Scottish audience—'Well, why don't ye dae it then—what are you staundin'
there talking English for?' And I had to say because it would be
hypocritical of me—I said, I spoke Scots until I was five, and I went
to primary school, and I was taught English—what I resent is that I
was taught English to the *suppression* of Scots. I think it was
necessary that I be taught standard English in conjunction, as a
harmonious marriage, with my own daily speech—it would have
been good! But that having happened, I couldn't sit here and say
'Well, we'll talk in the mither leid, Isobel.' Because it's taken me
about five minutes to work out the vocabulary for a start, so all I can
do, it seems to me, is inhabit the paradoxes as healthily as possible
and try to embrace the dichotomies. And I think there *can* be a
fruitful union between the two; it seems to me false to seek a
reversion, I think you have to inhabit the contemporary situation as
healthily as you can. When I taught in Ayrshire, I found that even
many of the words that had been absolutely natural to me like
'brace' for mantelpiece or 'assole' for the fireplace—I was speaking to working-class kids who came exactly from my kind of
background; it was, in fact, a former mining village that I was
teaching in, and they were totally baffled. You realised that a lot of
the phrases that had seemed to me—that *were* for me—natural, that
came, you know, off my lips like breath, they were just totally
natural, were already contained in glass-cases for them. And I just
think you have to confront what is truly happening and inhabit that,
rather than conceptually try to force things back to a time which has
gone.

IM I think so. There is also a problem, I think, for any writer actually
choosing to write in Scots. As far as I can remember I only have
found you writing in Scots in dialogue, where it would obviously
be, you know, hopelessly false *not* to, or in short poems, and I think
one of the problems is we all find it difficult to *read* any kind of
phonetic transcription of Scots, because we are so habituated to
standard English as the thing we read. We can read it in a Scottish
accent but that's the best we can do.

WM Yes, yes.

BT I notice actually about some of the poetry in the new collection that
    you are writing in a *kind* of Scots, but you're not obeying the rules
    of Scots orthography ...

WM That's right.

BT So what you're doing is transcribing, it seems to me, your
    Kilmarnock vernacular.

WM That's right. I mean, what I've been trying to do—

[IM Bob's speaking here as a Kilmarnock man himself.]

WM What I'm trying to do in these, Bob, is just precisely that—it's write
    in Scots which can inhabit the mouth. I think a lot of Scots writing
    that I have read and enjoyed the words on the paper does not survive
    as an oral phenomenon when you come to try to read it. So what I'm
    trying to do is to take the words as it were off the street, so that I do
    not impose upon them some intellectual strictures—some intellec-
    tual criteria. The thing that makes it valid for me to write them is the
    fact that they are there, not that I have thought it would be good if
    people would use them—but people *do* use them and it is an attempt
    to catch language such as men do use in Ayrshire, and women by
    the way.

IM Thank you! The first novels that you wrote, in some very, very
    general way seem to be inevitably I suppose, naturally I suppose,
    not exactly autobiographical but mirroring areas of your experi-
    ence; coming from that. Were you conscious of that?

WM Yes. I mean, I think that—I don't know whether it relates to the
    writing that influenced me early on. I mean the first example of
    what you might call demoniac possession by another writer (L) that
    I can think of for me is the short stories of William Saroyan when I
    was about sixteen or seventeen—things like *The Daring Young
    Man on the Flying Trapeze* or a title I love, 'The Barber Whose
    Uncle Had His Head Bitten Off by a Circus Tiger', which was one
    of the great titles for me. (L) I loved these so much that I was writing
    Saroyan stories, and that means they were highly, highly personal.
    In fact for a while I *was* Saroyan: he just thought he was; I was far
    more like him than he was. And then I suppose the next who really
    influenced me strongly was Hemingway. And I think there is an
    insistence in Hemingway which I would agree with, which is that in
    some form or other—of course you will, hopefully, transmute it—
    it will become something different—but in some form or other the
    seed of what you write, I think, has to come from personal experi-
    ence. If the art, if one could put that in quotes, you can't indicate
    quotes in this microphone here (L)—you know, when that is

brought to bear on it, it would transmute it. I think Eliot says something about the distance between the experience and the art— the bigger the distance the greater the art—and I think that there is something in that. All I'm saying is that I could never write without that initial autobiographical or personal impulse, but hopefully the finished product—it is impossible to tell in the finished product where the autobiographical elements are.

IM Yes, we are fairly sure that you didn't for example as an undergraduate commit murder ...

WM No, I didn't! I'm a bit short of experience in life you know ... (L)

IM Although the description of the, you know, the killing and the after effects in *Remedy is None* [London, 1966] is very powerful. And one gets the feeling, I suppose from your work generally, that *Docherty*—I come clean and say that so far to me is very much your most achieved book—*Docherty* springs to some extent from a complex of feelings about your own father? About the ways in which he was a fantastic man and other ways in which he was (I am guessing here) a defeated man, like Tom Docherty, defeated by the circumstances of the life which meant that he couldn't give his children what he'd like to have given them.

WM Yes, well, *Docherty* is an interesting example of what we are talking about Isobel, because, you know, there are undoubtedly many aspects of Tam Docherty which are simply grafted on from my father, but there are aspects which aren't. I suppose, what happens with that is in the compulsion—my father died of cancer when I was eighteen and that was obviously a trauma, and I suppose what happens with that is through the contemplation of—through the concern for—your father's experience—you hopefully see through that compulsion to a picture, maybe vision's too strong a word, but to a picture, a sense of, other men who had that kind of a life. And that's what I was trying to do; I mean *Docherty* is for me a celebration of, or if you like an elegiac celebration of that kind of man. I've had people say to me—I've had an ex-miner shake hands with tears in his eyes and say that, you know, the story of what he understood as his life had been written in *Docherty*. There were other people say that they knew men, either their own fathers or somebody that they had respected. and I think, you know, Tam Docherty *does* attempt to depict that kind of man, that's all. It was certainly through an understanding of my father that I arrived at the character of Tam Docherty, but in no way would I say that William McIlvanney's father and Tam Docherty are interchangeable. They're not!

IM And I was asking, Willie, about the sense—if any—or how many—
in which Tam Docherty is defeated in the book.

WM Yes, well, I think, for me, if you can use the term defeat about Tam
Docherty it is in a sense the defeat that is inevitable for all of us.
Because I find death—I don't think there is any way round saying
that death is a pretty severe defeat, you know, you don't come back
from that too strongly! And I think that if you want to call Tam
defeated it's in his awareness, and it was the intensity of the dream
which is unfulfilled which gives him the awareness of defeat. And
for me the heroism lies in being aware, and yet living on. I mean,
Tam doesn't degenerate into some totally wilful person who wishes
to practise ill upon others. You know, he may have fragmented, he
may have eroded a bit, but the central decency remains, and it is that
living on in that hard decency in the full awareness of the defeat of
his dreams and his ideals, that for me constitutes the heroism.

IM Yes, I think the dreams and the ideals constitute a kind of heroism
too—because he obviously transforms, transfigures the lives of the
people he lives with, not just his family but the men on the street
corner and everything else. The oddest literary comparison comes
into my head, with Jay Gatsby in *The Great Gatsby* because he just
by will power and a vivid imagination makes a whole world
happen, but when his world collapses and one is intensely sorry for
him, Jay Gatsby kills himself, and it seems to me that precisely Tam
Docherty's heroism is ...

WM No, Gatsby doesn't kill *himself*.

IM Oh, that's right. He gets killed! Sorry.

WM Gatsby, is shot by Wilson, the garage-owner character.

IM But what would have happened to Gatsby? You can't quite imagine
him living on and ...

WM That's right! That's right!

IM I made a gaffe all right, but I think my *sense* of it is right—Gatsby
was finished when his dream collapsed, whereas Tam's dream died
slowly, although seeing Mick in hospital was a very major puncture
to it.

WM In a way Gatsby had to die. Yes. I know what you mean, Isobel. In
a way Gatsby had to die with the dream. But I think that is for me the
difference of somebody like Docherty. I love *The Great Gatsby* as
a book, I'm not in any way trying to take from that, because it was—

IM But Tam's a greater guy!

WM Yes. I suppose that's what I'm trying to say. It's just one of my
favourite books, but I think that there's such a difference. I once
said, talking about *Nessus* when they put *Nessus* on the telly, I said

what was wrong with it was that they updated it, and for me the kind of moral dilemma represented in *A Gift from Nessus* [London, 1968] doesn't transfer too easily even ten years on. Because whether it works individually or not—you've got ostensibly a much freer—much looser moral framework in society, and I made the point that if you took a book of much greater substance, a much better book like *The Great Gatsby* and translated it into the '30s, it wouldn't work: it's got to be in the time of the '20s, because if you put it into the '30s it simply becomes a dreadful self-indulgence. And I think, great though the book is, I think there is that self-indulgence in Gatsby's dream, whereas I think Docherty's dream emerges from the earth below his feet, you know, Gatsby's comes down out of the air somewhere. (L)

IM After *Docherty* a lot of people were surprised or even disappointed that you should start writing quote thrillers, end quote. I'm not saying anything at all about the quality of the thrillers, which as you know I value. Could you tell us a bit about *why* you moved to the *Laidlaw* books, and what you're trying to do in them?

WM Yes, well again I think there is more than one reason, Isobel. One reason is the disappointment. I quite liked the idea of disappointing quite a few people, because some people had said, you know, you are the new Scottish novelist, and it was as if there was a niche, however small and cramped, already prepared for me, and I don't fancy inhabiting niches at any time, and especially not at my tender years! (L) I dinnae fancy it, so I thought it would be a good idea to offend, simply. I mean that wasn't ... that was merely an extra, a wee adrenalin boost in the motivation, I quite liked the idea. The main ideas were that first of all I had a kind of contemporary starvation after writing *Docherty*, because it took quite a while and it was ...

IM And it is set back a bit ...

WM Set in the first quarter of the century, and I thought, I've really got to engage with things contemporary. Secondly, my love-affair with Glasgow had blossomed even further by that time, and the city did and does fascinate me. And I wanted a medium that would allow me to write about Glasgow and yet give me the excuse for going into a lot of areas of the city. Now if you write a triangular relationship novel, you've maybe got half a dozen justifiable settings, but if you write a thriller you've got an excuse for going anywhere! (L) The guy needs to go and chap a door! And I liked that idea. So, you know, I had the desire for something contemporary, I had the need to find a way to write about Glasgow, and I had a character, because how the first *Laidlaw* book happened was not 'I will write a thriller:' it was that I had a character who kept—actually the first thing I did with *Laidlaw* was to make a lot of notes about somebody talking. I didn't know who he was. I'm not trying to be too Joan of Arc-ish, but I really *didn't* know who he was; (L) I just knew: this character fascinates me. And eventually—it was only eventually— I decided that I would make him a detective. And what I liked, what fascinated me about the character was that I wanted somebody who could, who would go to some kind of front-line of contemporary experience, who would have to subject his ideas, his attitudes, his morality, such as it was, to severe pressure. Because I think it's at the edge of things, I mean, the Balzac idea that if you want a character for a novel take anybody and push them to their limits. I wanted somebody who would, on our behalf, go to those limits of contemporary society and try to look honestly at it. Another point was that I've always felt that certainly in Scottish fiction the sheer variety of urban experience hadn't been, hasn't been, adequately explored, and I always wanted my writing to start from, and I suppose to finish confronting, the realities of what are around us, rather than sit in a room and unravel my entrails with fine artistic thoughts. (L) But to go out there and scuffle in the streets which is what *Laidlaw* was doing for me.

IM   And was part of it the thing you mentioned earlier, the desire, which must have been, on the whole, frustrated even with the success of *Docherty*, in that case the desire to actually write for and be *read* by the kind of people you're talking about?

WM   Absolutely.

IM   One might lure people into reading a thriller who don't read other books.

WM   Yes, that's right. I'm glad you mention that because that is, you know, in trying to recap on the reasons, that certainly *was* one, Isobel. What fascinated me was, here was a form which was popular, and therefore you had the chance that quite a few people might read it. Also it seemed to me a form which is frequently under-used. I mean, when I read somebody like Agatha Christie, I get reality starvation about page three—I just cannae believe it! (L) And I thought, here is a form which fights as a fly-weight, when it could at least fight as a middle-weight or maybe even a light-heavyweight. And I thought that was worth trying.

BT   On the other hand, you have been criticised for the use you make of the form, that you put more weight on it than it can bear, and as a result what you get is another problem of credibility about the

character: Laidlaw is altogether too much a heavy-weight intellec-
tually to be the policeman he has to be in order to be that character.
What do you say to that?

WM Yes, yes. I say 'Uhha!' (L) I say 'Oh aye!!' No, I think, that's a point
that has been put to me and I can see the validity of it. Again, I think
Laidlaw is feasible ... I mean I've had folk say 'oh, he could never
be a detective.' I would say that I *know*, not a lot, but I know
detectives, who are the embryo of my creation. After all, it is a
book. So in any book, you heighten the reality that's there. All I
would say is, I know detectives who are as intensely concerned
about the job, and I know a lot of detectives who are not: but I know
some detectives who are. And it's in them that I see the origins of
Laidlaw. The other business about it being heavy-weight: of course,
... as I say the book is heightened. I mean, I've taken a fair pounding
from some people for the last Laidlaw, *Tony Veitch*, because they
say 'Oh isn't it so desperately over-written and heightened!' I don't
think so, I think that my feeling when I finished *Tony Veitch* was
'Jeeze, that was a really tightly-written book.' Because I could
have—there are paragraphs in that book I wanted to write a novel
on, you know, it's very packed. And all I'm going to ask, person-
ally, about a book like that, is if it is written with that heightened
thing, that the heightening shouldn't be fake, and for me it's not. It's
like, the most intense language I know is probably Elizabethan
English, probably the blank verse of Shakespearean drama,
Marlovian drama and Webster and so on. And I suppose what I was
trying to do in *Veitch* was to deliberately heighten language, just to
let it go, to make everything as packed as I could. And obviously
that is a pain in the posterior to a lot of people, but these are the risks
you have to take, and I think you can lay that charge at Laidlaw, and
I just have to accept it, but it does not for me intimidate my sense of
what I want to do. I set out in *Veitch* to do that and as far as I'm
concerned it was an artistically appropriate decision for me. It runs
the risk of that. Another thing, as I said once not kindly, rather
heatedly, to somebody making that point, if you want to read grey
books read them. Grey books. If you want to read books, you know,
where you get an insight every twenty pages, read them! One thing
I would say about *Veitch* is it is awash with ideas and insights.
Maybe rather too awash. (L) But I would rather *try* to do that than
the other. In something you've read recently, I made the same
quote. [See McIlvanney's introductory essay, '"The Sacred Wood"
Revisited: An Essay', in *These Words: Weddings and After* (1984).]
That Roy Campbell quote seems to me appropriate here Bob, where

he says 'On some South African novelists':

> You praise the firm restraint with which they write.
> I'm with you there, of course.
> They use the snaffle and the curb all right.
> But where's the bloody horse?

All I would say is there's a horse in *Tony Veitch*: you might no' like it, it might be a bit overweight, but there's a horse there. (L)

BT   Another line of criticism about *Tony Veitch* in particular concerns the nature of the underworld milieu in Glasgow which you have depicted, and which has been complained of, as being rather peculiarly selective or just simply not representing Glasgow as it is, even its seedier elements. That you have created a sort of fantasy about Glasgow, rather than a realism, which people would rather you did, I suppose. Well, again, how would you tackle *that* criticism? Which has come from some writers *in* Glasgow, and who regard themselves perhaps as having a certain proprietorial interest in the mythology of the place.

WM   Yes, that's right. Again, I have been aware of that. I think the last point you make is a valid one. I'm not trying to dodge out of that wee door. But I think one thing you have to take into account is that Glasgow people for a start *are* very proprietary about the city, and the sense of it and the image of it, and presumably writers with their self-consciousness of the place are more so. I think one of the things, one of the qualifications you have to attach to such criticism of what I have done, is that you're certainly tramping on a lot of people's toes when you write about Glasgow. But that apart, the main area in which I suppose I've been aware of what you're saying is, that in *Tony Veitch*, for example, it was said that there is no mention, or no significant mention, of the drug scene. That is right, and the drug scene is very, very rife in Glasgow; I mean, there are pubs in Glasgow where you can simply go in and buy heroin now, which ten years ago was unthinkable. My answer to that is, first of all that they should realise that *Tony Veitch* isn't in fact a contemporary book. The first *Laidlaw* was set in 77. If you read this book, in fact Laidlaw is only about a year older, so we're talking about some years ago for a start. The second thing is that I had already planned a third Laidlaw, called *Rafferty's Answer*, which does in fact deal almost entirely with the drug situation. And what I had done was make an artistic choice which can be criticised. I want to concentrate that element in the next book. And I suppose what always happens with reviews is that obviously the reviewer has to judge it as of the moment, but I see the Laidlaw books as part of a sequence. And in fact, *Tony Veitch* is part of that sequence, and I think the sense of it will be different when the sequence is completed.

IM Tradition and the individual talent ... While we're on *the* things people have said, the inevitable charge that I think the woman must raise to allow you to tell posterity what you think about it, (L) is, William McIlvanney is obsessed with, peculiarly attracted by, *into* violence; hey, there's something funny about this guy! Emote.

WM Aye, I'll just punch the microphone, for starters, (L) I'll just batter this microphone immediately. No, it strikes me, glancing very briefly, as I do, since I don't like to read them, over my own books, (L) yes there is assuredly violence there. Now, you can say, is that just because I like it? But I mean I like sex. There's some sex in it, but there's not an awful lot of that, so I wonder is it merely a predilection? It's not a personal reality of my life, since I have very, very rarely engaged in fisticuffs, and it was too often for me any time I did. (L) But I think—what I always thought when I was doing it, is that violence seems to me a—back to the idea of a metaphor— violence does seem to me a very, very valid metaphor for a capitalist society. I mean, it seems to me quite honestly a fair metaphor in the sense of Heraclitus for living. I mean, I think that birth is a violence, I think that the act of sex is an act of mutual benign violence, but that doesn't mean that the violence is bad, obviously, and so I suppose that violence is, seems to me, a fair metaphor for life and certainly a good metaphor for life within a capitalist society.

For example the book I'm writing just now, has as its central image a bare-knuckle fight [*The Big Man*, London, 1985]. This is not because I love the idea of two men battering lumps out of each other. In fact, I hope, the whole point about the fight if it works is that it should be central to the whole narrative of the book, which is *meant* to be a kind of metaphor for a capitalist society. So the answer to that I suppose, Isobel, is that I think it is there as a fact in various sometimes muted or disguised forms, and through the exploration of that—I mean again it's the idea of edges, through the exploration of that edge of experience, you can reflect back on perhaps a deeper sense of the other aspects of experience. It's like writing towards an edge and from that edge, not writing towards an edge merely for the enjoyment of it. One thing I would claim for example in *Laidlaw* several people said to me there isn't really *any* significant violence in the book, you know, it's all implied, it's all—and it's true. If you read *Laidlaw*, you know, you read the *two* novels, Laidlaw hits one man who is a murderer and who is going to escape, and that is the extent of Laidlaw's violence; and Laidlaw is if you like the sort of compass for both books. And I think that's a fair explanation of what I'm trying to do. I'm trying to understand the nature of it, because I think it is *among* us in all kinds of forms, whether it's in the Tam Docherty sense a kind of legalised looting of people's lives. It's there in *all* kinds of manifestations, and I think it would be false to pretend that our lives are other than that. There is implicit in the nature of our lives a variety of sometimes very sophisticated forms of violence.

IM   Yes, I think that's a very interesting answer. Can I get a short point first, and that is that when you say that Laidlaw only hits one guy once, that doesn't seem to me to answer the charge at all; I think you *have* answered the charge, but I mean violence is not just to do with how many people hit how many people.

WM   Right, right.

IM   It's to do with how many people *intimidate* how many people, and how much fear there is: and there's a lot of *that* in the novel. You know, people constantly in fear from other people. I don't think it matters too much whether blows are actually struck.

WM   Sorry, you don't think that is, I think there are people constantly in fear from other people—

IM   I think that is violence.

WM   Yeh, but this is the point I'm making. I think that these realities are in our lives anyway. There are people, I mean I've known guys in a pub for example, who would dismember another man verbally, who didn't have the verbal capacity to cope with that, and would have been astonished and utterly dismayed if he had resorted to some mode of expression he could handle, like physical violence.

IM   One of the most violent things that happens in *Tony Veitch* is when one bully ...

WM   The pint yes.

IM   pours a pint of beer over somebody else—it's an absolutely an-guish-causing incident. But while there's more that we could obviously go on and talk about, basically we're agreeing about it.

      I was interested, I think you trailed your coat there when you talked about violence as a metaphor for life. I think you made a very good case for that, but you also, I think, twice talked about it as specifically life in a capitalist society.

WM   Yes.

IM   So you're crying out to be asked a question about politics, about violence in a capitalist society, about whether you think the nature of our society has a big impact on the kind of people we are and the kind of lives we lead.

WM   Oh yeh, absolutely. I write from *my* sense of you know, what is a socialist point of view. But I do not write as card-carrying party-member. Because I think that what you do, what *I* want to do with writing anyway, is to report from the front, and if you can, if you like, validate your socialism by putting it under pressure from the experiences that you contemplate, then fair enough. So, what I'm saying is that I write from a socialist standpoint, but I would claim that for me that standpoint has been *earned*.

IM   So you think that capitalist society in particular has a peculiar aspect of violence that is unique to it?

WM   Yeh, because I suppose the simplest way it occurs to me is in terms of injustice: it is a society *framed* in terms of specific injustice. The chance to fulfil yourself in a capitalist society it seems to me, depends upon the right to do so at the expense of other people. I mean one of the sort of small rubrics I worked out for myself once is that society can offend against its individuals in two simple ways: it can deprive them of necessary experience; in other words, if you're wealthy enough, you can buy a progress through life in which you do not have to come in touch, seriously, with many of the brute realities that encroach upon the lives of your fellows. And the second way is to inflict on you *unnecessary* experience; I think a lot of working-class people are simply given experience which is unnecessary; I mean, in a *just* society that experience wouldn't be something they had to go through. And in those two ways, I think a society which is *conceived* as a capitalist society, does offend against its members. Some it protects preposterously, and others it subjects ignominiously to, you know, unbearable pressures!

IM   Willie, you're obviously best known as a novelist; you have, though, published one book of poetry already—that rare volume called *The Longships in Harbour*, and now here you are visiting us in Aberdeen with a whole lot more poems in your pocket. [Many of these poems appeared in 1984 as *These Words: Weddings and After: An Essay and Poetry* by William McIlvanney, Mainstream, Edinburgh.] What do you think poems should be doing in this day and age?

WM   Well, I'm not sure. To go back to the very beginning of the interview, Isobel, if I have problems about writing prose, about justifying the writing of prose, how much greater must those problems be when it comes to justifying the writing of poetry? (L) I published that book what in—1970, and I've gone on writing poetry ever since without attempting to publish in a magazine even. And I think that indicates my own fairly tortured response to my own poetry. I suppose the reason that I still do it and the reason that I want *now* to publish another book of poetry, is that I see it simply as a valuable means of communication for us, and I think that what perhaps I'm trying to do in this book of poetry is to write poetry which *might*—or shall I say write myself towards poetry, it may not be there yet—write towards poetry which *might* communicate in the same way, for example, that some of the best popular songs do. Because I think that a lot of the energy that I used to believe— whether I was true in that belief or not is another matter—but I used to believe, resided in poetry, may have transferred—by that I mean, *popular* energy, to a medium like pop music, like whether it's the lyrics of Bob Dylan or Kris Kristofferson or Billy Joe or whatever, I think many of these men write what is for me poetry that is set to music.

BT   In actual fact, though, the way that *you* write poetry, bears, I think, some greater relationship to traditional or contemporary—but— traditional English prosody than it does to say the kind of lines written in the style of somebody like John Cooper Clarke whom as it happened we encountered with great pleasure for the first time ...

WM   With joy unconfined.

BT   Exactly, and my son knew all about him and we didn't, and we were astonished that a talent like that could have escaped our notice. What I'm saying is that sometimes in the way that you write lines you can hear echoes of songs throughout or occasional little allu- sions to them in rock mode, but at other times you're writing very literary poems, including using literary inversions and phrases such as 'certain it is that ...' Which puts you, stylistically, really quite a long way away from the public communication of such as Cooper Clarke.

WM   Yes, that's right. The thing I was saying before your remarks, Bob, was the expression of an endeavour, of an attempt, but obviously I bring with me a whole tradition of having read a great deal of poetry of the past and of the present which is not in that mode. And I suppose what I'm doing is trying somehow to move myself to- wards, perhaps with elephantine difficulty, (L) but move myself towards a point of what you might call popular comprehensibililty, without surrendering what I think is the true complexity of the things I'm trying to talk about. So I would agree with you. I think I am in some kind of halfway house: maybe I'll never get out of it.

IM You were talking when we started off about fiction about Saroyan and Hemingway; would you like to name any names of poets as you just said, of the past or of the present, who have particularly impressed you?

WM Yes. Instantly there are three poets, apart from the Scottish tradition, where I think simply that Burns has been academically drastically undervalued. That apart, I would say that the poets that have probably impinged on me most strongly and have suggested to me a way in which I might go would be Yeats, for a start. Another would be Wilfred Owen, who is, for me, central to what I believe might be achieved by twentieth-century poetry. Because I see Owen as somebody who went to the hardest place and as he suggested himself stayed human, and you know the Americans have got that phrase 'to have been there': he not only went there, he came back; which I think is part of the great secret. To take an example in prose, I remember reading a book, *Let Us Now Praise Famous Men*, Agee, and I thought that was a *marvellously* brave book, but that was somebody who had gone there and atomised: he just didn't come back. [James Agee, *Let Us Now Praise Famous Men*, 1941.] I mean I find that book for *me* simply doesn't work as a book: I think it's a massively brave failure. And it's in that kind of context that I find the depth of my admiration for Owen. Owen went there, brought some kind of sane truth back with him, and for me expressed it powerfully and beautifully. And the third one is I suppose somewhat different: I find myself very much in love with much of the poetry of Rilke in translation; I don't read German! And when I say that it's maybe a bizarre choice because I can see that Rilke was a very intellectual, very isolated poet, and Owen wasn't. And I suppose if I had a poetic ideal, it would be somehow in the marriage of those two things. And I suppose the poet I think who came nearest to it was somebody like Yeats.

IM We're talking now about this collection of poems, and we've been talking off the tape about just simply how you're going to put them on the page, because you've seen this collection as separate poems, but in some way juxtaposed to each other for particular effect. Is it because the collection, the poems, have that kind of unity that, as you say, you have eschewed magazine publication? You know, that you want to publish them altogether or not at all?

WM Yes, that's right. That, plus, to be honest, the continuing self-doubt that I have about them. I mean, one of the reasons I didn't put them in magazines was that I wasn't sure of my faith in them. I had to leave them there to either grow or diminish (L) in a dark room before I felt that I could publish them. And also, the first idea you mention, Isobel, is important. The idea that they are some kind of aggravated unity, some kind of, you know, unity through argument: they are in dispute with one another, I think, many of the poems. And that maybe relates to what Bob was saying about somebody like John Cooper Clarke. I think, one of the things that troubles me about myself trying to write poetry is that I don't want to profess a polished finality about what I am doing, and one of the ways to demonstrate that on the page is not to have each poem planted in a separate page as if here is a fulfilment, a final creation. But in the very tension among the poems, I hope, there is a kind of creative energy, you know, like electricity leaping gaps, and the reason I say that might relate to what somebody like John Cooper Clarke is doing, Bob, I think what he manifests is a terrific energy, that's the thing I feel about him more than anything else, a great verbal energy, a great desire to connect with what's happening around him. And so while the poems, as you say, may be within themselves, still rather literary, I suppose by breaking down that formal demand that each be seen as a fulfilled separate poem I'm hopefully moving some way towards the position you were talking about.

BT   Can I ask about energy in the context of your writing more broadly, because it does seem quite an important *thing* to you that life should be lived with a certain energy and indeed, quite a number of your characters seem to be almost crisis-seeking individuals. Would you say that is a fair comment? A characteristic of your writing is that characters seem to have to prove themselves by inviting crisis, which makes for a highly dramatic tenor to life and the way that they live it, and it would seem to me that maybe in a way that connects with a certain west-coast tradition of what it would mean to be, say, manly: you have to think in terms of experiences being dangerous. One can only really, as it were, *prove* one's honesty to life by these dangerous edges where one may break up, or, where one may *break* up relationships, families and so on and so forth.

WM Yeh, I think the sense of crisis is omnipresent in the books, but I think for me that doesn't mean that you go out and seek, deliberately seek, the edges. For me, perhaps in my naiveté, it seems that if you confront honestly your experience then these edges are there. I mean, to live in any society is to be aware of the lives of others within it and to share them. Therefore I think that if you confront your experience honestly these crises are present. I mean, the death

of a child for example is a dreadful edge of experience, and I
suppose what I'm really trying to say in the book is, you will not
avoid them. I would have thought the healthy thing is to acknow-
ledge that they're there and confront them and not build around
ourselves false fortresses of complacency and whatever.

BT But a lot of people, even if not trying to *avoid* such realities, would
really on the whole prefer that bricks didn't fall out of the sky on
their heid, and they would really hope that these crises would occur
only occasionally. I get rather the sense though that you say, well,
they're always there, and you'd be uneasy with yourself, or with
anyone else, who in a sense didn't look for them and that even
there's this element of bringing them on.

WM Yes, but I think Bob ... no, maybe there is. But in my own awareness
of it—the author's awareness of what he is doing, is by no means
perhaps the best awareness—but in my awareness it is simply a
matter of acknowledging that they're there. For example, if you are
living presently and you have avoided any kind of disasters for a
long time, it is a sure thing that around you many people haven't.
And all I'm saying is, or the point from which I think I am writing
is, that I would try to *insist* on that mutual awareness. If for example
I had a life which was safely constructed, financially secure, which
I do not—but if I did, I would find it hard to enjoy simply because
all around me there are people who are not in that situation. So what
I'm really suggesting is that I think the most important thing for me
that any person has, is the right to their own experience; is the
comprehension of their own experience, that freedom envisions,
the freedom involves the right to envision its own terms. And what
I'm suggesting is that people living in any society, if they are aware
of the others around them, *cannot* presume to enjoy some undiluted
happiness, even if their lives are secure, because the lives of many
other people aren't.

IM There's an interesting way in which though some people might go
from the other point and almost resent the books *because* of being
jealous of all this crisis, because there are people for whose lives
emptiness is a good word, I suppose. Characters like your Miss
Gilfillan in *Docherty* or by implication, I think, Jinty Adamson in
Tony Veitch, people for whom routine fills up most of the day, and
emptiness and vacuum is the order of the day. They might look at
the books and say, 'Life's not like that! Life's not *exciting* like that.
Life is harder than that!'

WM Yeh, I think that's valid. I think, being honest, one of the most
frightening places I have ever been in is a home for geriatrics,

because what I was aware of there was that many of these people, understandably, could no longer generate the passion even to be angry at, you know, the forms their lives took. And I mean, I suppose my answer to that if people say life isn't, is life *is* like that, if you subjectively make it so. That's why I say experience, your comprehension of your own experience is so important. The person who is crushed in a concentration camp, if they have the spirit, if they have the strength of will, can transform, you know, what the jailer does to them. That in fact—that I do believe—that if we can confront honestly our own experience, it gives us a strength to transmute what happens to us. And people who say life is boring and dull, you know, there are certain situations where *inevitably* life—a person is paralysed—I mean, I'm not presuming to judge these situations: I'm saying in a sort of average day-to-day situation, I think those who are bored with life secrete their own boredom. That the right that everybody has and which they have to maintain by daily injections of energy, is to transform their own experience through their understanding of it. And that understanding, it doesn't have to be a profoundly intellectual understanding, it's a question of spirit more than intellect.

IM   But you also, you can draw very sympathetic pictures of people who can't *do* this, I'm thinking again of Miss Gilfillan in particular. She's not paralysed physically, she's paralysed by her upbringing and the way she was taught to look at life, and her need to try and maintain middle-class gentility in Graithnock. You don't really criticise her in the book.

WM   No, no.

IM   You're very compassionate to the prison she's in as everybody else is.

WM   Yes, but then also, I have respect, because if you remember Miss Gilfillan dies on her own terms. They may be middle-class genteel, but I admire the way in which she inhabits them. She dies setting the table for meals which she cannot have. She dies fulfilling a code which is no longer real for her life, but she invests it, I think, with the dignity of her own energy. I mean, I don't find her *merely* pathetic, I find it all, you know, *all* of us in *that* sense pathetic— because we none of us controls in any complete way our destinies— but I have deep admiration for the way in which she continues to live in her own terms, to confront what must seem to her a very malignant fate, but to do it with her own dignity.

IM   OK. Can I move now and really invite possibly negative responses, because I want to approach an area we have approached once or twice before, and that is to sound you out on *your* general response and reaction to the whole notion of the academic study and teaching of literature?

WM Yeh, well, I suppose it goes back to the beginning of this interview, Isobel. Coming from the background that I come from, having the ambitions that I have, academicism is for me not a significant aspect of those ambitions. What worries me about academic criticism is that it is frequently, as I've suggested to you about Eliot for example judging Villon, it's frequently like a chemist analysing a cupful of cataract and purporting to give you some essence of the phenomenon. The biggest objection I have to what I *understand* about academic criticism is that it tends to treat the books and the words as some kind of closed circuit, and to me the words and the books are only significant in so far as they relate to our lives, not as some phenomenon separable and judgeable for itself. I mean, there's a moment in *Tony Veitch* which—for which you have chastised me previously—(L) in which Laidlaw makes a point, certainly a point which is valid for me, that books are a kind of psychic energy, we absorb them and they, in whatever small way become a part of the way we live or the way we think about how we live, and that is to me crucially important. Now I suppose the element I find frequently missing from academic criticism is simply how the books relate, or how any writing relates, to some kind of reality of our experience. I know that's a difficult one to grasp, but it's nevertheless something that I would wish to stumble towards for good.

BT Is your objection to academic*ism* not even more specific though, in that you do have this liking for people who live in the existentialist sense authentically and this does often mean living dangerously?

WM Yes.

BT So would your objection to academicism be itself represented by say this kind of thing, where one maybe gets lectures on somebody like Baudelaire with no *sense* coming through that the person lecturing on Baudelaire is aware of just how dangerously, emotionally and physically, Baudelaire lived his life?

WM That's right. Yeh, I think that's true. I think that they—and again in danger I don't mean in some heroic Hemingway sense, I think that the dangers are around us daily, and I think that is a valid expression of how I feel, that frequently they criticise from a position of safety those who live dangerously. I mean dangerously in a psychic way, not necessarily in a specifically physical way. And also the other aspect is that they frequently—inevitably—write within a career. I

mean, for me, writing never has been and never will be a career. I
mean, at one stage I gave up teaching to try to write, but it's not that
I see that I will have a successful career as a writer; for me, the
success is in hopefully getting some of the words right, hopefully
some of the books right. And I think very often academics function
within a system where the strugglings, the dangerous, the psychic
dangers run by others become a means to the fulfilment of career,
and that troubles me.

IM Did you enjoy your own university education?

WM It was very interesting, aye. The thing I enjoyed most about it, as I
said earlier, was that it demystified universities. The aspect of it I
enjoyed most, was other students. The most educational aspect, I
believe, of my university career was the Union. *Amazing* arguments
for hours in the Union, you know, so then as I said in an essay once,
when I came out of there sometimes I was so unsure of myself that
if I'd looked in the mirror I wouldn't have been surprised if there
was no reflection, you know. We argued about everything! God was
summoned to the meetings frequently (L), and I found *that* the most
exciting aspect, you know. Just the sheer clashing of, sometimes
not awfully well-informed minds, but intense and eager minds.

IM Did you meet any informed academic minds that really made a
difference to your understanding?

WM Oh absolutely! There is one, a man called Jack Rillie who was a
lecturer at university and he was utterly important, he was one of
the men who helped me, he probably doesn't know it, but he helped
me to go through university without cracking up! You know, there
were stages when I thought I would just pack up. But I found *him* a
representative of something I believe in. A marvellously informed
man, but who continued for me to relate literature to the realities
around him, and there is just no way I could thank him enough for...

IM That's a point of *hope* to end the discussion about academics. We
can all hope to be like Jack Rillie. Thank you very much!

A BARFIT LOON

DAVID TOULMIN

We interviewed John Reid, 'David Toulmin', at his home in Pittodrie Place, Aberdeen, in April 1985.

IM   Mr Reid, where did the name David Toulmin come from, and why do you not write as John Reid?

JR   Well there are hundreds of John Reids, in fact there were three of them quite prominent in literature when I started, and I wanted to get something more unique. I had two pen-names before then, one was Mark Meadows which I thought was a bit too illustrative of what I was doing, working on the land, *in* the meadows. Another was John Longside, because I lived near the village of Longside and that again seemed too parochial, or too obvious, and I searched around for the most unusual name in the Parish. And it belonged to a crofter called Tolmie which I think is a highland name. I choose Tolmie and the name of my foreman which was David, the Christian name, David Tolmie. I wrote a story for *The Farmer and Stockbreeder*, and sent it off under this pseudonym. They sent me— they accepted the article and sent me a—what I believe is called a galley-proof—and I thought 'Oh heavens, here's a misprint for a start!' Because Tolmie had become Toulmin. David Toulmin. However, I let it go, and later on reflection I discovered it was a corruption of Tomintoul. If I'd called myself Tom Toulmin it would have been a complete corruption. Anyway, it was a misprint, and fortunate that it was so, because I was rummaging in a bookseller's dustbin in Rosemount Viaduct many years later and I came across a book *Anthology of Poetry* and this David Tolmie was very strongly represented. I wouldn't have been unique but for the misprint, so I stuck to the name and it has been good to me.

IM   That's a splendid story. I'd like to hear what—anything you'd like to tell us about your childhood, Mr Reid.

JR Well, I thought you was maybe going to ask if I had been a happy child, which I was not. Until I was about twelve I couldn't stand reality without its refinement. The dreaming and the arts. An escapism I discovered when I read my first books and saw my first movies. Almost coincident and the film driving me to the book, which was invariably better and gave me greater joy than the cinematic effort. This was an emancipation which enhanced and brought sunshine into my childhood which previously had been a somewhat miserable existence filled with fears and depressing thoughts I couldn't understand. Fortunately, my childhood notion for the arts has remained with me all my life and still continues to brighten my darkest hours.

    Puberty was another depressing time for me and reaching manhood was a traumatic experience, preceded by depression, and culminating in epilepsy; a period when even my enchantment with the arts was sometimes of little avail in providing relief from my obsession. I have always been an introvert. Most things that have happened to me have been affairs of the mind; spiritual adventure without stirring a foot. I have never been a globetrotter, or an explorer in search of life; it has all happened to me within the citadel of the mind; an exigency which has furnished me with a lively sensitivity and keen refinement in cultural taste. A mental equilibrium demanding trapeze precision and tightrope agility which has often occasioned me to miss my footing, with calamitous results. Yet, this suppression of spirit has not been without its other extreme, and an idyllic perception of life which perhaps would be denied the more pedestrian or mundane person.

IM That's very interesting. It's not something that comes very much into your books is it?

JR No.

IM The depressed side, the melancholia. You mention it a few times but when you write about your childhood, you manage to pick out the good things, don't you? The books, the toy-theatre, things like that. I mean, these stories about young boys are mostly you, are they?

JR Yes.

IM So what hobbies most gave you most happiness as a child?

JR These stories refer to the time after I discovered the literary, cinematic side, you see, and there's a brighter environment about these stories than there would have been earlier in my life.

IM So, earlier on, did you get on well with your parents?

JR Oh yes. Oh yes. The trouble's always been within myself, not really to do with anybody else, except on an occasional—you met an odd character who took the rise of you, or bullied you or something, which is common to all children.

IM And like the boys in these stories you were liable to miss school because you were more interested in your own hobbies than what they taught you at school. Is that right?

JR Yes. Literature, history, geography were my three subjects, and I hated everything else. Algebra, geometry, arithmetic, and I just played truant to get rid of them. Which was worse the next day when I went back and had missed a lesson in the arithmetic or whatever: it didn't do me any good but it still didn't stop me from playing truant.

IM And did you enjoy playing with the other children? Did you make good friends with them, and enjoy games like football and so on?

JR I played with the other children in the playground, yes. I was never interested in sport. Couldn't play football. It wasn't—the only time I did play they had to put me in goals, I could do that, but I wouldn't go out in the field and dribble and all this sort of thing—I just wasn't interested.

IM Well, we've heard that you became very early interested in reading, and that it changed your life: could you tell us some of the reading that was most important to you?

JR Well, one of the very first books I read was *John Halifax, Gentleman* by Mistress Craik. Then *Reginald Cruden* by Talbot Baines Reid; the Ballantyne books, *Coral Island, Gorilla Hunters, The World of Ice*, etc. And Stevenson's *Treasure Island*; Defoe's *Robinson Crusoe*; *Crusader and Saracen*; *Robin Hood*; *Buffalo Bill*; Dixon Hawke; Sexton Blake. *Adventure, Hotspur,* (weeklies of course), *Comic Chips* and *Comic Cuts*. And in manhood, I went on to books like *She* by Rider Haggard; *The Life of Napoleon*; *The Story of San Michele*; Johnson's *Lives of the Poets*; Voltaire, Sheridan, Wilde; most of the English dramatists.

IM You mentioned that book by Talbot Baines Reid, how did you get hold of that? *Reginald Cruden*?

JR Well, I got it in the school library, which wasn't much of a library in those days. It was just a small bookcase filled with books provided by the J. & P. Coates firm of thread-spinners, or whatever they were, I got the books there from the Headmaster. We had one hour's reading time in school a week, and of course I couldn't get far into my book in an hour, and I asked the schoolmaster if I could take the book home, and he gave me permission to take any book I was reading home with me, and that was the only way I could get books. There was no such thing as a mobile library in those days, and to be perfectly honest I didn't know there *was* a library in the town, in Peterhead. I didn't know that these sort of things existed, you see. Books were very difficult for me to obtain. There wasn't a book in the house—there *might* have been a Bible at *one* stage, and I think my mother once borrowed a copy of Burns from somebody, but not permanent—it was never in the house permanent, and my father could neither read nor write.

IM   Was that common?

JR   No, most people could read and write at that time. He left the school when he was twelve, and he'd never mastered reading, and I noticed when he looked at the newspapers it was just the pictures he looked at.

IM   Yes, no wonder he found it difficult to understand you with your literary interests.

JR   When he became pension age, I had to put my hand over his hand holding a pen, to get him to sign his name for his pension. Otherwise he probably would have got away with a mark, I don't know, but that was a fact, that he couldn't sign his own name, and this was the sort of environment or background I was brought up in, you see.

IM   Which makes it all the more impressive the road you've come since then.

JR   Yes. Well now, my mother was a reader. Not a heavy reader. But she read the usual, *People's Friend* stories, you know. The weeklies, the newspaper serials, and she was what you might call an inveterate letter-writer; she was a very good letter writer—but a very bad speller.

IM   And did she write in the Doric?

JR   Occasionally she dropped into the Doric, I think, quite unconsciously, because she didn't know the English equivalent, but all throughout our married life until she died, she kept sending these letters, and they were quite unique, you know, so any talent I may have inherited would be from her, I think.

IM   Yes. I seem to remember, though, that in Paul Dukes's introduction to *Hard Shining Corn*, he says that you destroyed her letters when she died because she wanted you to.

JR   Yes. ...

IM   Why do you think she wanted them burned?

JR   Because there was a little malice in some of them, and we were afraid that they might drop into the hands of some of the family and offend people you see.

IM I see entirely, yes.

JR So she requested that we destroy them. I kept back a few which are really humorous, and unharmful and these I still retain, and I've copied out one or two of them for my diaries.

IM Yes. Because in a way it's a priceless thing to lose, isn't it? I think it was very good of you to obey her instructions.

JR Well I was cheating in a way by keeping back the half dozen, (L) which I thought would be interesting to anyone to follow up.

IM So, we've talked about a very small number of books available at school through the Coates' library, and magazines through your mother, but there was another source of books as I remember later on, when you went to the cinema, and you saw the film of *Jane Eyre*, and you wanted to read the book. Could you tell us about that?

JR It was during the war, and very few books were being printed, or even reprinted or re-issued. I had seen the film *Jane Eyre*, it was Joan Fontaine and Orson Welles, I think, that were the stars, and I so enjoyed it that I wanted to read the book. This quite often happened in my life, that I'd seen the film and wanted to read the book, which is still done apparently, judging by the number of paperbacks that appear whenever a big movie or a television series appears. I was doing this sort of thing fifty years ago. Anyway, it's about forty years ago that I seen this film on *Jane Eyre*—I couldn't get a copy anywhere. So I advertised in the press. Only one reply came from this. 'J. J.' as I call him. He had a copy, and I went round to see him and he gave me the book—wouldn't take anything for it—and we established a relationship which continued until he died. And he gave me books that I didn't know existed. *He* knew. He was a literary man. He was a civil servant in real life, and he knew literature and he knew the sort of books I should be reading. I gave him some of my material to read, and he knew the sort of books I should be reading, and he gave me the books. He had a good library which he had inherited from his father, and but for him I would never have reached the status that I did when I got into book print. He supplied me with the most unusual books, like for instance, *The Journal of a Disappointed Man* by Barbellion; the plays of Sheridan; Pepys *Diary*, the *Story of San Michele* by Axel Munthe, you know, I think he's a Swede. I still pick up his books, he has been dead now for twelve years, I still pick up one of his books from my collection and refer to them. They have been a tremendous influence on my literary achievement.

IM Since you had no real formal teachers, he must have been the nearest thing to a philosopher, guide, friend, teacher, the whole thing.

JR   Yes. And he wrote to me three times a week. Enormous, voluminous letters about literature, and all that was going on in the publishing world and he just staggered me with what he wanted me to read—I couldn't keep up. I couldn't even answer his letters, because I was working a nine-hours day, sometimes seven days a week. And Margaret, my wife, here, used to get on to me: 'you haven't written to J. J. yet' (L), and so I said heavens, I haven't had time, but he persisted in writing and he still sent another letter, and eventually, before he died, I returned all his letters to him, but he burned them. They were not letters that *any*body would read; they were in a category by themselves; they were absorbed in literature, to the point of dryness to the ordinary reader, not for me but for the ordinary reader. Thus, I think, they were deprived of value, but I didn't mean him to burn them; I just returned them for safekeeping, because I as a cottar moving about couldn't always guarantee that I would preserve them, and I wanted him to have them back, but this is what he did with them.

IM   J. J. was what you called him, but would you mind telling us what his name was?

JR   His real name was John James Sangster.

IM   And where did he live?

JR   Peterhead.

IM   Ah, well that's fine. One of these days somebody will bring out a footnote on him, I think.

JR   In fact he lived at I think it was 27 St Mary Street. That's his address. Peterhead! I should have added that J. J. retired quite early from civil life. He had plenty of time on his hands—he seemed to have plenty of money. I think he dabbled in shares, and time was no obstacle.

IM   One of the fascinating things about your stories, Mr Reid, is that they all seem so authentic, and real life, that it's very hard for the reader to know which things absolutely happened, and which of them either you invented or you've perhaps transplanted from one place to another. Shall we take an example of the story 'The Dookit Fairm': how near to real life is that story?

JR   Well, if you could say that 'The Dookit Fairm' was written from personal experience, where the youth on the farm shoots his girlfriend the kitchen maid, it just can't be true, because there she is, sitting there, as my wife! (L) The thing is the editor of the *Evening*

Express sent a reporter out to interview me, and when the chap returned with his write-up he sent him out again to ask me to write a story in the Doric for his readers. Now I had 'The Dookit Fairm' in manuscript, but I could never find a satisfactory ending for it, but seeing that I had got an opportunity to present the story, I re-wrote it. I did it in two evenings. I wrote it as near the Doric core as I could. The Editor wanted something in the Doric, and I went ahead and this story of the youth shooting the girl had been in my mind from years before, when a blacksmith accidentally shot his wife from the henhouse, where he was baiting rats, and she came within his sights at the moment he pulled the trigger, and he killed her. So I transplanted that incident from the next parish to 'The Dookit Fairm' and that was how it was done. It was fictionalised.

IM Yes. The farm was absolutely as it was in real life, and you were working there as you did in real life, and now your wife was also there. What about the woman who was in charge of the farm at the time? The very religious lady who didn't like sex, was she real or...?

IR She was real. I think I called her Elsie Wabster in the story. She is an exact replica of the woman she was and this business about her going to have a child was a fallacy, but it *could* have happened by a hormone change. But I found it difficult to introduce the word hormone in a Doric story!! (L) But I wanted to say 'Anither doo at the Dookit?' [See 'The Dookit Fairm', in *Hard Shining Corn*, p. 63.] Because this was what the neighbours *would* have said. One of them started off my story just weeks after I'd got to this Dookit Fairm. I'd been there about a fortnight and I'd met him across a fence, he was working in his own croft, and he said 'Foo div ye like the Dookit?' I says, 'I hinna been awfa lang there to find oot!' He says, 'It's an awfa big Dookit for jist twa doos!' [*Ibid.*, p. 54.] There was jist the man and his wife you see, no children, and I wanted to bring this out in the story that there would be another doo at the Dookit so therefore I engineered this what I thought would be plausible, a hormone change in the woman, because she takes such an interest in the young couple. So that's how much these stories are fictionalised.

M That woman spoiled and indulged and encouraged the young couple, very much as the lady farmer's wife does in 'Moonlight Flitting'. ['Moonlight Flitting', in *Straw Into Gold: A Scots Miscellany*, 1981, pp. 26-60.] The story about Gertie who loses her baby.

IR Oh yes. I changed the name of the Dookit Fairm to Slabsteen and used it again.

M So that farmer's wife is in some ways the same person?

JR   Yes. Again, the lady dies in the 'Moonlight Flitting', but she's still
     here, you see, so this is fiction [Mrs Reid]. (L) Again, she doesn't
     like this, she was not expecting a child when we were married.

IM   No I think you made it quite clear somewhere else that the first child
     was fifteen months after you got married. (L)

JR   I spoke to a lady who had read the *Straw into Gold*: in fact I used to
     work in her garden, and she spoke about reading the book. She says,
     'You know, that story 'Moonlight Flitting', you had me in tears,'
     she said, 'I was weeping. But I just don't see how I could ask if it
     was true.' And I says, 'Well, we'll just leave it at that!' (L)

IM   Mind you, it is a *very moving* story, because you've crafted it so
     much, the way in which all these bad things about premature birth
     and the cattle and ...

JR   I deliberately set out to do that.

IM   Yes.

JR   To show the crude lifestyle that we endured. I deliberately did that
     and, it's not exaggerated, in no way, and Margaret very nearly died
     of childbirth-bed fever. She was just in time. I said why not make it
     a reality and get a story out of it! See?

IM   Yes. In that story as you say, the circumstances that you live in are
     seen as being very brutal: not just other *people* being brutal, but
     nature herself. For example, when you tried to help the heifer
     calving and you actually tear the calf's legs off.

JR   We dismember the calf. That is not the only instance of that
     happening. I might explain these were Ayrshire cows sired by
     Ayrshire bulls, big animals, therefore in a heifer the calf was too
     big. If the cow was serviced fairly early when she was in season
     which could happen, she was not quite matured, and the animal was
     too big: we often lost a calf that way. Now, the farmers discov-
     ered—and I think it referred to short-horn cattle as well—the bulls
     were big you see, the farmers discovered that if they sired their
     heifers with a black Aberdeen-Angus bull, the calf was smaller and
     it was easier on the mother, and that's how they solved it. All these
     animals now are usually sired with the black bull. But it hadn't got
     to that stage when I was writing that story and this is what was
     happening.

IM   But it's an interesting example of savagery in Nature itself, not a
     question of human malice, just Nature itself being cruel. You've
     also in that same story got a chap who is on the whole quite a
     likeable neighbour, McPhee, but the narrator takes a scunner to him
     and he finds the way he kills premature calves is positively cruel.

JR   Yes, I thought it was cruel. I'd never seen it before. I suppose nowadays the vet would inject them with something to put them out of the way, but that just wasn't done. These calves, they were aborted almost, they were premature: they couldn't suck, some of them couldn't stand, how you was going to get them to take milk was a problem. The best thing to do was to *get* rid of them, but how was it to be done? The farmer wouldn't have thanked you for coming in to the phone and getting the vet to put a calf out of the way. He'd have had to pay for that! So, the cattleman just used his own discretion and put it out of the way. This chap did it with a hammer!

IM Although you describe it very briefly, this is something common in your books. When you come to something really unpleasant you don't hide from it, you tell us about it, but usually very briefly: you don't glory in the violence. But there is quite a lot of violence and quite a lot of cruelty from time to time in the life that you give us in the stories, perhaps the most shocking examples being the way that Joyce is treated in *Blown Seed* by her daughter-in-law and son. But there are other examples. Do you find that you have to write about this degree of cruelty because you've come across it in real life?

JR The story of Joyce's cruelty was related to me by my mother. In fact, most of the story of *Blown Seed* has been built up from things told to me by my mother among the neighbours, and I've moved things around a bit to disguise the story. But much of it I believe, was true, loosely based on fact. I've used that, and I've transplanted farms, mansion houses, and changed names, so that it takes a wee bit of figuring out to pinpoint them, although the locals can do it for me, oh yes they can do it no bother.

IM I'm sure. When I gave you an idea of the questions I was going to ask I'd only reread some of your books: in the course of rereading the others, I realised that Mattock Hill was Mormond Hill for example, the white stone deer makes it very clear. What about Lachbeg House and the various dotard laird stories?

JR Well Lachbeg House would have been Cortes House which is nearest to Mormond Hill, but it is not palatial enough for my taste. So I moved to the big house of Cairness. Do you know where it is? It is a huge mansion house in the Lonmay area, but I had to bring it nearer the hill so that the dotard laird could hear the pipes you see, so I had to transplant it! (L) And Lachbeg Woods of course and the lake are the Cortes area: it is a bit nearer the hill as well. There is a reality in the background which has been transplanted to suit the incidents in the story narrative. That's all there is to it.

IM And what about the Handerson family who, I think, they're mainly in *Hard Shining Corn*, the piper himself, Gleg, and the son with the wooden leg: were they real?

JR   Yes. I wrote *Blown Seed* first, but it was rejected so many times, and lay so long in a drawer, that I took the short stories out of it and published them.

IM   I see.

JR   I got them accepted and I thought this was a short cut to getting into print, you see. But always the novel came back, so when I wrote the final draft I had used these, 'My Uncle Simon', 'Folks in Black'; 'Sarah and The Angels'. [See *Hard Shining Corn*, pp. 74-79, 88-95, 111-17.] These stories should have *been* in *Blown Seed*, but I had used them to get into print in a shortcut you see, so when I came to write the final draft I had to change the name of Uncle Simon to Riach, Gleg Handerson to Craig MacKinnon: that's how there are twins, there are two supposed uncles with wooden legs, and two grandfathers who played the pipes. This is how it happened. The pillaging of *Blown Seed* to get the short stories. In fact, if I had reached a stage of recognition much earlier in my life, the short stories I've written since *Blown Seed* would have been novels.

IM   I was wanting to ask you about that. Did you think of writing any more novels, or did you just settle for ...?

JR   It's a hard job writing a novel. To write another one at my age—I'm almost seventy-two—I don't want to punish myself in my latter years. I've been disciplined, and I've had to work to a timetable all my life, and I feel that I'm off the hook. Why should I punish myself like Sir Walter Scott did? I'm not in debt as he was, (L) so I think I'll stick to the shorter, more documentary stuff, I've had my fling at the fiction.

IM   But it wasn't a punishment when you did it, was it? I mean when you wrote *Blown Seed*, which must have been unbelievably difficult in the circumstances of your life, you must have wanted very much to write a novel.

JR   Oh yes. In fact, I went to hospital once, and I was feeling so bad when I went into hospital I told Margaret to burn *Blown Seed*; it was still in manuscript. I told her I didn't want to come back and see it; if ever I came back, I didn't want to see it again. But she didn't burn it, and about nine-ten months, well maybe two years after I came back from hospital, I took another notion to *Blown Seed* and I rewrote the whole thing. It took me a year. And polished it up you know, and added things that I'd learned from life since, and that was the thirteenth offer to a publisher when it was accepted. People don't realise that. Some people tell me they can't understand how

they refused a book like that! Well it's happened. The last reject
was from Routledge and Kegan Paul, quite a reputable house, and
they have published Scottish stuff; but then—Paul Harris—he took
it.

IM   He took it after the success of *Hard Shining Corn*, would it be?

JR   That might have influenced Paul Harris, yes. But it didn't cut any
     ice with the London publishers.

IM   But once Paul Harris had taken the risk, the London publishers were
     very happy to come in and publish the paperback?

JR   Yes. Pan had the paperback before the hardback appeared! Yes. In
     fact, the rep who first read the manuscript told me he read it in bed
     one night, and he said 'it was in a long roll of toilet paper', he said,
     'and I was throwing it over there, this span of paper onto the carpet
     and I couldn't get stopped,' he says. 'Well,' I says, 'it was a dirty
     story anyway!!' (L)

IM   So it's been the bestseller of your books, would you say?

JR   It's completely out of print. It has been my bestseller, it's well over
     twenty thousand. At a guess, 25,000 copies. Now completely out of
     print. But it's not my best lending book. My best lending book from
     the libraries is *Harvest Home*. Second in the list is *Travels Without
     a Donkey*. *Blown Seed* is well down the list, probably because it's
     getting scarcer, I don't know. But there was a time in Aberdeen
     when they were queueing up at the libraries to get a copy, putting
     down their names for it.

IM   I believe that you actually began writing as early as—oh, fourteen,
     or so?

JR   Earlier than that. I was about eleven or twelve when I became aware
     of the pleasure I could get from reading, and my regret now is that
     more of the classics of literature were not available to me at that
     early age, when I had the opportunity to study them. Within a year
     of starting to read I had begun writing myself, and by the time I left
     school I was attempting a history of Roman Britain.

IM   Good heavens!

JR   Which my work on the farms squeezed completely out of me. I just
     didn't have the heart.

IM   After that there'd be quite a long time when between your work and
     your marriage and so on, you wouldn't have a lot of time to think
     about writing?

JR   No, that is true, but I think fate had a hand in it. By the age of
     fourteen I was on the fringe of emancipation. And *could* have been
     a writer by the time I was twenty. The only snag being, that for lack

of experience in life I wouldn't have had much to write about! I think fate had other ideas for me, and gave me a further twenty years of life before she opened my eyes to the talent I possessed, and what could be done with it. At the age of twenty-nine a serious illness drove me deep within myself, and triggered off the thought processes that launched me into literature in a period of two years of serious practice. My first article was published in 1947.

IM Where was that?

JR When I was at Cairngall Farm, Longside.

IM And what was it about?

JR Animal husbandry. The advice to a novice always is, write about the things you know about, and this was something I knew about, being a cattleman. That was twenty years after I left school, and my first attempt took me nearly to the top of the ladder with *Farmer and Stockbreeder*, a national weekly journal, from which position I had to descend to the local press when I couldn't conform to the standards required by the paper.

IM The standards, or what you wanted to write about, perhaps?

JR What I was writing about in article form was sometimes not written to a theme, as they required it. I just didn't have the training.

IM Or perhaps you really wanted to write about something slightly different?

JR I wanted to bring the human element into it more, you know.

IM Well, first of all you began by writing the odd article on animal husbandry: were you writing stories for your own pleasure at the same time?

JR No, the stories came later. From the age of fourteen when I started on the farms until about twenty years later I hadn't written very much at all, the occasional letter to the Press was about the stretch of it, but still the reading went on. And the cinema-going, but this illness I endured at twenty-nine changed my life pattern. It induced me to think deeper about life, and I sought a solace in this, or an identity with something, a sharing of endurance or suffering, and I found it in Shakespeare, in the tragedies. And this took me deeper into literature—or wider shall we say: you cannot get deeper than Shakespeare but perhaps you can get wider. It brought me on to the English dramatists, from the Elizabethans down to Sheridan and Wilde, and included most of the English poets. Milton. It led me on to the English poets such as Wordsworth, Campbell, Tennyson, Hood, Milton, Spenser, Cowper, Shelley and of course the American Longfellow and Whittier, and the Greek Homer and the Roman Virgil.

IM   To name but a few! Now, it's interesting that it took this illness to change your reading habits, or to make you find time to read some literature that can't have been just easy, as a rest from farm duties; but it also led you to think more seriously about writing yourself?

JR   Yes, I suppose you could say that. I wanted to get on to the human aspect of literature, to write the short story. And it took a lot of practice. I could never get the story to end properly. There was never a plot came out of much of what I wrote. In fact, I think I got a real push when I read Lewis Grassic Gibbon's *Sunset Song*. This Long Rob of the Mill. I knew a character a bit like Rob of the Mill. He was Rab of the Barnyards. [See 'Rab o' The Barnyards', in *Hard Shining Corn*, 1971, pp. 26-36.] I wrote that story very much with Grassic Gibbon in mind. And it was successful right from the start. I sent it to the local paper, and they published it, and I sent it to the *Scots Magazine*, and they took it right away and paid me fifteen guineas. This was the first big sum I got. Usually before that from *Farmer and Stockbreeder* they paid me five guineas for a one-page article. For short paragraphs they paid me, oh, thirty bob or something, you know, but I went on from there and I wrote *Blown Seed*, sporadically, if that's the word, intermittently, when I could get at it, it took me many years to complete the first draft, and I couldn't type at that time. I sent it in to Aberdeen, I think it was to Alice Copeland's printing office where she had about a dozen typists hammering on all the time, and she typed it for me, and that cost me a bit of money. Well, it seemed a bit of money in those days, it might have been fifteen, seventeen pounds or something: but nobody would accept it. Collins, for instance, said that the Doric dialect wouldna bring it over the Tweed, so that soured me a bit, you know, and in an effort to break into print I pilfered from *Blown Seed* and wrote the short stories from incidents in the book, and these were successful, so when I came to write the final draft of *Blown Seed* these stories had to be kept out. Looking back, I think they should have been left in the book, because a lot of people wouldn't have read them in the short story form anyway. However, I was completely honest with myself, I thought that they shouldn't be repeated and I kept these short stories out of *Blown Seed*, and that is why I have duplicated some of my characters.

IM   So, *Blown Seed* for a time wasn't getting you anywhere, and these stories did get published—in local papers basically?

JR   Yes, and broadcast.

IM   And broadcast. Was that somehow easier? Was it easier to get things on the radio than into print even?

JR   I found it easier to get on radio than to get into print. But perhaps
      that was by outside influence. I knew Arthur Argo.

IM   Ah, yes.

JR   I knew him when he was a reporter with the *Press and Journal*, he
      worked up in Elgin, and he used to visit me and research for his
      folklore stories, and we shared this, and when he moved from
      Aberdeen Journals to radio in Glasgow he took the half dozen of my
      published stories with him, and passed them round the producers.
      Gordon Emslie I think was the producer who picked on 'Dookit
      Fairm'. Absolutely delighted he was with it! And he had it broad-
      cast; the reader was Victor Carin, now dead. And they also broad-
      cast the title-story from *Hard Shining Corn* read by Douglas
      Murchie. Brian Murdoch read 'Touch and Go'; a chap MacDiarmid
      read 'I Wadna be a Loon Again'. I think I had five broadcast,
      because as I said I had a little help from Arthur Argo, and of course
      when I offered the book to Paul Harris the fact that the stories had
      already been broadcast encouraged him to go on with it.

IM   Well, let's start the Paul Harris story at the beginning. Who *was*
      Paul Harris, and why did you go to him?

JR   Well, Paul Harris, he was an Englishman really, from London. He
      came up here to Aberdeen University, I suppose for the sort of
      education he wanted, I don't know. He went to Elgin first and
      moved down I think to Aberdeen University, and he was still in
      Aberdeen when the Garvie murder trial came up, and he wrote an
      account of the trial, but he couldn't find anybody at all to publish it.
      But he was so determined that it should see the light that he set up
      his own publishing equipment, in an office in Guild Street, and
      went ahead and published the Garvie trial himself. And he pub-
      lished another book, I think it was called *The Old Man of Ben
      Macdhui*, I forget the author's name. [See Affleck Gray, *The Big
      Grey Man of Ben Macdhui*, Aberdeen, 1970.] The third book he
      published was *Legends of the North-east* by Fenton Wyness. [See
      Fenton Wyness, *Spots from the Leopard: Stories of Aberdeen and
      the North-east*, Aberdeen, 1971.] I read this in the papers, just when
      I had my manuscript in book form, and I thought now this chap, this
      Paul Harris, if he can publish a book with a title like *Legends of the
      North-east* maybe he'll publish a book with a title like *Stories of the
      North-east*! So I went in to him with the manuscript, but I learned
      later that it lay in a drawer for four months, he'd just glanced at it,
      couldn't understand the Doric, and forgot about it. Until his char-
      woman, I suppose we should call her, Mistress Blair, opened the
      drawer and came upon the manuscript; had a glance at it, thought

she would like it, took it home and read it, and she was absolutely delighted with it. She took it back to Paul Harris and told him what she thought, and that she—in her opinion—it was worth publication. Paul yet wasn't convinced. He had a schoolmaster read it, and he had Mrs Blair's son Donald Blair read it. He was a journalist, I believe, with *The Scotsman* at the time. Curiously enough, Donald had read another story of mine in the *Buchan Observer* just two days previously, that was 'Aikey Brae', the story of 'Aikey Brae'. [See *Hard Shining Corn*, pp. 80-87.] He'd read this in the *Buchan Observer*, and now he saw this manuscript and he noticed that the author was the same person, David Toulmin. And he got interested and read the manuscript and advised Paul to publish it, and that's how it all started. But still relevant to the fact that if Mrs Garvie hadn't arranged to have her husband murdered, I probably would never have been in print in book form. (L)

IM   That's a lovely story. It's interesting because it's something you seem to have felt a few times, it's almost as if there *is* a fate somewhere, deciding what you're going to do. There was one point you talked about in one of your books where you'd got a job—I think it was in 'Brain Scar', and you'd got a job on a farm and it was a nice farm and a nice job, but you only stayed there a month; and if you had stayed there, then you wouldn't have met Mrs Reid, and you probably wouldn't have written, and all the rest of it. [See 'Brain Scar', in *A Chiel Among Them*, Aberdeen, 1982, p. 214.]

JR   Perfectly true. I feel I have a guardian angel somewhere who looks after me. When I think I'm doing the wrong thing a few years later I realise this is how it should be! Although, mind you, at the time I thought it drastic!

IM   Fine. Well *that* kind of fate that directed your life is obviously something you think of quite seriously. There's a *different* element that comes into several of the stories, where we have dreams that mysteriously come true, or almost visions, superstitions, like the lady in 'Snowfire' who was always terrified that somebody would be ill when an ambulance couldn't come to the farm, or that there would be a fire when the fire-engine couldn't come, and it's you know one of the very dramatic elements in the story that both of these things happened. Do *you* find yourself particularly interested in that kind of coincidence?. Or is it more that you found the people you write *about* were very interested in dreams and so on?

JR   This is touching on the supernatural, shall we say. Well, touching on that, on ghosts, dreams, superstitions, most of that came from my mother. She told me a lot of these happenings. For instance, the story of the 'Folks in Black'.

IM   The dream of the coffins?

JR   Yes, that's her story. And 'Sarah and The Angels'; that's also my
mother's story. As regards the farmer's wife who had a fear of snow
blocking the roads, it's real. It's my experience. This lady always
had a fear that she would take ill in a snowstorm and that a doctor
or an ambulance wouldn't be able to reach her. She seemed to have
a foreboding, and actually she *was* ill, although it was not apparent,
but the crucial stage of her illness was reached in a snowstorm. The
actual thing that she dreaded, happened! And the farm was isolated
for a week, and they had to dig their way through to reach an
ambulance with the farmer's wife. That was true. There's quite a lot
happens in that story, that's 'Snowfire!' [See *Straw into Gold*,
Aberdeen, 1981, pp. 61-83.] People have said that I have brought
too much into it, and yet there's so much truth in it that I aye do this.
I haven't interfered with truth; why should they accuse me of
accumulating the circumstances?

IM   Yes. It is, of course, a very dramatic story, because it has the fire at
the farm as well as the road blockages, but as I think you suggest
with the historical references you bring in, to Napoleon and so on,
there have been outstanding periods and moments in human history
when precisely a whole number of things come together like that. It
just does happen, doesn't it?

JR   Yes. Yes. I have trifled with some things—for instance, in the story
it says that eight people were smothered in the snow. That didn't
happen for a year or two later in a later storm, but it happened. As
regards the cattle being machinegunned by the German airman: that
happened on the *next* farm, and the cattleman was walking through
the cattle on his way to the turnip field and the bullock next to him,
dropped dead from a bullet from a reargunner's post. So I transferred the incident to the farm I was working on, and the cattle *were*
thirsty; they had to be watered; no water available anywhere, until
the farmer—he saw me smashing turnips with a mallet—they
wouldn't go through a cutter—he had the bright idea of the mallet,
that I take it down to the river and break the ice, which was seven
inches deep. And it took a bit of hammering to get a wee hole
enough for one animal to drink. Of course, we couldn't herd the
whole sixteen heifers away, and they just sprawled over the ice and
I had the plane come at this crucial moment to give my story a
dramatic twist. So, it's not so very far from the truth. I think, I
should get away with it! (L)

IM   Oh I think undoubtedly you do! And you do prepare us for a bit of

a striking, an unusual story by the way you introduce it, I think it's
perfectly fair.

A minute or two ago you were talking about Lewis Grassic Gibbon,
and he has always been used as somebody to compare you with, for
all that you lived through the work on the farms and he carefully got
away from it. Apart from the figure of Long Rob in *Sunset Song*, has
he been an important influence in your writing?

JR   In giving me a start with the short story I would say he had.
Otherwise, there are other Scottish writers who have inspired me
more so than Gibbon. For instance, J. M. Barrie with *A Window in
Thrums*. That was the first kailyarder I read. In fact I read it in bed
while I was recuperating from pneumonia, the serious illness that
affected me in 1943. I had double pneumonia and I was supposed to
die. But I didn't.

IM   Fate again!

JR   That was when I read J. M. Barrie's *A Window in Thrums*, the first
kailyarder I'd ever read. And I was *so* surprised to find that in
literature I could come *so* near my own life, you know. This was
something new to me, that this could be done.

IM   Though perhaps the harsh and violent bits of realism that you give
us when you write about life on the farms is just a little polished
before Barrie uses it? I mean he gives us very real-looking people
but he doesn't give us the very dramatic or cruel or violent times,
does he?

JR   No he doesn't, he's genteel, shall we say. But he does have a ghost
story I think on one of the farms that's brought into it. Anyway, the
Window in Thrums and then I was greatly moved by A. J. Cronin's
Hatter's Castle. A tremendous book, I thought, when I read it. And
George Douglas Brown with *The House with the Green Shutters*. I
think that inspired me to write 'Playing Truant'. [See *Hard Shining
Corn*, pp. 19-25.] Because the son in *The Green Shutters* plays
truant if I remember. I thought now *I* could write about this!
      Another Scottish writer who greatly influenced my style, even in
the Doric, was Joseph Laing Waugh with the Robbie Doo books,
Robbie Doo and *Cracks with Robbie Doo*. That gave me a ground-
ing in how the Doric could be used in the dialect of the stories, and
I went on and *did* use it from something that I'd read there. [See
Joseph Laing Waugh, *Robbie Doo: His Reminiscences*, Dumfries,
1912; *Cracks wi' Robbie Doo*, London 1914.] I had written the bulk
of my stories before I read *Johnny Gibb of Gushetneuk*, so I don't
think I could be blamed for copying either *Gushetneuk* or the other

Doric masterpiece *Eppie Elrick*, because I haven't read it yet!

IM It's not just a question of who influenced you, but also who you enjoyed—you enjoyed *Johnny Gibb* when you came across it?

JR Oh yes, yes. In fact, all this Scottish writers I'm mentioning, I enjoyed them all. I suppose the inspiration would come from the enjoyment. If you'd found them boring they wouldn't have been inspiring. So I think I enjoyed them all and Lewis Grassic Gibbon, as I've said, encouraged me to write this 'Rab of the Barnyards'. Now another Scottish writer is Jessie Kesson. She is my female equivalent and contemporary, and one time cottar neighbour.

IM Really, when was that?

JR In Foveran parish. Although we have never met.

IM Really?

JR No!

IM So how near a neighbour was she?

JR About three miles, as the crow flies.

IM It's quite a long way, maybe.

JR And she was writing in the *People's Journal* at that time. Some of her Gibbon-style short stories, which were also published in an Aberdeen publication, was it *North-East Review*? I think they were published there. She was writing these at that time and I was reading the *People's Journal*, and I was still in practice writing my diaries, and we certainly didn't know that each other existed until Margaret, my wife, took ill with lubella, is it you call it?—German measles

IM Rubella, I think!

JR Rubella! Margaret took ill with rubella and the doctor came, Doctor Martin from Ellon, and he said a few words to Margaret and told her what was wrong with her. He came through to the kitchen—no, I had a book lying on the bedroom table—it was Tolstoy's *Diaries*, no—it was Arnold Bennett's *Journal* was lying on the bedroom table and he says 'Who reads this?' 'Oh,' she says, 'It's ma man.' 'Good gracious!' So he came through to me and I also had Tolstoy's wife's diary lying: he was amazed you know that a cottar body should bother himsel wi' this. He says, 'The only other time,' he says, 'I discovered something o' this sort was when I visited a lady at the farm, I think it was called "Watridge Farm", a Wishart farm, on the Wishart estate,' and he said, 'this woman had books piled all over the place,' he said, 'I couldna' get a chair to sit on, it was heaped with *Scots Magazines*! And she was jist an ordinary cottar wifie,' he said. 'And I says, "Do you read all this stuff?" "Oh, well, aye, Doctor," she says, "I dinna only read them, I write in them!"

"Good heavens," he said, "I got the surprise of my life!" And he
says, 'This is another case! How far have ye got?' And I said, 'Oh,
not very far, doctor. A few articles in the *Farmer and Stockbreeder*
and I'm stuck! I'm dried up!' 'Oh, but you must keep at it, Mr Reid,
you can't let this thing go!' And gave me all the encouragement he
could. So that is how near I got to Jessie Kesson without knowing it.

IM But you have met her now?

JR Never met her!

IM Never? Ha, but you've certainly, I think by this time, both admired
each other's work?

JR Well I certainly admire hers! I don't know her opinion of me, but
we're both in common with that—the fact that neither of us were
educated. [In fact, Jessie Kesson *was* educated, as far as the Higher
Leaving Certificate.] We're just from the soil, you know. What
education we have is our own endeavours from reading books, and
taking an interest in things in general. But the difference is, the
learning we've done, we've done it on a voluntary enthusiasm.
Whereas I sometimes go into the reference department of the
Library, and it's crowded with students all hard at it you know,
pegging away, and I could guarantee I've more enthusiasm than
quite a few of them. It's a shame to say it, but maybe it's forced
labour with some of them, whereas with me I want to do it. That is
the difference!

IM John R. Allan wrote a very short Preface to *Hard Shining Corn*. Do
you know him?

JR Yes. Margaret and I have both been to visit John R. Allan when he
lived at Little Ardoe at Methlick when he was farmer there. I took
my diaries to him, oh, in the '50s somewhere and he tried to publish
them without success. And he felt, and his wife felt, that they should
have been published. Anyway, they were not, and never have been.

IM Yet!

JR So yes, I knew John R. Allan.

IM And he clearly admired your work. Did you enjoy *Farmer's Boy*?

JR Yes, but more so *The Seasons Return*, and I've been dipping into
The Lowlands of Scotland, I think he called it—

IM *North-east Lowlands*

JR Yes, *North-east Lowlands of Scotland*. I liked *Farmer's Boy*. I see
it's being reissued again. This must be about the third or fourth
publication. But my favourite is *The Seasons Return*. It's the way he
describes the farm workers, people like myself. How we would
have had all our jackets hung up in the garage expecting the worst
weather conceivable. This was an instinct with the farmworkers, to

keep his oilskin suits and wellington boots handy, you know. And he has a fine way of describing how we surrounded ourselves with these rags. (L)

IM   He's got a slightly cheeky thing in his introduction to *Hard Shining Corn* about how you've left out the very common swearwords. I think it's cheeky, because he obviously does *exactly* the same in *Farmer's Boy*, doesn't he?

JR   He misses the swearwords? Yes, I suppose he does.

IM   So I mean it's just a sensible measure any writer has to take and rest easy.

JR   Yes, and when I reflect on the fact that *Hard Shining Corn* is very much used in schools, I'm rather glad that I kept out the swearwords. Whereas if it had been written later, in the more permissive age, I'd have probably delighted in putting them in! (L) But in *Harvest Home*—that other collection—there's some pretty near-the-bone in there.

IM   Yes. 'Mother Nature had pished herself and the sun came out to take a wee-wee,' Yes. [See *Harvest Home*, Edinburgh, 1978, p. 8.]

JR   And when I learned it was going into schools I was worried, you know! (L) Because of the kids reading it. And I explained this to the headmaster down at Linksfield here, and he says oh, don't worry they know it all nowadays! (L) So I haven't worried since.

IM   *Harvest Home* was a collection I particularly enjoyed, because it was still short stories: it wasn't a novel, but it was given a kind of unity because so often the narrator was the same chap, and he had the wife and in this case Mrs Reid's name is Kathleen (L) and a wee boy called Brian, and somehow these characters coming up several times in the course of the collection gives you a feeling of you know, knowing the whole milieu ...

JR   It shows how easily that book could have been written as a novel.

IM   Oh yes, yes.

JR   But then I was still working when I did it, my time was somewhat limited; and Paul Harris wanted the book, and I just carried on in the usual form, the short feature.

IM   So, what made you decide to give up life in the country and to come and live in Aberdeen?

JR   Mainly because of the rat-race that farming was becoming. Mechanisation had pushed the manual worker aside. I was a manual worker. I *did* go on to a tractor to retain my job, and stuck it for four years, but I was just getting in the way of the younger chaps. I *felt* redundant, and as things have turned out I *was* redundant, so I decided to move into Aberdeen and look for a job in the city. We

bought this flat, which we couldn't do nowadays: we just happened
to buy it at the right time when we could, with a scrape, afford it,
and I got a job at the Marts at Kittybrewster which I considered to
be the fag end of our industry you know, farming, I didn't like it at
all. In fact I made myself ill by persisting with it, you know. So I got
a job as a landscape gardener with W. Smith & Son, at Hazlehead;
and for me, this was a more refined method of farming. It had an
artistic touch which appealed to me, this landscape gardening, and
I *really* enjoyed that. I did it for six and a half years until I was sixty-
five, and retired. Now I've been retired for seven years.

IM   But not exactly idle!

JR   No, never idle! In a literary sphere I'm always involved, you know.

IM   Yes. In fact you were telling me off the tape that there is a
collection, another miscellany, with your agent and *nearly* ready to
go to a publication now?

JR   Yes, that's true.

IM   So that's at least one other book we have to look forward to. Is there
another one after that?

JR   You missed out one *before* that. *The Tillycorthie Story.* It should be
out in the summer I would think.

IM   This was a story that was published in *Leopard* magazine. Could
you tell our listeners what it's about?

JR   It's aboot a barfit loon fae Leeds. New Leeds in Buchan. A barfit
loon, which is a loon that hidna on shoes or stockings. His people
couldna afford them. And he got a job as a herd, looking after cattle
for somebody. When he grew a bit bigger he got a horseman's job;
driving a pair of horse on a fairm you know. And then he moved to
Fraserburgh and went on the fishing boats. I think it was the days of
the Fifies and the Zulu boats you know. Quite a while back. And
from there he emigrated to Bolivia, where he had quite a struggle
with other associates in the tin mining in Bolivia. But after about
twenty years there—I forget the exact period of time—he hit the
jackpot with a very wealthy mine, and became by modern standards
a multi-millionaire. He came back to Scotland and built this huge
mansion at Udny called Tillycorthie and brought up his family, and
died an old sick man.

IM   And you have in fact used part of this story in one of your own
fictional short stories, haven't you? [See 'The Secret of
Tormundie!', in *Straw Into Gold*, pp. 84-95.]

JR   Yes.

IM   But he didn't really marry the kitchie deem when he met her again
in Bolivia? Was that a bit of ...?

JR   No, he did! He met her out there and they married. Yes, that is the
     dramatic fact of the story.
IM   So, that's a very interesting occasion, when you start off by writing
     a fictional story, and quite a long time later you find the man so
     interesting you come back and write the true story of his life. [See
     The Tillycorthie Story, Aberdeen, 1986.]
JR   Yes. I don't think that has happened to me in any other instance. If
     I have, I've forgotten, but that is a fact. It has been written as fiction
     and then as biography. And of course there's such a thing as I call
     faction, which is a mixture of truth and fiction, as you might say. I
     think I go a bit for that nowadays too.
IM   I think you always did! Insofar as it doesn't matter how imaginary
     your stories are, your backgrounds are so real there's always a lot of
     fact there, isn't there?

     Although it's not *very* obvious in your early stories, there's just the
     occasional time when you're told that the narrator goes to church
     and then perhaps the farm wife likes him better because he does.
     But more recently there have been stories with more religion in
     them; I'm thinking particularly of 'One-Armed Bandit', where a
     character gets very much reformed and through losing his arm
     becomes a very dedicated Christian. [See 'One-Armed Bandit', in
     A Chiel Among Them, Aberdeen, 1982, pp. 35-55.] There's quite a
     bit also in your very serene and happy travel journals *Travels
     Without a Donkey*, and you talk about praying in churches from the
     top of the land to the bottom, so would you like to tell me a bit about
     religion, is it important to *you*?
JR   How it affects me? Well, I'm not an atheist. I believe there is some
     unseen power at work. I can't define it, but its greatest appeal to me
     is in what has been written about it. I mean directly, in the Bible. It's
     the Bible poetry that captivates me. I keep an open mind on
     religion. I have sometimes used it in my stories to expose the
     snobbery and hypocrisy in our farming hierarchy in the period of
     which I write. Particularly so in 'Man in a Loud Checked Suit' from
     the *Harvest Home* collection. I think it's brought out quite specifi-
     cally in that story. The other one referring to church, referring to
     religion, 'One-Armed Bandit', was written as an excuse to express
     my ardent love of Scripture and Bible phraseology. Loosely based
     on fact, but replacing a blacksmith with a farmer. It was the
     blacksmith who became the minister. But for reasons of identity I
     used the farmer. That would be faction, would it?
        As for church lore, this comes across as you say, and I agree, very

much in *Travels Without a Donkey*. This is a fervent love I've got for churches, even though they are in ruins. And again I suppose the poetry comes into it. And all the generations who have worshipped in these places and lie under the gravestones outside. Their histories—their lives—but there's less acrimony if that is the word, among the churchgoers in the North-east than there would be in the south of Scotland. In spite of that, isn't it not so that the Disruption started here, perhaps engineered from Edinburgh, but actually got into motion here, so there must have been a more hard core church society in that period.

IM   I was wondering though, whether a bit like the politics, the way you talk about that, perhaps the farmers were the leaders in religion, and the cottars more or less did what they were told?

JR   The hangers-on as you might say. Yes. A great many of the farmers were elders, church officers or whatever you call them, and they went every Sunday, and I think they expected you to do the same. And the difference is that the farmers could dress themselves in the morning and remain dressed all day. With us, the workers, we were in our working togs all morning until nine o'clock, we had to go home and get wir tea, change into wir Sunday-best, go to the church, with the farmer, or on our own motivation, come back to dinner, take off the Sunday-best clothes and get into the togs and get back to the byre again. It was all a bit of an effort on our part.

IM   It sounds very much like the farmers suddenly taking you to the poll to cast your vote, and giving you the first ever hurl in their car.

JR   Exactly the same. The fact that they had the conveyance—the car—privileged them; to bias their choice of candidate, you know.

IM   And you actually admit that you voted Tory to please a farmer on one occasion, really against your own ideas?

JR   Yes, I was a Labour man at that time, not really heretic about it or anything you know, but if anything ... John R. Allan was a Labour man and I voted for him you see, because he was a bookie man! (L) But, I've always declared in politics, I'm not politically minded by any means, but I prefer to be considered as an Independent, not adhering very much to *any* party, and I would greatly approve of a permanent coalition government for this country.

IM   So there's a sense in which you're some kind of an Independent not only in politics but I think also in religion. The John Reid who has a wee bit of time and peace to go on holiday in *Travels Without a Donkey*: loves going into churches, loves reading from the Bible and looking where the minister's left it open, but the other places where he uses words like 'shrine' and 'pilgrimage', it can often be where a poet was born, or where a poet flourished, so that almost it's the religion of a literary man ...

JR   Yes. And thou shalt have no other Gods before Me still has to be adhered to! (L)

IM   But poetry is a pretty good second. Poetry is something that means a great deal to you?

JR   Oh a great deal, tremendous! Although, mind you, I'm not a poet myself.

IM   You've published *very* little poetry.

JR   Very little poetry! I've got one or two at the end of *Straw into Gold*, but I find poetry in prose. That's what I look for. And as I said my latest library book is on show-business, the life of Katherine Hepburn and I like the literary quotes. How the critics accept what she's done in a film, all this sort of thing, I think there's a turn of phrase in these thumb-nail sketches. They appeal to me. I like to build pictures with words, or form an opinion with words. I like to use words. Although, mind you, after all my experience, there are quite a number of English words that I can't pronounce properly, because I haven't had the proper schooling for it, you see.

IM   I don't think it's as simple as that. I think there are a lot of words that all of us know from books, that we don't use in conversation.

JR   That's right.

IM   So when they suddenly come up, you know, I think that's a common thing.

JR   Therefore, it would be a common error and not only on my part, others, yes. I can pronounce all the Doric words of the mither tongue, they give me no bother, there's just one we used yesterday: Margaret's sister was round, and we were talking about what sort of food we liked, and what we didn't like, and I says I'm always pleased that I can enjoy my food, I'll eat almost anything you know, I'm not difficult to please. I says I don't like these people who say I don't like this, I don't like that. Of course they're entitled to their taste, but they should be thankful that they can eat and enjoy what they're eating. Now, Margaret's sister came up with something that she didn't like and I got the word for it and I said you're 'skaichin'.

IM   That's nice.

JR   Now that's the Doric for 'choosey' or 'put off' or 'scunnered'— that's another Doric one of course.

IM   'Picky' even, I suppose.

JR   What was that other word—eh—it was fastidious! 'Skaichin'! Fastidious in her food. So that was the proper word for that. But there's some of the English words I can't pronounce them in speech, but I've only to go to the dictionary to get—when I'm writing—to get the proper spelling. I know the word, it's just that I'm not sure of the spelling, and it's quite easy for me to defer to the dictionary, whereas in pronunciation and speech I just blunder.

IM   Yes, I think we all know that one.

You've had quite a lot of illness and difficulty, and yet as I see it you've never sat down under it for any length of time. You've mentioned already on the tape that when you were, I think, sixteen, you had this epileptic seizure. Could you tell us about that?

JR   Well, I think I've written quite in detail about it in 'Brain Scar'. Anyway, for about a year before that I had lapses of consciousness, just momentary. I would have been driving into Peterhead with a load of oats for the granary, sitting on top of the cart you know with the one horse, the orra beast, and very suddenly I forgot where I was and just a strange numbness came over my brain you know, and I got a bit frightened. However, it left me and I probably wouldn't have had another seizure that day.

IM   And you were depressed as well?

JR   Oh yes, this thing was depressing me, you see. And it always seemed to be worst in the afternoon after I'd had my dinner. This numbness of the brain came over me, you see. Anyway, I put up with it. I didn't know what it was, and I was turning into a man. I found it very difficult to become a man! Anyway, I left this farm, and went to live with my parents. They were cottars, and I was a single man boarded with them you see, which was just as well from what happened. Because my father and I were digging peat in the evening, in the moss, which I've said in the story, and this young hare came over the bank, and my father killed it with his spade, you see. A hare to these people was something to eat! So he took it home and my mother made hare soup with it which was a delicacy in a cottar-house. Maybe even yet it would be a delicacy if people knew how to do it. And I was spooning my—when this jaw just suddenly—and I can't remember which side it went to—and I lost consciousness and fell off my chair, and I knew nothing more for about two hours. And I woke up and they had me on the bed with my clothes on, and my jaw was still twisted round you see. They'd got a doctor by now. But he couldn't tell what it was. And my mother wanted an answer to it. And I'd just had a cousin died from the same thing, you see, this convulsion. And she took me to this Dr Yule in Peterhead and he felt this, you can feel it yet, just slightly, there's a scar there, maybe you can see it.

IM Yes, just slightly.

JR A bit deeper then. He says that's an obstetric injury. You know, and
he says, a scurfulous wound on the inside and it's touching the
brain, that's why you're having these numb feelings you see, and he
gave me this mixture to take which apparently had been a marvellous thing. I don't know, but it was supposed to dissolve this scar
which it eventually did, and I never had another seizure.

IM So everything apparently then was fine, and from then on you had
fine health?

JR Oh yes. About a year after the epilepsy I grew very sturdy and
strong and could take anything in my stride. Until this pneumonia
struck me at twenty-nine and that really floored me! It just knocked
all the stuffing out of me, you know, and the doctor told mother that
I was going to die. There was no hope for me. But he gave me a
heart injection. He says, 'We'll see; I don't think there's much
hope!' And I just passed out. I could be dead; I didn't know
anything about it! And I woke up next morning and I knew I was
going to get better. I was past the—the climax?

IM The crisis!

JR The crisis. I was past this, and I recovered. But, as I say, it deepened
my thoughts considerably. And sent me deeper into literature,
especially Shakespeare, when I encountered all these passages in
Macbeth, and guilt, and all the rest of it. I suppose, it triggered off
my literary career?

IM Yes, that's right. So it was useful from that point of view.

JR And then again the other thing you referred to; the mental illness: I
feel that that's part of it as well.

IM When did that happen?

JR The first time was—I was about forty, I think, when I had the first,
and they had to take me to Kingseat you see and get this electrical
treatment.

IM It must have been pretty horrifying?

JR Oh yes, it was quite an experience! And then in 1970 I went in
again, and I was in the last time just four years ago! As recent as
that. But somehow I always managed to climb back. This is the
beauty of it! And the convalescence from mental illness, it's an
elevating experience. You can see that you're going to get better;
the world becomes marvellously beautiful again, you know. And I
think I had to have one before I could have the other. I don't know,
but you see they say that Churchill had the black bear on his
shoulders, is that what they call it? Well, it's maybe the same thing,
you see.

BT It was a depressive illness?

JR A depressive illness, yes, yes! Maybe you don't get the gift without the curse, I don't know. As I've said it, is it destiny is blind—or one of them is blind. Destiny: she can't see what she's giving you, you see?

IM But I think it would be marvellously reassuring for anybody listening to you that on each of these occasions well-spaced throughout your life you must have felt really defeated when it came back, but each time you've come back from it. With an enhanced enjoyment of life?

JR Yes, the depths of despair—the slough of despond—is really a harrowing experience—just—I don't know how to describe it— you're just overwhelmed, you know! You've nothing further to live for—nothing—you feel like walking into the sea, and things like this. It's really horrific! But if you get over it the other extreme is just as delightful.

IM I think somebody who had only read your stories would hardly know how much you have experienced depression, but I think they do get the feeling of somebody who is broad-minded and tolerant and quite *likes* his fellow human beings. Is that fair?

JR Yes.

IM Although you said to us when the tape was off that there was an awful lot of malice in the world, yet I think your working attitude is quite an open and positive one, isn't it? Is there anything at all that makes you—I haven't warned you about this question at all but it doesn't matter—is there anything at all that makes you *really* angry?

JR Angry? Careless workmanship, I'm a perfectionist, you see. If I see careless workmanship, especially on our own property, I really get rattled at that. Because I was a conscientious worker myself, and I like to see things done properly—although mind you I do admit mistakes. Anybody can make mistakes, and I can forgive these. But if something is just slipshod, carelessly done, that's one thing that nettles me, if you want to know.

IM That's a very good answer from a man who's liable to rewrite a story I don't know how many times until he gets it absolutely the way he wants it.

JR On the same, or on the other hand, I'm a very tolerant person. It takes a lot to anger me, you know. And Margaret and I have a marvellous relationship. Some people might say 'She's haen some life wi' that bugger!' You know. (L) You know, from my mental condition. But you ask Margaret and she'll tell you I'm one of the pleasantest persons to live with, and gives her no bother at all. We can have the odd argument, I'm sure you'd have too.

IM You'd have to be half-deid if you're not having arguments.

JR Och, you wouldn't be human if you didn't! But I'm quite rational in my behaviour. And a man, an old farmer once said to me, he'd been in the mental hospital, this was *years* ago, when these institutions were really barbaric you know, he says there's two kinds of lunatic: there's the devil lunatic, and there's the angel lunatic. Now I'm the angel one! You see. There are the other type who are incurable. It's an illness: they can't help it. They'll never change them, I suppose, but there's all different types of it, just as there's physical illnesses that are all different and complicated. I would say, with a mental illness, in comparison with physical illness, you've got a fighting chance. You really have! If I'd gone into hospital with cancer or heart trouble or something, I've no chance, very little fighting chance. If you go in with a mental illness you have a fighting chance.

IM And you're a fighter if you're nothing else.

JR Well, I'm a very *quiet* fighter but I'm very persistent and very determined: it takes a long time but I win in the end you see. Typically British!

IM Scottish!

JR No, I'll give England the honours, English as well, it's the British this, win the last battle.

IM Well, thank you very much indeed, we've very much enjoyed this conversation. Thank you.

JR Well, I've done my best.

IM You've done splendidly!

Printed in the United Kingdom by
Lightning Source UK Ltd., Milton Keynes
142268UK00002B/118/P